At Home
Among Strangers

At Home
Among Strangers

JEROME D. SCHEIN

Gallaudet University Press
Washington, D.C.

Gallaudet University Press, Washington, DC 20002
©1989 by Gallaudet University. All rights reserved
Published 1989.
Fifth printing, 1997
Printed in the United States of America

Library of Congress Cataloging-in-Publication Data

Schein, Jerome D.
    At home among strangers / Jerome D. Schein.
        p. cm.
    Bibliography : p.
    Includes index.
    ISBN 0-930323-51-3
    1. Deaf—United States—Social conditions. 2. Deafness—Social
aspects—United States.   I. Title.
HV2545.S29   1989
362.4'2'0973—dc20   89-35384
                                                  CIP

Contents

Preface

When they become mindful of my career, people sometimes ask how I became interested in deafness. They seem to expect an account of some personal involvement with Deaf people—relatives or friends. But my answer does not meet these expectations.

I grew up knowing nothing about deafness, let alone about Deaf people, Deaf culture, and the Deaf community. The universities I attended provided no courses about deafness. None of my friends or relatives was deaf. My original interest was strictly academic: while a professor at Florida State University, I was offered a position as a clinical psychologist at what was then the only institution of higher education for Deaf people in the world—Gallaudet College. When I arrived at the college, in 1960, I had only curiosity about, and no knowledge of, deafness.

That lack of background—of negative prejudice, if you will—was my good fortune as a researcher. I escaped the notion that Deaf people were somehow inferior to other people. How could I hold such beliefs when the first Deaf people I met were college professors, skilled craftsmen, professionals, and well-placed government officials? When I needed to discuss demographic techniques, I called upon Wilson Grabill, an international authority on fertility statistics, in the Bureau of the Census, who was deaf. Two early research collaborators, Suleiman Bushnaq and John Kubis, were deaf. Poker games with professors of business administration, economics, English, history, and mathematics—all of whom were deaf—kept me humble. To learn manual communication, I had a daily round of Deaf tutors whose knowledge of the language of sign was vastly superior to mine, and it will remain so for all my life.

Shortly after beginning to work at the college,[1] I became aware of the Deaf community. It did not occur to me then, as it does not now, to question its existence. Thanks to the good-heartedness of academic colleagues and local Deaf leaders, I found myself living in the midst of the Deaf community. It became the subject of some of my earliest research.[2]

Also important for my personal development was the close friendship that arose between me and one of the most effective Deaf leaders of that, and possibly any other, time—Frederick C.

Schreiber, the first full-time executive secretary of the National Association of the Deaf. Until his untimely death, I lacked awareness of his profound influence on me, but I now realize that he did more than anyone else to shape my understanding of Deaf people and of the Deaf community.[3]

When I left Gallaudet College in 1968 to become dean of the College of Education at the University of Cincinnati, I maintained my relations with the National Association of the Deaf (as chair of its Research and Development Committee) and I continued to direct the National Census of the Deaf Population that had begun the same year.[4] Fred and I remained close friends and colleagues for almost twenty years, literally to the day he died, on 4 September 1979.

In the years since his death, I have considered over and again the nature of deafness and pondered the structure of the Deaf community. This study is a further attempt to answer the many questions that arose in those years of my association with Fred and the many other Deaf people with whom it has been my great privilege and deep pleasure to have been associated. Living within and alongside of the Deaf community, I have often felt that I did indeed comprehend it. But that has been an elusive feeling. What is more, how to convey what understanding I did have has been a problem. This book is my latest effort to solve it.

Science fiction writers sometimes base a story on the idea that another world exists parallel to our own. The heroine or hero accidentally crosses over into an invisible society that occupies the same space we do but of which we are unaware, because it functions in another time dimension. This book also describes parallel societies; but societies that are real, not fictional. The stories it recounts are true. The history is as accurate as my research permits; the people about whom it speaks live or have lived. You may challenge the text's theories, dispute its conclusions, and doubt its predictions, but you can be assured that its facts are facts, not inventions of a sci-fi novelist. Being true, however, does not deprive this account of its potential fascination. To the contrary, the people and their exploits excite more interest for having occurred rather than having been invented.

This book is about the Deaf community in the United States. You need no time machine to find it: you need only open yourself to people and events whose presence lies on the periphery of the majority's experience.

To Fred and to deaf people, I owe more than I can repay. Learning about them became a major focus of my professional life quite by accident and without their bidding. Having taken so much from working with them, I feel an obligation to share my observations in the hope that what is written here will assist Deaf people in attaining their deserved role in society.[5]

I also owe a great debt to Gallaudet University for giving me the opportunity to take a year off for this study. In 1986–87, the university awarded me the Powrie Vaux Doctor Chair of Deaf Studies, a great honor and an exceptional opportunity for research. I was particularly pleased to have that chair, because it was named in honor of the late Powrie Vaux Doctor, a Gallaudet College professor with whom I worked on a number of projects, including the International Congress on the Education of the Deaf in 1963, and whom I regarded as a friend.

While at Gallaudet University during 1986–87, I had assistance from many people who made the year a celebratory, as well as productive, one. Raymond J. Trybus, Sally W. Dunn, Michael A. Karchmer, Frank R. Zieziula and the entire Counseling Department, afforded me great academic and personal courtesies for which I am deeply grateful. Robert R. Davila, through Peter Goodman and the housing staff, made life on campus a model of hospitality. Eugene Peterson, who preceded me in the Doctor chair, took pains to smooth my reentry into the Gallaudet milieu. Linda L. Delk and her fine staff provided stimulation and support throughout the year. The Gallaudet Learning Center houses one of the finest collections on deafness in the world. Under the masterful direction of John M. Day, it affords scholars interested in deafness a unique opportunity to work in a most congenial atmosphere. Many other faculty and staff members extended warm cooperation and made the research a most enjoyable task.

Edward C. Carney, Mervin Garretson, Paul C. Higgins, Ivey Pittle, Kathleen B. Schreiber, and my wife, Enid, took the time to read drafts of some or all of this book, an arduous task for which I am hard-pressed to find adequate words to thank them. At least I must say that they are not responsible for any errors, omissions, or other deficiencies that may remain in the text. They tried to steer me right, so they cannot be faulted for my obtuseness.

Lastly, I must thank those Deaf people and normally hearing professionals who allowed me to interview them and wished to remain anonymous. Since I promised them complete confidentiality, even though several indicated that they had no reservations about being quoted directly, I can only express my gratitude by saying, You know who you are, and you know how much I appreciate your patience at my probing and your wisdom in responding.

To all of these good friends and colleagues, I express my thanks and my fervent desire to meet their expectations in this and all future endeavors.

NOTES

1. In October 1986, by act of the United States Congress, Gallaudet College became Gallaudet University.
2. Schein, 1968.
3. For Schreiber's biography, which is intertwined with a brief history of the National Association of the Deaf, see Schein, 1981.
4. Schein and Delk, 1974.
5. An astute scientist writes, "As sometimes happens in anthropology, the professional observer doesn't much like the members of the society he has joined, and as also happens . . . they don't much like him" (Thomas, 1987, 10–11). I hope that has not been, and will not be, the fate of this participant observer.

At Home
Among Strangers

INTRODUCTION

The coincidence amazed me.

I was reading Harlan Lane's *When the Mind Hears* and was struck by a passage written over one hundred years ago by a young deaf man raised apart from other deaf people. He heard about the Hartford Asylum, a new school for deaf children, and arranged to visit it accompanied by his normally hearing older brother, Charles. Here is what he wrote after his first meeting with deaf people when he was sixteen years old:

> Charles and I went into the boys' and next the girls' sitting room. It was all new to me and to Charles it was amusing, the innumerable motions of arms and hands. After dinner he left and *I was among strangers but I knew I was at home.*[1]

That last phrase sounded familiar. Turning to my bookcase, I found a pamphlet published in 1973 and in it these lines from a speech by a young deaf man describing his first encounter with other deaf people:

> My sister told me about the Maryland School for the Deaf. My immediate reaction was one of anger and rejection—of myself. I reluctantly accompanied her to the School one day—and at long last began to come *home.* It was literally a love experience. For the first time, I felt less like a *stranger* in a strange land and more like a member of a community.[2]

Though separated by more than one hundred years, the two teenagers, Edmund Booth and Frank Bowe, neither of whom had ever before been with people who shared their deafness, both described their feelings at that first meeting in similar words expressing their sense of comfort, relaxation, and familiarity. They felt *at home among strangers.*

Deaf women and men have come together for at least the last two centuries to form their own communities within the larger communities in which they live. From time to time, the general public becomes aware of deaf individuals and of deafness as a condition, but seldom, if ever, is it aware of the Deaf community. In 1988, students at Gallaudet University—the only institution of higher education for deaf students—demanded that the next president be deaf. The "Deaf President Now" movement emerged in newspaper headlines, radio commentaries, and television features. Not only in the United States but also throughout the world, the general public observed Deaf people struggling for a cause that was seen as a civil rights issue. The stereotype of Deaf people as intellectually limited faced a sharp challenge. The courageous student leaders, backed by the Deaf community, conducted a brilliant public relations campaign and emerged victorious against a prejudice dramatized by the university's own board of directors. This one event may effect a long-term change in the general public's attitudes toward Deaf people. It will not, however, educate the public about their nonhearing neighbors, especially about their culture, their organizations, and their everyday social lives.

WHO IS DEAF?

The little child swinging in the park, that lovely lady walking into the supermarket, that gentleman standing at the bus stop—nothing about their appearance tells you they cannot hear. Deafness does not show. Only if you attempt to engage them in conversation will you realize that they are unusual. If you speak to them when they do not see you, they will "ignore" you. When you do attract their attention, their intent stare at your face may disconcert you. Often their voices, if they answer you, will be unusual, monotonic, nasal, poorly articulated. With all of these clues, will you guess these people are deaf? Or will you have other, unflattering ideas about why they differ from your expectations?

DEGREE OF IMPAIRMENT

Definitions can mask theoretical presuppositions. To achieve a theoretically neutral definition of deafness, I have focused on the role of hearing in communication. After all, hearing losses can occur in high and/or low frequencies, at greater and lesser degrees, affecting one or both ears the same or differently. These are all considerations that audiologists and otologists must take into account. In the end, for the individual, the important question is how has the hearing impairment affected the ability to communicate. Hence, my definition is in those terms: Deaf people cannot hear and understand speech through the ear alone, with or without amplification.[3]

The corollary to that definition is that deaf people are visually dependent; they cannot carry on a conversation with their eyes closed. To communicate on a one-to-one basis, they must be able to see the other person.

This definition eschews the medical view of deafness as a disease. It does not treat deaf people as pathological. Their condition makes them different from the majority of people, but that difference does not make them inferior beings. However, while we point out the absence of functional hearing, we should hurry on to state that the deaf person may in all other respects be unimpaired. Being deaf should not imply anything but the inability to hear. Deaf people have fought against the use of "deaf and dumb" for the very reason that it implies that those who are deaf are also mentally incompetent. As the former director of the National Association of the Deaf often said, "It's not the ears that count but what's between them."

AGE AT ONSET

Having defined deafness in terms of its behavioral consequences—specifying that the hearing impairment affects human communication—the point in individuals' development at which they become deaf is indicated by a modifier, thus: *prelingual* deafness (occurs before three years of age), *childhood* deafness (occurs before adolescence), *prevocational* deafness (occurs before nineteen years of age), and so forth. A variety of modifiers can be, and have been, used to indicate individuals' ages when they became deaf. The unmodified term encompasses all ages at onset.

Specifications of age at onset and degree of impairment, critical as they are for maintaining communication between researchers and their readers, do not exhaust the connotations of the word. Roslyn Rosen, a Deaf educational administrator, sagely observes, "Deafness is much broader than just a hearing loss; it is a complex sociopolitical reality that permeates one's life."[4]

Until recently, society almost invariably considered deafness to be a pathological condition. Its management fell in the physician's province. As a medical problem, its social implications tended to be lost. Yet, from time to time, scholars have noted that deafness does not hurt, is not fatal, and is disabling only in particular situations. Deafness alone does not prevent one from learning, working, raising a family. The medical model—the view of deafness as a pathological condition—obscures rather than aids deaf people in making a successful adaptation to their circumstances. The definition of deafness selected for this study remains neutral with respect to a particular disciplinary allegiance; it can be as successfully applied by educators, physicians, psychologists, rehabilitationists, social workers, sociologists, and other specialists interested in studying the condition and/or working with Deaf people.

Another way to define Deaf people is in terms of their preferred mode of communication. As one anthropologist has noted,

> Indeed, what makes Deaf people a cultural group instead of simply a loose organization of people with a similar sensory loss is the fact that their adaptation includes language. An environment created solely by a sensory deprivation does not make a culture. Blind people find themselves in a visual void. This similarity in circumstance certainly provides for a strong group bonding of individuals of similar experience; it does not, however, form a culture. Blind people are vision-impaired members of the variety of America's linguistic communities. What does form a culture for Deaf people is the fact that the adaptation to a visual world has by human necessity included a visual language. In the United States this is American Sign Language.[5]

Deafness in the Deaf Community

Members of the Deaf community vary in the extent to which their hearing is impaired, from mildly to profoundly. Their losses are similar in that they will have occurred early in the deaf person's development, with most arising before eight years of age. To distinguish those who are members of the Deaf community from those deaf people who are not, writers in this field have adopted a simple convention that has been widely adopted. When capitalized, Deaf refers to members of the Deaf community. Written in lower case, deaf refers only to the inability to hear and understand speech, and it carries no further social connotations, no indication of the age at onset, and no implications of membership in the Deaf community.

STEREOTYPES

In this century, scientists have struggled to escape the stereotypic thinking that defines people by their physical characteristics. Some folk sayings seem innocuous ("Fat people are jolly") and some not ("Left-handed people are erratic"). Regardless of pejorative intent, such generalizations encourage mental laziness that, by itself, is debilitating to the thinker. The classic treatise by Donald G. Paterson, *Physique and Intellect*, destroyed with scientific precision myths about the relationship between physical features and personality that ranged from "redheads are fiery tempered" to "Chinese people are inscrutable." Yet some stereotypes persist.

Would it be better not to define deafness, not to differentiate those with extreme hearing losses from the rest of the population? Would that avoid stereotypes? No, deafness would not go away because we did not use that name. The evil of stereotyping does not reside in the naming but in the associations that the naming implies—the generalizations about the behavior of those who are named. Deaf people would object to banishing the term, because deafness is a part of their identity. They have a history, a culture, a community, and they wish to preserve the bases of their self-concepts. To deny deafness would, in effect, deny a major portion of their existence. Deaf people's objections come not from being called deaf but from being considered mentally incompetent, clannish, socially inept, lacking in refinement, and hosts of other calumnies that do not correctly apply to them as a group. Yes, some Deaf people are boors, stupid, and even criminal, but the majority—the overwhelming majority—are not. Thus, to do away with a term does not eliminate the stereotype. Even worse, abolishing the study of deafness would perpetuate ill-founded legends by preventing the corrective facts from emerging.

HOW MANY DEAF PEOPLE?

Knowing the size of the Deaf community is fundamental to understanding it as will be discussed at length in chapter 8. Here we will deal with that question descriptively, to orient the reader.

STEREOTYPES

Perhaps no single example demonstrates more dramatically the arbitrary character of the able-bodied world's perception of handicaps as biological conditions than the impact of success upon the way in which almost any disability is perceived and remembered. We do not think of Franklin D. Roosevelt as a great crippled president: we think of him as a great president who, among many other things, happened to be crippled. Nor do we customarily think of John F. Kennedy as a handicapped president cut down before he could redeem his promise. Yet he suffered from Addison's disease, a chronic illness that qualifies its bearer to carry the handicapped label. And while both Alexander the Great and Julius Caesar were epileptics, it takes Jorge Luis Borges (himself blind but not considered handicapped) to remind us that in Caesar's case, a handicap changed the course of history. While swimming in the Rhine, Caesar had an epileptic fit and nearly drowned. Only the presence of a soldier on shore saved his life. As a result of the incident, Caesar decided not to mount a major invasion of what is now Germany.

Nor do we remember that Lord Byron had a clubfoot and Alexander Pope had curvature of the spine. Elizabeth Barrett Browning was a paraplegic. Milton was blind when he wrote *Paradise Lost*, Beethoven was deaf when he wrote the Ninth Symphony, Nietsche was a syphilitic, and Dostoevsky was an epileptic. Edison was deaf, and Freud spent the last sixteen years of his life wearing a prosthesis on his jaw. To speak of these men and women as handicapped seems a contradiction in terms. It seems so, we believe, because success defines a chronologically adult individual as carrying out certain adult functions so well that his inability to carry out other adult social functions is judged irrelevant. We remember FDR's cigarette holder better than his wheelchair.[6]

The number of Deaf people is very small relative to the general population. It is smallest when one adds to the definition of deafness the age at onset. Table 1 shows deafness occurs at a rate of 873 per 100,000. This yields a sizable number of people (over two million, if the rate is applied to the present population of the United States) but as a proportion of the general population it is small. Pre-

Table 1 Prevalence and Prevalence Rates of Hearing Impairments in the Civilian, Noninstitutionalized Population, by Degree and Age at Onset: United States, 1971

Degree of Impairment	Age at Onset	Number[a]	Rate per 100,000
All degrees	All ages	13,362,842	6,603
Significant bilateral	All ages	6,548,842	3,236
Deafness	All ages	1,767,046	873
Deafness	Prevocational[b]	410,522	203
Deafness	Prelingual[c]	201,626	100

SOURCE: Adapted from Jerome D. Schein and Marcus T. Delk, Jr., *The Deaf Population of the United States* (Silver Spring, MD: National Association of the Deaf, 1974), 16.

[a]Do not add numbers in this column. Each category includes those in the succeeding category. "All degrees" includes all of the people in the remaining four categories. Of the 1,767,046 who are deaf, 410,522 had an onset before nineteen years of age and 1,357,324 had an onset at or after nineteen years of age.
[b]Onset prior to nineteen years of age.
[c]Onset prior to three years of age.

vocational deafness—on which this text focuses—occurs at a rate of 202 per 100,000 persons. Rarest of all is prelingual deafness, which occurs at a rate of 100 per 100,000. Thus, in a town of one thousand people, only one would be prelingually deaf, another one prevocationally deaf, and two or three more deafened later in life, for a total of eight or nine. Clearly, deaf people are a minority of the population, and the earlier they are deafened, the smaller is their proportion of the total population.

Incidentally, the figures in Table 1 make a point unrelated to population size. Note that the data are for 1971. The study that yielded those numbers was the first in over forty years, and it is the most current study that provides estimates of the size of the Deaf community.[7] This gap in information about the Deaf community indicates how little attention deafness is given by the government and provides a bit of evidence for the alienation felt by Deaf people. Not counting a group diminishes its social and political influence. The establishment by Congress in 1988 of the National Institutes of Deafness and Other Communicative Disorders recognizes the oversight and mandates that steps be taken to correct it.

THE DEAF COMMUNITY

A community is made up of persons who have a common characteristic.[8] The Deaf community consists of Deaf people who communicate visually and who share a wide variety of interests based on their loss of hearing ability. Along with these shared traits have grown organizations, mores, and literature that are special to Deaf people. Higgins, in his book on the Deaf community, specifies that "communities consist of people in social interaction within a geographic area and having one or more additional common ties."[9] My own definition eliminates any reference to geographical limits because I do not believe that a Deaf community is physically constrained. Deaf people seek (or indicate a preference for) each other's company, remain in contact with each other, share common interests, and act in concert on some significant issues, even though separated by hundreds of miles.[10] Thus, their social groups meet the criteria for a community.

Recognition of the Deaf community grew slowly among scholars studying deafness. Until recently, they have not perceived the social structure that Deaf people have built and nourished over the last century and a half. The experts' emerging awareness of American Sign Language (ASL) as a true language, independent from English, enabled the concept of the Deaf community as a linguistic entity to emerge. Members of the Deaf community use sign language—usually ASL, in the United States—to communicate with each other, making social interactions much easier than they are when the Deaf person must depend on lipreading and speaking in English. But Deaf people share more than a language; they have common interests, similar ways of behaving, and similar backgrounds.[11]

The Deaf community is not geographically bounded, a characteristic usually included in definitions of community. They are not deterred by great geographic distance in their efforts to interact with those whom they regard as their peers and colleagues. Surprisingly, they do not share the same degree of hearing disability. Deaf community members differ in the extent to which their hearing is impaired, from mildly to profoundly, while their hearing disabilities are usually similar in that they will have occurred early in their development.

Some authorities have looked upon the Deaf community as an ethnic group, even though its constituents do not have a common heritage; quite to the contrary, many Deaf adults are alienated from their parents, with whom they have great difficulty in communicating (see chapter 2). As more and more parents learn manual communication, that situation is changing, so that many Deaf children are now better integrated into their nuclear families. Whether seen as a linguistic, ethnic, social, cultural, or disability group—and granting that its members do not live in physical proximity to each other—*the Deaf community exists.* As the next chapters seek to demonstrate, Deaf people in the United States have built a comprehensive organizational network that fills the gaps that would otherwise be left in meeting their psychological and social needs and that preserves their culture. Lest this discussion of the Deaf community sound too utopian, recognition must be given to racial, sexual, educational, and economic distinctions in the Deaf community. They exist and they are no less troubling in the Deaf community than they are in other communities. They will be discussed in the following chapters.

DEAF VIEWS

What do Deaf people think about the Deaf community? Several Deaf writers have commented on the Deaf community without explicitly defining it. Its reality must seem palpable to them, rendering unnecessary any effort to define it.[12] Even two sociologists concerned about deafness do not define it, although they write about it.[13] However, Roslyn Rosen, an educator and Deaf leader, views a Deaf community as principally identified by its use of sign language.

> The Deaf community is a microcosm of any community of people, a cross-section of society at large, in its heterogeneity of physical builds, races, religions, intelligence, interests, and values. The common denominator is the inability to hear and its ramifications.[14]

Unlike an ethnic community, Deaf people are remarkably diverse in their origins. They vary by race and parents' country of origin. Unlike members of the Polish community, for example, they do not share a nationality. Unlike members of a religious community, they do not require the same church affiliation as a condition of membership. Deaf people are not even entirely alike in their inability to hear, which ranges from some to virtually none. Furthermore, all persons who cannot hear do not belong to the Deaf community. Membership is a matter of choice. Why some join and others do not is a fascinating topic for research—research that has not been done.

CRITERIA FOR CONFIRMING THE
DEAF COMMUNITY'S EXISTENCE

As the foregoing makes clear, the Deaf community is a concept, not a place. It is a name given to the tendencies of Deaf people to seek each other out, tendencies that are manifested in the organizations and guides to behavior that facilitate such interactions. Hence, the Deaf community is real—as real as any other community.

Its existence is attested to by the various authorities cited. They point to folkways, shared attitudes, organizations, and specific behaviors as the means of identifying the Deaf community. Most do not define Deaf communities geographically. The magnetism that draws one Deaf person to another is not greatly attenuated by distance. As the subsequent pages unfold, the criteria for establishing the existence of a Deaf community are its distinct culture and its formal organizations.

COMMUNITY OR COMMUNITIES?

Some theorists question the use of "community" as opposed to "communities" of Deaf people. They regard the sense of homogeneity that the singular form suggests as misleading. Carol Padden, for example, notes, "Thus, there are many different deaf communities across the United States, but there is a single American Deaf culture with members who live in different communities."[15] Certainly, the white and nonwhite Deaf communities have substantial differences. Whether these differences are sufficient to warrant conceptualizing separate cultures remains open to research. Ernest Hairston and Linwood Smith ask, "Are we [blacks] that different?" Their explorations bring them to conclude "that deafness has the same effect on a person despite racial, ethnic, or cultural background, but where Black deaf persons are concerned, the differentiating factor lies in being Black rather than in being deaf."[16]

My own view is that the within-group similarities among deaf people outweigh the differences in the adaptations they choose to resolve common problems. While not disagreeing about the heterogeneous nature of the Deaf community—see especially the variety of organizations that Deaf people have created to accommodate the differences they find among themselves—an argument can be made for holding to the singular concept.

First of all, the Deaf community is singular in the same sense that the United States is singular. Within the United States, one finds a bewildering array of political, social, and ethnic subdivisions. It is as valid to speak in the singular about the Deaf community as about the United States. That obvious argument aside, one must ask if the singular concept is useful. For the answer to that, I beg the reader's indulgence until the next six chapters have been read. If from accumulated observations common threads are found, then the Deaf community as a singular entity deserves to stand. But if no valid generalizations about it can be deduced, it should be cast aside. Let utility, then, determine this issue. At the same time, however, let us not overlook the correctness of Padden's and Higgins's contention: within the Deaf community reside numerous distinguishable communities of Deaf people.[17]

THE SELF-HELP MOVEMENT

One might also think of Deaf communities as self-help groups, as people with similar problems banded together for mutual support. Viewed in that way, the Deaf community is more than one hundred years old. That it has been highly effective in serving its members will be discussed in later chapters. That it should serve as a model for other disabled groups has apparently escaped the attention of most rehabilitators.[18]

Deaf people have evolved their own society to attend to their own needs, to serve their own ends, to manage their own problems, and to provide points of interchange with the general society of which they are a part and yet from which they are apart.

The fierce independence of the majority of Deaf adults confronts popular conceptions of disabled people as weak and demanding of sympathy and aid. Those characteristics fit some chronically impaired persons, but they do not represent the majority of people deafened in childhood. These individuals tend to join the Deaf community, that is, to associate mostly with other persons who have been deafened in childhood. Conversely, those who become Deaf in adulthood seldom become members of the Deaf community; they strive to retain their lifelong relations with friends and relatives whose hearing remains intact. These tendencies—of early deafened persons to seek each other's company and of late deafened persons to remain aloof from those who are early deafened—provide a significant clue for those seeking to understand the behavior of Deaf people.

TERMINOLOGY

Misuse of language may reflect abuse of people. Certain terms and common usages do unintentional violence to attitudes toward Deaf people.

GHETTO

Such a term is "ghetto." Its application to the Deaf community creates a non sequitur. It is a nasty term for the section of a city in which Jewish people were confined by decree. Jews did not volunteer to live in these often-walled quarters; they were forced to do so. In current parlance, "ghetto" has also been used to characterize urban areas inhabited by minorities, usually black or Puerto Rican. The implied coercion is economic, not legal. To speak of the Deaf community as a ghetto suggests that it is a place and that its members are forced to live with each other. Such implications defy the truth: Deaf communities arise from the decisions of Deaf people to interact with each other. A distinguished Deaf leader expressed with suitable irony his resentment at that inapt term by recounting an incident at the 1972 convention of the National Association of the Deaf, in Miami Beach, Florida, held at the then-luxurious Deauville Hotel.

> Watching the multitude of the Deaf guests who were dressed in the latest fashion—women in low-cut, clinging gowns with glittering jewelry and men in formal attire of varying colors, animatedly chatting in the expensively decorated and furnished hotel lobby, an officer of the Association remarked, "And they call this a Deaf ghetto!"[19]

SUBCULTURE

Often in the professional literature, references are made to "the Deaf subculture." The "sub" in subculture or subgroup is condescending. It connotes inadequacy, something that is beneath (i.e., inferior to) the majority culture or group. Those who use the term may protest that they meant only to indicate that, as a minority group, Deaf people's culture differs from that of the majority, that it is, at least in some ways, unique. But for such purposes other terms are available, terms that do not carry the dictionary meaning of "beneath" or "lesser."

NORMAL

From time to time, writers use "normal" as a term contrasted with "hearing impaired" and/or "deaf." "Normal" can have all sorts of connotations; it is a term that drags a great deal of excess baggage with it. To avoid implications other than that "normal" refers solely to hearing ability that characterizes the majority, this book uses "normally hearing," "general," or other designation for the majority. If the majority were deaf, deafness would be normal or general. Thus, in place of "normal," one should not read "good," "preferred," "moral," or any other laudatory adjective; it refers only to the most numerous group. If one acts like the majority, dresses like the majority, hears like the majority, then one behaves normally, dresses normally, and hears normally. Nothing more; nothing less.

THE DEAF

One last word on nomenclature. Characterizing people by using a descriptive adjective in place of a noun is a destructive verbal habit. In this context, I urge conscious avoidance of "the Deaf." Its brevity alone is offensive. It denies Deaf people a measure of humanity, their personhood. For a scientific text, it inexcusably lacks essential precision. When it is used, does "the Deaf" refer to deaf children, deaf adults, deaf students, or what? In this book, use of "the Deaf" will occur only in quotations from others and in established names; for example, National Association of the Deaf (not National Association of Deaf People) and Texas School for the Deaf (not Texas School for Deaf Students).

PLAN OF THE BOOK

What is the Deaf community? Where is it? Who are its members? How did they come together? Why have they created the society in the way they have? How do they conduct their affairs? In what direction is the Deaf community moving?

To answer these and many other questions about the Deaf community, this book divides roughly into two parts. The first seven chapters describe the Deaf community, beginning with this introduction. Chapter 2 takes up Deaf culture, a phenomenon not even considered as recently as two decades ago. Chapter 3 looks at the structural underpinnings of the Deaf community, its organizational base. Chapter 4 probes family life—both the families from which Deaf people come and those they create. Chapter 5 discusses education and rehabilitation, while chapter 6 examines the economic consequences of deafness. Chapter 7 looks at the Deaf experience with law, medicine, and other societal agents. These chapters intend to establish the existence and importance of a phenomenon that has had scant attention in the literature on deafness, to extract generalizations that can be useful to scholars without losing the specificity that piques general readers' interest.

The second, and much shorter, part of the book attempts to explain why the Deaf community exists, and why it has developed as it has. The explanation centers on five factors. Chapter 8 discusses these five factors in detail, along with an explanation of how they interact with each other. Using the five factors in tandem with information about trends in and around the Deaf community, chapter 9 then makes predictions about the future of the Deaf community.

A brief presentation of the five factors appears here to provide the reader with a framework on which to arrange the ensuing description of the Deaf community. If these descriptive chapters have been rendered with appropriate objectivity, then a number of theoretical explanations may be suggested by them. Being even sketchily acquainted with the five factors—demography, alienation, affiliation, education, and milieu—the reader can test their explanatory power as the description of the Deaf community unfolds.

DEMOGRAPHY

The most fundamental point about Deaf communities is that they can only come into being if there are enough Deaf people. How large that number must be has not been studied, but it is already clear that numerosity has two faces: one absolute and the other relative. The absolute number of Deaf people needed to form a community is certainly greater than two and less than a million or even a thousand. Precisely what the Deaf population size must be has not been ascertained. But the absolute number alone will not determine the presence of a Deaf community. The number *in relation to the size of the general community* constitutes another important determiner. Ten Deaf adults among fifty normally hearing persons might not generate a separate Deaf community, whereas ten among a thousand might. The enigma, if there is one, will be resolved in chapter 8. At this juncture, it is sufficient to note that both actual and relative numerosities are fundamental to determining whether or not a Deaf community will develop at any given time in any given place.

ALIENATION

Rejection by general society drives Deaf people to join with other Deaf people. Instance after instance alienates Deaf people from society. The general community's lack of acceptance of Deaf people—whether actual or only perceived to be so by Deaf people—accounts, in part, for the formation of Deaf communities. In the chapters to follow, how alienation manifests itself in this country will be detailed.

A BREED APART

The following is a portion of a story that appeared in the *Portland Oregonian* and was reprinted in *The New Yorker*, 22 August 1988.

Meanwhile, some 60 pro-North marchers held their own rally nearby, featuring signs such as "Pardon North—Indict the Linders," a reference to the family of Ben Linder, a former Portlander killed in Nicaragua last year. The supporters played flutes and guitars while stressing the broad base of their point of view.

"All Republicans aren't white people," said Sharon Caldwell of Newberg. "We have all kinds of people here—blacks, Hispanics, Jews, and the hearing impaired."

Affiliation

Deaf people have a mutual attraction for each other. The single word "communication" cannot adequately convey the depth of feelings aroused in Deaf people by the relaxed, sympathetic interchanges they have with others who share their deafness. Thus, both centrifugal (alienation) and centripetal (affiliation) tendencies play major roles in development of the Deaf community.

Education

The initiation and continuation of a Deaf community also depend on both formal and informal teaching that Deaf children receive. Their education comes not only from schools, but also from peers, family, and others whom Deaf children encounter while growing up. Cultural knowledge derives as much, if not more, from experiences outside the classroom as from instruction within it. How Deaf culture is transmitted is a major consideration in the study of Deaf communities.

Milieu

The politics of the general community affect all of the groups within it, but the relationships are not necessarily reciprocal. The social climate created by the larger society in which a Deaf community arises determines to some degree its structure.

Interactions Among Factors

To be complete, a theory must account for the interactions among the five factors. They are not independent of each other. Numerosity affects the public attitudes to Deaf people. As their numbers grow, Deaf people are more able to defend themselves against majority impositions and their attractiveness as a market for goods and services increases. Numerosity also interacts with the way Deaf people regard their own Deaf community, and the number of Deaf people influences educational policies. Since these factors are not played out in a political vacuum, the milieu must enter into understanding the various combinations of the other four factors.

PREDICTIONS

The theory seeks to ascertain the likely course of the Deaf community *given* various sets of economic, political, and social conditions. To the extent that it is valid, the theory will correctly anticipate how the Deaf community will respond to conditions that may soon arise. That is one of the theory's functions. It should also be useful to Deaf leaders and those who wish to influence the Deaf community by making accurate predictions in response to "What if?" questions.

A BIT OF LEAVENING

Describing so complex an entity as the Deaf community risks two dangers. One is that concentrating solely on the Deaf community's positive attributes justifies the criticism that such an account patronizes Deaf people by making them into "Barbie and Ken" dolls. After all, why should Deaf people have to be any better than people in general? The other is that painting too dour a picture of life in the Deaf community makes deafness into a living horror, a constant burden of near-intolerable weight. Both approaches lie. The Deaf community is not heaven on earth; it is the adaptive response of a minority group, hence it reflects unfavorable conditions surrounding it. It is populated with people, not stereotypes. Difficult as it is to sail between these two descriptive rocks, we shall endeavor to steer a careful course. Imagine describing the United States by focusing on a farm community in Iowa or, conversely, on a family living on Manhattan Island. Neither selection could convey to the proverbial Martian visitor the essence of this nation. Yet there is a society that is defined by the political boundaries of this country, and it can be described in terms that do the diversity of the nation justice.

Deaf people belong to more than one community, even though our interest in this book is on their membership in the Deaf community. They are like other Deaf people in some respects, but not in all respects. Deaf culture has distinctive features, though not all aspects of Deaf culture differ from the majority culture. The importance of the generalizations we seek lies in the assistance they can give to predicting how the Deaf community will react to future conditions. Prediction is the essence of science. Prediction also provides the key to explanation, another goal of scientists. When we are able to predict a group's behaviors, we are a long way—some philosophers would say we are all the way—toward an understanding of that group. The broad survey of the Deaf community in the following pages concentrates on its central tendencies, what the *average* Deaf person is like. It seeks generalizations about the Deaf community. But, in doing so, it recognizes that the Deaf community, like any large group of people, is not homogeneous. So this book strives to achieve balance by presenting more than one view of the phenomena that collectively make up the society of Deaf people in hopes that the composite will do justice to it.

NOTES

1. Cited in Lane, 1984, 233. Italics added.
2. Bowe, 1973, 9. Warfield (1957, 60, 76, 78) also expresses the "at home among strangers" feeling, though she considers herself hard of hearing, not deaf.
3. This discussion is based on Schein, 1968, and Schein and Delk, 1974. Deafness has been so variously construed that its very use in technical writing has been questioned (Barker, Wright, Meyerson, and Gonick, 1953). Yet the term is embedded not only in common parlance but also in the technical literature of a wide variety of professions. The meaning cannot be understood by reference to a dictionary. Here are two definitions among many: "partially or wholly lacking or deprived of the sense of hearing; unable to hear" (*The Random House Dictionary of the English Language*, unabridged, 1983); "totally or partially unable to hear" (*Webster's New World Dictionary of the American Language*, 2nd college edition, 1970). Since the degree remains unfixed in these two definitions, mildly hard-of-hearing people would also fit the "partially," hence would be "deaf"! Nor can we turn to laws for a definition of deafness for two reasons. Until very recently, there was no legal benefit or penalty for being deaf, so there was no legal need to define the term. In the last few years, however, "deaf" has appeared in laws establishing services (e.g., Captioned Films for the Deaf), creating commissions (e.g., Texas Commission for the Deaf), and requiring specific treatment

(e.g., Public Law 94–142, "Education for All Handicapped Children Act of 1975"). The latter does have a definition that is basically the same as that used in this book: "Deaf means a hearing impairment which is so severe that the child is impaired in processing linguistic information through hearing, with or without amplification, which adversely affects educational performance." The first two laws do not define deafness, apparently relying on common usage for its meaning.

4. Rosen, 1986, 241.
5. Rutherford, 1988, 132.
6. Gliedman and Roth, 1980, 28–29.
7. Schein and Delk, 1974.
8. Schein, 1968. While the phrase "Deaf community" has only recently appeared in the literature, the concept dates at least from early in the nineteenth century, when it was used by Jean-Marc Itard not as a description of an existing entity but as a suggested solution for the social problems of Deaf people (cited in Lane, 1984).
9. Higgins, 1980, 38.
10. Cohen (1985, 7) writes, "The concept of community has been one of the most compelling and attractive themes in modern social science, and at the same time one of the most elusive to define." He continues, " 'Community' is one of those words—like 'culture,' 'myth,' 'ritual,' 'symbol'—bandied around in ordinary, everyday speech, apparently readily intelligible to speaker and listener, but, when imported into the discourse of social science, however, causes immense difficulty. Over the years it has proved to be highly resistant to satisfactory definition in anthropology and sociology, perhaps for the simple reason that all definitions contain or imply theories, and the theory of community has been very contentious" (11). Cohen does not attempt to formulate a definition of community; rather, he proposes to follow Wittgenstein's advice and avoid lexical restrictions initially and seek meaning through use of the term. A reasonable interpretation of the word's use implies two related suggestions: that the membership of a group of people (a) have something in common with each other which (b) distinguishes them in a significant way from the members of other putative groups. Thus, community implies simultaneously *similarity* (with members of the community) and *difference* (from other communities).
11. Higgins sets forth the membership criteria: "Deafness is not a sufficient condition for membership in the deaf community, though some degree of hearing impairment is a necessary condition. . . . [Membership] is not an ascribed condition. [It] is achieved through (1) *identification* with the deaf world, (2) *shared experiences* that come of being hearing impaired, and (3) *participation* in the community's activities. Without all three characteristics, one cannot be nor would one choose to be a member of a deaf community" (Higgins, 1980, 38).
12. Jacobs, 1974, 1980; Schowe, 1979.
13. Nash and Nash, 1981.

14. Rosen, 1986, 241.
15. Padden, 1980, 93.
16. Hairston and Smith, 1983, 81.
17. Higgins, 1980; Padden, 1980.
18. Rhoades, Browning, and Thorin (1986) and Cohen and Livenah (1986) regard self-help groups as relatively new phenomena. The latter authors note, "The Self-Help Movement began in the 1930s as a response to several factors that were making general counseling services unavailable or unresponsive to those who needed them" (8). They appear totally unaware of organizations like the National Association of the Deaf and the National Fraternal Society of the Deaf.
19. The quotation is from Jacobs (1974, 70). Kenner (1986) holds a contrary view about using the word "ghetto" to describe the Deaf community. In his essay in the *New York Times Book Review* on the book by Walker (1986) he writes, "No, 'ghetto' is not too strong a word. 'I didn't think mutes were allowed to have driver's licenses,' a man in a gas station grumbles as early as the ninth page [of Walker, 1986]. That is but one slight among thousands; later, a psychiatrist, a specialist in the Deaf, refers offhand to his patients as 'defectives.' And in New York major agencies serving the blind are found 'on the genteel upper East Side or on tree-lined streets in Chelsea,' but the Society for the Deaf 'in a place the police had forsaken.' "

2

DEAF CULTURE

Human infants enter the world defenseless. To survive, someone must feed them, give them shelter, and protect them from the elements. Compared to other animals, they mature slowly, and as they mature, they require instructions on appropriate behaviors that enable them to fit into society. How they are succored, what they are taught, and the means by which these activities are carried out, the specifications of needs and the acceptable ways of satisfying those needs—all of these add up to what we call culture. It is the accumulated wisdom of the group, providing the basis for its survival and the survival of its members. Culture encompasses institutions, folkways, mores, art, and language.

In defining Deaf people,[1] we said that they are not distinguished by their appearance, except when they communicate. The same might be said about their culture: at first it might seem not to differ sufficiently from that of the majority culture to justify a separate designation. Close scrutiny, however, reveals a unique culture, the American Deaf culture.[2] In what follows in this chapter, its distinctiveness will be emphasized. It is not, of course, completely different from the surrounding culture, but sufficiently so to warrant its designation as a separate culture.

BRIEF HISTORY OF THE UNITED STATES DEAF COMMUNITY[3]

"A people can face the future only when they have fully and imaginatively lived their past, and if the literature does not exist it has to be made—even a hundred years later," writes the Australian poet and novelist David Malouf.[4] He is writing about the Australian people, but his words apply equally well to the Deaf community.

When did the Deaf community start? Intimations exist that it preceded the establishment of the first permanent school for Deaf children, in Hartford, Connecticut, in 1817, but determining "firsts" with regard to the Deaf community is frustrated by the scarcity of written accounts of Deaf people in Colonial times and shortly thereafter. There may have been formal organizations of Deaf persons before 1817, but no information about them has surfaced. Since sign languages have no generally accepted written form, we lack records about Deaf people in that era. As for written material, whether written by Deaf or nondeaf authors, an absence of interest by the general community probably discouraged publication of any writings that might have been made about the Deaf community, if it existed at that time.

The school in Connecticut and those that soon followed in the other states became focal points around which Deaf people could organize; they served as the places where Deaf people met other Deaf people, often for the first time. By 1836, a mere nineteen years after the first school for Deaf children was established, some Deaf adults in New England formed the first recorded organization of Deaf people in the United States, the Hartford school's alumni association. Shortly thereafter, other alumni groups sprang up throughout the nation. Having easy communication with each other and sharing common interests, Deaf students usually developed strong bonds that persisted into adulthood. The relationship between the schools that Deaf students attended and the organizations they joined as adults continued throughout the nineteenth century, as state after state opened schools for Deaf students and the graduates of those schools set up structured means of continuing to meet socially.

In 1850, a national meeting of Deaf people took place in Hartford, Connecticut, to honor Laurent Clerc and Thomas Hopkins Gallaudet, founders of the Hartford Asylum. The death of Thomas Hopkins Gallaudet shortly thereafter stirred Deaf people to convene another national meeting, in 1853, in Montpelier, Vermont, for the purposes of raising money for a monument to him. Laurent Clerc was selected to head the Gallaudet Memorial Association. At that same meeting, a permanent organization of Deaf people was proposed, and a year later, in March 1854, in Henniker, New Hampshire, the New England Gallaudet Association came into being, the first regional organization of Deaf people in the United States. State

An Auspicious Occasion

Harlan Lane, writing in the guise of Laurent Clerc, describes a meeting of Deaf people.

In the fall of 1850 Thomas and I were honored by a large gathering of Deaf people at the asylum at which each of us was presented with a silver pitcher and tray, a gift of those throughout the United States who had been educated at our school. With two hundred visitors and the two hundred pupils enrolled, it was the largest Deaf convocation up to that time, ever, anywhere. The participants' general appearance was of intelligence and respectability, industrious habits, comfortable circumstances. The event was the forerunner of conventions and associations of the Deaf that have sprung up in the twenty years since—and the countless more sure to come. It was modeled on Berthier's Central Society of the Deaf, which counted members from diverse regions, schools, and professions and held annual banquets in honor of Epée, beginning in 1834. . . . Hundreds of visitors came from as far as Virginia for the ceremony.[5]

associations followed rapidly. Sixty-three years after the Hartford Asylum's founding, the New England Gallaudet Association of the Deaf celebrated its twenty-sixth anniversary, and New York, Wisconsin, and Indiana had state associations of the Deaf. By 1890, there were state associations in Arkansas, Iowa, Kentucky, Michigan, Minnesota, Pennsylvania, Texas, and Virginia. The first national organization, the National Association for the Deaf, came into being in 1880. In 1899, the Gallaudet Alumni Association became the second national organization of Deaf people.[6]

The organizational trend nearly carried to its ultimate conclusion—a separate territory with its own government for Deaf people alone. A fascinating account of the early years of the Deaf communities in the United States and Canada tells about Deaf Mutia, the plan for a state, all of whose members would be Deaf.[7] A similar idea for a Deaf township was proposed in France.[8] That the idea foundered in the face of practical arguments does not detract from the evidence it provides of the seriousness with which Deaf people regarded their alienation from the general community and of their devotion to the Deaf community.

By the beginning of the twentieth century, Deaf people had capped the pyramid of Deaf organizations with the National Fraternal Society of the Deaf, founded in 1901. Throughout the years from 1815 to 1880, the Deaf community grew with little active resistance. The centripetal factor—pleasure in joining with others like themselves—prevailed. With the 1880 Milan Manifesto[9] and the attacks on sign language that followed it, the centrifugal factor—alienation from the general community—became the dominant force shaping the Deaf community. Opponents of Deaf people not only fought against sign language, they opposed the very existence of the Deaf community. Eugenics arguments were marshaled against schools for Deaf children on the grounds that such educational arrangements led to marriages between Deaf persons, and these, in turn, would eventuate in "a race of Deaf people."[10]

Technology, without intentional malice, further alienated Deaf people from the general community. The invention of the telephone placed Deaf workers at a great disadvantage in the labor market. Radio, and later television, were largely inaccessible to Deaf audiences until well past mid-century. Even motion pictures, which Deaf people could enjoy as long as they were "the silents," moved out of reach with the advent of "the talkies."

The response of Deaf leaders to the progressive decline of the Deaf community's fortunes was typically to caution against too blatant reactions. Aggression turned inward in the form of attacks on deaf peddlers—persons who put Deaf people in a poor light by begging from the general public. In 1945, National Association of the Deaf's president, Byron B. Byrnes, appeared before a Senate committee considering an extra income tax exemption for deaf people, as it had already granted blind persons. Byrnes surprised the committee by testifying *against* the exemption. He argued that Deaf people did not want to be singled out; they preferred improved education that would enable them to compete equally, rather than to appear before the public as less capable than others. At the time, Deaf people had little difficulty finding work in defense plants at good wages. Also, the meaning of "being singled out" had connotations of the Nazis' systematic annihilation of "undesirables," news of which was just becoming known in the United States. The correctness of Byrnes's decision is a matter of debate even today. Contrast his approach to Congress with that of Edward Miner Gallaudet, in 1864, when he succeeded in getting it to approve of a college for deaf students, despite the pressures of the ongoing Civil War and the prejudices against any education for children who were born deaf.

Beginning with the civil rights movement in the 1950s, the Deaf community began to adopt a more aggressive stance. Rather than continue a passive course of accepting whatever befell them, Deaf leaders moved out of their previously low-profile strategy into a more openly demanding one. Led by NAD's reinvigorated leadership, the Deaf community made known its frustrations. The two decades beginning in 1960 produced many notable new ventures: National Technical Institute for the Deaf, Captioned Films for the Deaf, National Theatre of the Deaf, and National Captioning Institute, to name but a few. As the Deaf community nears the close of the twentieth century, it has reasons to be optimistic— but guardedly so. It has participated in many welcome changes, but many barriers remain up, and many disabling factors continue unchanged.

LANGUAGE[11]

Deaf culture's most distinct feature is American Sign Language (ASL). If one regards culture as providing the means of adapting to the environment, then sign language exemplifies the genius of Deaf people: it provides for rapid, efficient communication without the use of sound and with no special devices or bodily modifications.

Sign languages in each country are, with few exceptions, unique to that country, much as most spoken languages are unique to particular countries. Within countries, the national sign language has dialects. Thus, the varieties of sign languages parallel the varieties of spoken languages. It stands to reason, then, that as Deaf cultures vary from the general cultures in which they are embedded, so will they vary from Deaf cultures in other countries and, to a lesser extent, within a country.

In the Deaf community, ASL dominates as the preferred language. Its grammar and vocabulary are distinct from English. But only recently has ASL been accorded the status of an independent language. The "discovery" of ASL ranks among the great twentieth-century advances for Deaf people. Before 1960, ASL was considered merely a means of manually encoding English. The recognition that ASL had a grammar and vocabulary separate from English was due largely to the research of William Stokoe, then an English professor at Gallaudet College. Stokoe's doctorate in linguistics and his professional commitment to the education of Deaf students prepared him to study the communication by Deaf people from a scientific

The Bandwagon

The following excerpt is from an editorial in *Dee Cee Eyes* (15 June 1974), a publication of the District of Columbia Club for the Deaf.

Once upon a time sign language belonged to Deaf people. It was like the bunny that tried to associate with the antiseptic baby and the prophylactic pup in the sense that it wasn't carbolated and it wasn't sterilized but it belonged to us. And we loved it and cherished it despite all efforts of our all-knowing mentors to convince us that it was a crutch, a liability and a wall that prevented us from becoming "normal," whatever "normal" was supposed to mean. And for close to 100 years we have resisted all effort to make us into something we are not and never wanted to be in the first place. Then suddenly Sign Language was "IN." It is the thing today decorated with cherries and whipped cream and now we call it "total communication." Of course, we are glad that finally after all these years of frustration and dogged determination to keep what was ours we have achieved recognition. We have overcome to the extent that education finally has come to grips with the problem and agreed that we, the Deaf people, were right after all.

If that were the end of the matter, it would be great. And as in the fairy tales, we could all "live happily ever after." But that isn't all. With the acceptance of signs, everybody got on the bandwagon. So many people got on this bandwagon that there suddenly were too many and some had to be pushed off and guess who the "some" were? The Deaf, of course. Now everybody is in the business of improving sign language, everybody knows more about it than the people who have been using it for a hundred year and more. It was bad enough when we found that every Tom, Dick and Harry was inventing signs for words without regard for the Deaf community and for that matter without regard for each other, but it became the height of the ridiculous when they began to "improve" on signs that were already in existence. It seems high time that the Deaf community ought to get up in arms and suggest politely or not so politely, if you wish, that this is our language. We can and do appreciate help in speeding its growth, but leave what we have alone. We do not need or want improvements on the signs we already have, and if you want to add or help add to our vocabulary, fine. But where does the Deaf community fit into this project? Like it or not, you can invent every kind of sign imaginable but they are only as good as the people who use them. If we are to use them, then we must approve of them, and in some cases it seems we do, but in the long run it should be noted that we are not even asked, and by and by the worm will turn.

stance. He noted the regularities in Deaf students' mistakes when using English, and he had the acumen and objectivity to realize that their grammatical errors arose from differences between ASL and English. Each manages the major functions of languages—conveying time, person, number, direction of action, and so forth—in their own ways; each has a different syntax and grammar. Stokoe's paper on the structure of ASL and the dictionary that grew out of his research conquered the linguistic profession on behalf of ASL.[12] Soon thereafter, ASL moved from the status of a curiosity to a formal language in its own right.

Even before ASL was given scientific status as a separate language, Deaf people developed the same attachment to it that their normally hearing fellows had toward American English.[13] It might be strange to hear normally hearing people speaking about "our beloved language," but not so Deaf people. This is not to say that either group loves their language less, but English speakers do not need to express their attachment to their native language; it is taken for granted. Not so with Deaf people. ASL has been attacked. Serious efforts have been, and continue to be, made to eradicate it.[14] Rightly or wrongly, Deaf people see these assaults on sign as assaults on themselves, much as any minority language group regards efforts by the majority to impose its language on the minority as a personal and cultural assault. Wars have been fought over language dominance, and political struggles have focused on language choice.[15] Deaf people also resent the subtler efforts by well-meaning innovators to modify ASL until it becomes "English on the hand." Frederick C. Schreiber, when he was executive secretary of the National Association of the Deaf, spoke out against such approaches (see box, "The Bandwagon"). He welcomed the general community's acceptance of the legitimacy of sign language but not its tinkering with the language that Deaf people "love and cherish."

VARIETIES OF ASL

For simplicity, we talk about *a* Deaf community and *a* Deaf culture. But that view is challenged by other observers, as well as by the facts (see chapter 1). What about ASL? Is there a single sign language used by Deaf people in the United States? James Woodward[16] finds considerable differences in ASL across the United States. Edgar Shroyer and Susan Shroyer[17] report numerous variations in signs for the same concept. They asked thirty-eight native signers from twenty-five states how to express 160 different English words in sign. For 130 of the 160, their informants gave 3 or more different configurations. They showed 24 signs for "cheat," 17 for "Halloween," 16 for "hot dog," 12 for "light," 17 for "perfume," 22 for "picnic," 18 for "slippers," 10 for "soon," and so on (see Figure 1). No question of the regional variations. The question that does remain is how readily Deaf persons from one region can understand the signs from other regions. So far, the answer appears to be that Deaf people have little difficulty in adjusting to signs from other regions, just as speakers with one regional accent can be understood by listeners from other parts of the country. Within the same region, more than one sign may be used depending upon the nature of the occasion (i.e., formal or informal). The same is true of English; one uses slang at some times and not at others. Thus, it would appear that, as with English, we can speak of ASL in the singular without overlooking the variations within the language.

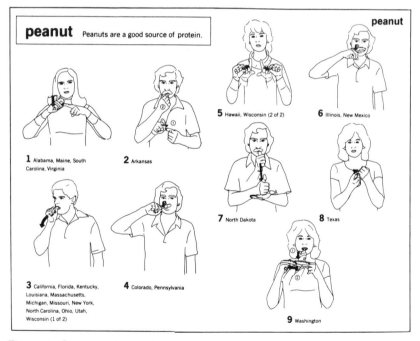

Figure 1. Sign variations of *peanut*.

NOTE: Reprinted by permission of the publisher, from Edgar H. Shroyer and Susan P. Shroyer, *Signs Across America* (Washington, DC: Gallaudet University Press, 1984), 170–171.

A SMALL QUESTION

Albert Pimentel tells this story about an incident that occurred when he was director of the Registry of Interpreters for the Deaf. He had just concluded a forty-five-minute speech on interpreting when an elderly Deaf man approached the podium, waited politely for others to conclude their interchanges, and then signed to Pimentel:

"I very much enjoyed your speech. It was very good, and I learned a lot. But I was puzzled by one sign you used."

Al was pleased by the man's flattering remarks and, eager to help, he asked, "Which sign was that?"

The man quickly replied by making the sign for *interpreting*!

SPEECH AND SIGN

The majority culture emphasizes spoken communication. Speaking is a prerequisite to social participation in the general society. What is more, members of the majority culture judge others by their speech and language. The Irish playwright George Bernard Shaw based his most famous play, *Pygmalion,* on this thesis (see "On the Kerb"). The fact that our society looks down on those who speak poorly or use substandard English applies with equal force to those who do not speak at all. This prejudice has economic consequences, too. Being "a good talker" gives one a competitive edge in the marketplace, as well as in social gatherings.

It should not be concluded from the foregoing that all Deaf people do not speak. To the contrary, many do. But being forced to depend upon minimal auditory cues and less sensitive kinesthetic feedback to monitor their speech, Deaf talkers often sound odd. One attractive, early deafened woman who has worked very hard to develop her speech remarks, "I am tired of being asked by strangers I meet, 'What country are you from?' " They assume that her imperfect speech must result from foreign birth, though she was born in Virginia; deafness does not occur to most people as a cause of poor speech.

Deaf people are further betrayed by the phonetic inconsistency of English orthography, so they often pronounce words as they are

ON THE KERB

Professor Henry Higgins, George Bernard Shaw's fictional linguist in *Pygmalion*, act 1, on seeing Eliza Doolittle, the Cockney flower seller, pontificates to his companion as follows.

You see this creature with her kerbstone English: the English that will keep her in the gutter to the end of her days. Well, sir, in three months I could pass that girl off as a duchess at an ambassador's garden party. I could even get her a place as a lady's maid or a shop assistant, which requires better English.

written. A native American speaker sees "tow" and pronounces it to rhyme with "go," but pronounces "cow" to rhyme with "ow." English pronunciation makes no distinction between "bear" and "bare" but does between "dear" and "dare." Despite different spellings, "pique," "peak," and "peek" have identical pronunciations. Confusing? Yes, if one does not constantly hear the accepted pronunciations in association with the printed forms. What are the rules? None cover the innumerable exceptions. G. B. Shaw jokingly suggested that the correct spelling of "fish" should be "ghoti": "gh" as in "tough," "o" as in "women," and "ti" as in "relation."

A critical factor in determining whether or not a deaf child will develop usable speech is age at onset. Those children born deaf or deafened before speech has emerged (the prelingually deaf group) will seldom have intelligible speech. The later people are deafened, the more likely they will develop and retain their speech. How is Deaf speech received in the Deaf community? A linguist who was born deaf explains that

there is a general dissociation from speech in the Deaf culture. Some Deaf people may choose to use speech in community activities that involve non-Deaf people, such as mixed parties, parent education programs, or while representing the community in some larger public function. But on the cultural level, speaking is not considered appropriate behavior. Children who are brought up in Deaf culture are often trained to limit their mouth movement to only those movements that are a part of their language. Exaggerated speaking behavior is thought of as "undignified" and sometimes can be interpreted as making fun of other Deaf people.[18]

Educators who adhere to the "simultaneous method" practice speaking and signing at the same time. It can be done relatively easily, provided that Manual English is used, rather than ASL, because the latter has a different sentence structure. Trying to speak in English and sign in ASL is a little like patting the head while rubbing the belly but much more difficult. The adherents of the simultaneous method also require Deaf children to speak as they sign. Those with poor voices learn to mouth an approximation of what they are signing. The practice of signing and speaking, or mock-speaking, arouses negative emotions among many in the Deaf community, representing as it does another imposition of an insensitive general society.

Deaf people in conversations with nondeaf people usually tense up. Speaking is difficult when you cannot monitor your own voice and when you have only the feeblest of cues to enable you to know how you sound to others. As one Deaf person has put it, "For me, speaking is like walking about in public naked." There are Deaf people who regard a Deaf person who has usable speech and who uses it prominently as subversive, as showing off. Marlee Matlin signed her acceptance of the Academy Award for Best Actress of 1987. As the presenter of an award in 1988, she chose to speak. The reactions in the Deaf community were mixed—some cheered her

To Speak or Not to Speak

The attitude of Deaf people toward speech reflects another aspect of alienation. A linguist who was born deaf stated the Deaf community's attitude succinctly.

Mouthing and the use of speech represent many things to Deaf people. Since speech has traditionally been forced on Deaf people as a substitute for their language, it has come to represent confinement and denial of the most fundamental need of Deaf people: to communicate deeply and comfortably in their own language. Deaf people often distrust speech communication for this reason. In speaking, the Deaf person feels she will always be at a disadvantage and can never become fully equal to hearing people who, from the viewpoint of the Deaf person, are always the more accurate models of speaking.[19]

for showing what a Deaf person can do, and some chastised her for deserting her less vocally articulate fellows. Regardless of the emotion directed at Marlee Matlin, their printed remarks revealed the depth of feelings that surrounds speaking, a function that the majority culture takes for granted.

An Open Letter

The following letter was addressed to Marlee Matlin by Don Brown, director of Social Services for the Hearing Impaired, Flint, Michigan, in the agency's March 1988 newsletter, *Vibrations*.

This past month we saw the drama of *Children of a Lesser God* played out again at Gallaudet University. This time your part in the movie was played by a cast of thousands, mostly students. And, like the movie, America watched with fascination. Both the movie and Gallaudet have used language as a vehicle for conflict. It is not something new to deafness. *Children of a Lesser God* and Gallaudet University have wrapped it in a cultural package and placed it on America's conscience.

In America today there exists a form of communications apartheid directed at deaf people who use American Sign Language as their method of communications. It is obvious in education. It was obvious at Gallaudet. . . .

Your Oscar performance in the movie and the student victory at Gallaudet University must be metaphors for equality. Deafness contains new names now that go alongside of Clerc. They signal a new era, just as he did long ago. It is alive with the energy and enthusiasm of youth and inquiring minds that dare to take exception. It is based on deafness with dignity. It has stirred our passion for what is right. As you take the envelope to announce a winner during the Academy Awards remember your heritage. Let "your body, face, and hands shape the miracle of recognition."* Let it recognize the memory of those gone before you with dignity. Let it recognize those students who will define deafness not by default, but by direct participation. To give voice to your script dulls the Oscar-shine and diminishes the success of these students. To sign your script allows Alice to grow up.*

*References are to the poem published alongside the letter, "Grow Up Alice," urging Alice to lose her inhibitions and use ASL.

PARALINGUISTICS

Communication involves far more than language. It can occur without language. A shrug of the shoulders, a smile, an abrupt gesture with one finger, orienting one's body toward or away from another person—these unspoken messages can be understood throughout a culture and, sometimes, across cultures. Particular greetings—the Asian bow, American "high fives," the European buss on both cheeks—tend to be culture-specific, and their use in other settings might provoke unexpected responses. Just so, in the Deaf community, nonverbal behaviors have meanings that are different from the meanings assigned by the general community. To draw upon just one behavioral category, eye movements, the direction of gaze in ASL serves the function of pronouns in English. Where it is acceptable to glance away from normally hearing speakers while they are speaking, doing so while a Deaf person is signing interrupts the conversation. Indeed, the general community regards intensely looking at another person as rude, whereas it is essential in the Deaf community. Dependence on vision alters the relations between two people engaged in a conversation. Deaf people in conversation keep a greater space between themselves, because they need to observe more than the head of the person speaking, since important signs may involve areas around the beltline and occasionally the thighs.

The majority culture in the United States considers gesturing and overly expressive facial expressions to be vulgar. Quite the opposite is true in Deaf culture—and for very good reasons. The "gestures," of course, are frequently signs in ASL. The facial expressions provide much additional information, just as emphases in speech do. A "deadpan" signer is the equivalent of a monotonic speaker. Even more, some facial expressions have the equivalent functions of adverbs and adjectives in English; they modify the meaning conveyed by the manual signs. Thus, in their bodily positions, their use of their hands, their facial expressions, and many other detectable and decipherable physical features, signers differ from speakers. The known paralinguistic features appropriate to signers and not speakers, and vice versa, are already large, and they will likely grow as linguists continue their investigations.

BILINGUALISM

Living, as they do, surrounded by speakers of English, Deaf community members almost always learn at least some of the second language. It will be the basis of their instruction in school, even though it may be delivered manually. There are no books printed in ASL; most hearing instructors lack ASL fluency; as a language independent of English, it will rarely be taught to Deaf children. They will be expected to learn the language informally through usage; it is passed from child to child, with only occasional interaction during the formative years with Deaf adults—hardly an efficient means of maintaining linguistic purity. Accordingly, ASL suffers from considerably more regionalism and a great deal more social variability in its use than does English, which has gained homogenization from radio and television, as well as from the availability of print forms.

A growing movement within the Deaf community favors bilingualism in recognition of the facts. Deaf people need two languages, ASL for their interactions with other Deaf people and English for interactions with the larger society. Hence, it is argued, they should strive for competence in both languages. This situation

ASL First, English Second

The author of the following revelation holds a doctorate in sociolinguistics.

I had a tremendous conflict in my self-concept—my perceptions of myself were positive within the community of Deaf persons, but negative within the hearing community. Although I was born Deaf to Deaf parents, and although I grew up learning ASL as my native language, it took me many years to recognize exactly how this early language experience affected my identity as a person. All my life, I was not aware that American Sign Language was my first language and English my second language. I always felt inferior when I wanted to communicate with hearing people with my English, but I noticed that I felt comfortable communicating with Deaf people. . . . once I learned that ASL is my native language, I developed a strong sense of identity as a Deaf person and a more positive self-image. Once I accepted ASL as my native language, I became eager to improve my English because I was then able to accept hearing people as equals. i found myself enjoying teaching hearing people ASL as their second language. And I like having hearing people teach me English as a second language.[20]

is not unique, and it is workable. Indeed, the United States, unlike the older European countries, does little to promote second-language competency in its schools. Most of the technologically advanced countries of the world insist that children acquire at least one other language. All that the proponents of bilingualism urge for the Deaf community is that Deaf children study ASL along with English. One counterargument—that learning one language conflicts with learning another—has been discredited to the bilingualists' satisfaction.

A more emotional issue that has also failed to pass objective scrutiny is that if Deaf children learn to sign they will not learn to speak. The confusion between speech and language muddles the issues. Nonetheless, there is no scientifically acceptable evidence that signing and speaking cannot coexist. Thus, two arguments against bilingualism (that learning one language interferes with learning another, and that signing inhibits speaking) lack scientific support.

CENTRALITY OF ASL IN DEAF CULTURE

Is a favorable attitude toward ASL held by all deaf people? No, though deaf people who denigrate it are exceptions. Gilbert Eastman, a professor of drama and a playwright, recounts in his memoir an early conversation between himself and another Deaf instructor at Gallaudet College (see "Stubborn"). Eastman's colleague did not hold ASL in high regard, though he unconsciously used it; he parroted majority attitudes, identifying himself with the "elite," as he perceived normally hearing people. Eastman, to the contrary, recognized that ASL is another language and that calling it ungrammatical because it deviates from English was as silly as calling French incorrect for placing adjectives after nouns and German wrong for putting verbs at the ends of complex sentences. Such arguments between educated Deaf people should diminish now that the independence of ASL from English has been established. Eastman's point, however, is that even those Deaf people who ostensibly do not have high regard for ASL typically use it.

For many members of the Deaf community, they and ASL are indistinguishable. Their self-concept is based on being Deaf, and being Deaf, to them, means using ASL. Their feelings about ASL comfort them, just as using ASL in communication with other Deaf

STUBBORN

Gilbert Eastman, a Deaf Gallaudet College professor, recounts
a conversation with a Deaf colleague—all, of course, taking
place in sign language (Eastman, 1980).

FRIEND: Listen to me carefully. I'll explain to you the dif-
            ference between the Sign Language we are us-
            ing and the Sign Language others are using.
EASTMAN: I know Sign Language.
FRIEND: You don't understand this.
EASTMAN: Neither do you.
FRIEND: Wait a minute. Let me show you. What we use
            is like this: *"Hey, Gil . . . I would like to take you
            out for a drink . . . How about it?"* See, I use a
            sign for each word. That is one Sign Language.
            Or better to say, that is English.
EASTMAN: Yeah, I know that.
FRIEND: Another Sign Language . . . I don't like to
            use . . . is like this, "Me think car red expen-
            sive." That is not English.
EASTMAN: But it's Sign Language . . . ASL.
FRIEND: No, no it's not. It is a low language.
EASTMAN: It is not a low language.
FRIEND: Damn! You not understand. Stubborn always
            you.
EASTMAN: See! You're using ASL.
FRIEND: I never use ASL.
EASTMAN   Good grief!

people is made more comfortable by ASL. Barbara Kannapell expresses these sentiments from the stance of a Deaf professional:

> What gives me special insight as a sociolinguist is the fact I was
> born into, and grew up as a member of the community of Deaf
> people. So I know that a critical factor in understanding ASL is
> understanding that ASL is very much a part of a Deaf person. If
> you want to change ASL, or take ASL away from the person, you
> are trying to take his or her identity away. I believe "my language
> is me." To reject a language is to reject the person herself or him-

self. Thus, to reject ASL is to reject the Deaf person. Remember ASL is a personal creation of Deaf persons as a group. Perhaps those hearing or Deaf people who cannot deal with ASL are really saying they cannot deal with or accept the Deaf person.[21]

This strong feeling about ASL has probably existed among Deaf people for a very long time. The NAD's establishment, in part, arose from the desire of Deaf people to defend sign language. Their allegiance to ASL did not become overt until after 1960, as it became clear that ASL was a true language, not a degraded form of English. Since that time, more and more Deaf people have become outspoken proponents of *their* language. Once ASL was recognized as a legitimate language, the Deaf community shifted from being a disabled community to being a linguistic community. Deaf people did not talk with their hands because they could not otherwise communicate, they signed to convey a language, ASL.

HEAVEN CAN WAIT

A deaf woman writes,

The difference between a deaf and hearing point of view became clear to me recently at a funeral of a deaf man. During the eulogy, the preacher remarked that this man was now in Heaven with his Lord and he was now "communicating with his hands in his pockets." He no longer needs sign, the preacher continued. He can now speak. He can now hear. He is now healed. The preacher's bias was caught by an astute deaf woman who wondered why he assumed that deaf people go to Heaven and learn speech but not that hearing people go to Heaven and learn sign. "Does he think that when French people die, they go to Heaven and learn English?" she asked, annoyed also by his assumption that deaf people are defective and that when they die they are "healed" and become hearing people. This deaf woman, who had been a close friend of the deceased man, asked to say a few words at the grave site. Speaking through an interpreter, she remarked that this man had signed all his life and that signing was his preferred mode of communication. She even suspected he was already at work with Laurent Clerc developing yet another kind of sign, Heaven Sign Language (HSL).[22]

TELECOMMUNICATIONS[23]

Many of the technological advances for the majority in our society
have penalized Deaf people. This irony emerges most clearly in
telecommunications. The invention of the telephone made it difficult for Deaf people to compete in the labor market. Radio became
an important means of broadcasting information, whether commercial, political, governmental, or whatever, further cutting off Deaf
people from the larger society surrounding them. Television did little to improve the situation, though it embraced the technology that
could have (and to some extent now does) include Deaf people.
Talking pictures were a blow to the entertainment and education of
Deaf people; they could enjoy the "silents" on a par with the rest of
the audience. But Deaf people and their supporters have not passively accepted the status quo. They have taken steps to reduce the
handicap the new technologies have imposed.

A pattern has emerged in this century. First, an advance in
communications technology enters the market, an advance that
puts Deaf people at a disadvantage. For a period of time, nothing is
done to redress the social injury. Then moves are made to overcome
the handicap imposed by the technology, sometimes initiated by
Deaf people and sometimes by those interested in their welfare. In
time, the modifications help Deaf people catch up with the majority, though not completely.

TELEPHONE

The telephone, as originally conceived, depends upon the user's
speech and hearing, hence it disables Deaf people. Its ubiquity imposes an economic burden. Because so much commercial activity
occurs via telephoned messages, Deaf people are denied many employment opportunities and much market information that is easily
obtained by calling. Deaf people depend on others, in order to telephone. A hearing intermediary makes the contact and interprets
the incoming message. The intermediary may also voice the Deaf
person's response, if the Deaf person prefers not to speak. The arrangement is awkward, but it does provide access, especially for
Deaf professionals and executives who can afford to employ secre-
taries who double as telephone interpreters.

In 1964, a Deaf engineer, the late Robert Weitbrecht, invented a
system that enables Deaf people to use existing telephone lines. The

Deaf person types a message into an electronic unit that interfaces the telephone via a modem that transmits the auditorily encoded information to the receiving end, where a similar machine decodes the auditory signals and displays them visually or prints them on paper. The generic term for the many versions of this system is "telecommunication device for the deaf" or TDD. A TDD overcomes the telephonic barrier, but only when both the sender and the receiver have TDDs.

With the technical difficulties solved, Deaf people still do not make as extensive use of the telephone as their normally hearing peers. Why? For one reason, because using a TDD requires English, and most Deaf people have painful attitudes toward English, having been told again and again in school that their usage is incorrect. The TDD demands that they put their English out where everyone can see it! So many Deaf people avoid using a TDD, preferring, instead, to drive over to see a friend rather than telephoning. It is an aspect of Deaf culture that is likely to change over the coming years as more and more Deaf children become accustomed to using TDDs at an early age. Like their normally hearing peers, they will probably become telephone-TDD addicts.

For another reason, TDDs are far more expensive than telephones, costing hundreds of dollars to purchase. Some states have adopted legislation requiring their telephone companies to provide TDDs on the same basis as telephones are provided; i.e., to make them available on a per-month rental. California's legislature mandated the provision of TDDs without charge to deaf persons. Other states have followed with their own variations. However, the availability of rental TDDs is not nationwide.

Another limiting factor in the use of the TDD is that two are required, one at each end of the telephone line. Deaf people cannot call a place—store, utility company, person, airline, or whatever—unless that place has a TDD to receive and respond to the call. While the number of TDDs operated by businesses, police stations, fire companies, and others whom Deaf people may wish to contact are increasing, the probabilities are still small that a Deaf person's TDD call can be handled properly. One enterprising solution is the relay service: Deaf people call a central number by TDD; the central operator receives the Deaf person's message on the TDD, relays the call by voice, and repeats the spoken message to the Deaf caller on the TDD. It's a bit slow and awkward, but Deaf people welcome relay services because they open the entire voice network to Deaf people. Telecommunications for the Deaf, Inc. (TDI) has lobbied for increased and improved relay services throughout the United States. TDI cites many government-financed toll-free numbers—few of which provide access by TDD. Similarly, many companies provide an 800-series long-distance number for inquiries and complaints, and again none of them is accessible to Deaf TDD users.

In a letter to the Federal Communications Commission, a Deaf woman recited her terrifying experiences in attempting to contact a hospital to get assistance for her ailing husband. She was unable to do so in time, and he died. She wrote, "As a deaf, gainfully employed U.S. citizen and taxpayer, I am discriminated against and denied my legal and inherent right to communicate by extremely limited and ill-defined (and in many areas nonexistent) TDD relay services."[24]

RADIO

Can Deaf people use radio? As it is presently configured, no. Radio use depends upon the transmission of audible signals that are meaningless to those who are deaf. But a project conducted in Philadelphia between 1975 and 1979 demonstrated the use of a subcarrier radio frequency that is inaudible on the regular frequencies and does not interfere with their clear reception. This signal drives a TDD as if the signals were sent over a telephone line. The idea has proved technically feasible. This method of transmission frees the TDD from the telephone lines, enabling Deaf people to have TDDs in their cars, as those who can hear use cellular telephones and citizen-band radios. Is the system inexpensive? Yes, the signal that drives the TDD is "piggybacked" onto an existing radio signal. Adding the energy to activate the TDD in no way interferes with the regular broadcast, since only those who have special receivers can detect it. What would be broadcast? In Philadelphia, news and weather programs and special features about matters of health made up most of the material. However, there are no limits to the content that might be sent, and two-way transmission is possible, though it would require additional equipment. The system can be activated anywhere in the United States. So far, it remains dormant. Whether at some time the Deaf community will seek its rejuvenation is conjectural. Perhaps that movement must await some disenchantment with television viewing that has only recently become accessible to Deaf people.

THINGS TO COME

Philip Bellefleur, an educational administrator, predicts:

Often I am asked, "What is the future of telecommunications for the Deaf?" A better question would be, "What will its impact be on the growth of the Deaf community?" In answer to the first question, humanity's progress in technology is in direct proportion to the tools at its disposal. When there was only a hammer, people could only pound on things; when the knife was developed they began to cut; and when the telephone was invented, they began to communicate by wire over long distances. The future of telecommunications, in order of probable appearance: . . . [Unimpressive list follows.]

Obviously, the future holds concepts such as a "time operator," "weather operator," "dial-a-prayer," or "dial-a-poem," and other bourgeois services available to most people now. But the future of telecommunications for the Deaf will be more than machines and more than dial-a-prayer services. The TTY [TDD] will have a total impact on the growth of a community that has been unparalleled since the invention of the hearing aid at the turn of the century. A network of communication will develop that brings together a mini-society within the larger one and facilitates an exchange of information between the members of both groups. It will motivate Deaf students and stimulate achievement—but most of all, it will bring Deaf and hearing persons closer together.[25]

TELEVISION

For Deaf people who had looked forward to it with pleasant anticipation, television's actuality proved to be a disappointment. One Deaf leader describes it as "radio with a few pictures," emphasizing the fact that the speaker is often not shown. The frequent use of reaction shots, in which the camera moves away from the speaker to the person being addressed, makes speechreading impossible. Television programs are designed as mixed-media presentations that depend upon seeing and hearing. Seeing alone is seldom adequate for appreciating a television program. From the introduction of television until 1970, that was the situation.

One solution to Deaf viewers' frustrations arose in a round-about manner.[26] When the National Bureau of Standards proposed the use of the vertical blanking interval, line 21, to carry information, such as weather reports and time signals, the idea occurred that line 21 could also be used to broadcast captions. The federal government supported the research that led to the present system of captioning and then appropriated funds to activate it. The principal organization involved is the National Captioning Institute (NCI). NCI is a private, nonprofit organization whose owners are not deaf. It has received multimillion-dollar support from the federal government, as well as fees from the networks and from advertisers, who pay to have their programs captioned. NCI does have an advisory board of members of the Deaf community and it employs a number of Deaf people in such roles as public relations and research; however, its control rests outside the Deaf community.

A counterapproach to captioning is to provide manual interpreting of the spoken dialogue. Before captioning became widely available, some local television stations employed signers to interpret the news as it was read. Many religious broadcasts include signed interpretations ("Christopher Closeups" was the first national program to do so, beginning in 1971). A brief vogue for programs of instruction in sign language in the 1960s and 1970s was led by New York University's award-winning "Speaking with Your Hands," whose twelve lessons played on NBC stations for a dozen years after their initial broadcast. It has become increasingly popular for candidates for office to have their speeches interpreted. In the more successful uses of interpreters, the interpreter's image is inserted in a corner of the screen and is visible throughout the broadcast, regardless of what the other cameras may be focusing on.

Occasional programs incorporate signs in the production. The National Theatre of the Deaf has been telecast nationally on several occasions. The voice-over interpretation is only necessary for those who do not understand sign. *Love Is Never Silent*, a made-for-television movie about a Deaf couple and their hearing children, featured Deaf actors playing Deaf people. As noted below in the discussion of motion pictures, having Deaf actors fulfill such assignments was a rare event. True, some programming has featured Deaf performers (e.g., Bernard Bragg's long-running series, "The Quiet Man," on San Francisco's public television station, KQED, and Linda Bove's regular appearances on "Sesame Street"), but often when scripts of a television play have called for a Deaf person, the role has been given to a hearing person. Furthermore, the audiences for these programs are not Deaf people, but general viewers.

Interpreting broadcasts gives Deaf people access to general programming, but Deaf people would also like programs that concern their affairs directly. Variety shows, like "Silent Perspectives" and "Rainbow's End," have enjoyed popularity, some for years. "Deaf Mosaic," seen largely in the Washington, D.C., area, won Emmy awards for high-quality programming in both 1987 and 1988. These programs are designed for Deaf audiences and presented entirely in sign. Silent Network Satellite Service (SNSS), which began in 1982, has found its place on cable television. With its potentially vast capacity, cable can accommodate special interests in a manner that the limited broadcasting capacity cannot. SNSS has taken advantage of the two technologies—cable and satellite—and developed educational and entertainment programming aimed at Deaf people and those interested in them, such as, "Aerobisign," "It's Music to Your Eyes," and "Say It with Sign." This program array demonstrates the feasibility of targeting a segment of mass media specifically for Deaf people.[27]

MOTION PICTURES

"The silent movies created the largest mass audience for public entertainment in the nation's history, and for a brief time the Deaf community participated fully in the mainstream of this popular cultural form."[28] Not only could Deaf people enjoy silent movies on a par with the hearing audience (with the exception of the piano accompaniment), but Deaf actors had an equal opportunity to earn a livelihood by appearing in them. After all, the audience could not distinguish hearing from Deaf actors, nor did the actors have to react to spoken cues. The result was that a number of Deaf actors did have feature roles in silent movies. The public remained unaware of the deafness of Granville Redmond, Tommy Albert, David Marvel, and Albert Ballin. Helen Keller played herself as a young adult in the film about her life, *Deliverance*. Not only were her deafness and blindness obvious, but also she became the first, and probably the only, deaf-blind actress ever to appear in films.

The participation of Deaf people in the movie industry ended with the addition of sound to the movies. For the half century from the introduction of voice to film until 1987, no Deaf actors succeeded in motion pictures. The few times a character was supposed to be deaf in a movie the part was played by a normally hearing person (e.g., Jane Wyman played the deaf girl in *Johnny Belinda*.) Then, in 1987, Marlee Matlin won the Oscar as best actress for her leading role in *Children of a Lesser God*. Matlin has several other movies scheduled, so it is possible that her triumph will not be a rare exception. As with television, motion pictures may now open more opportunities for qualified Deaf actors.

Once sound took over the movies, many Deaf people became devotees of foreign-language films because they were captioned. Realizing the situation, Congress, in 1958, created Captioned Films for the Deaf (CFD). CFD captions entertainment and educational films under licensing agreements that promise the filmmakers that only Deaf people will view the captioned versions. The selections of adult entertainment films are made under contract with the National Association of the Deaf. The captioned films are distributed without charge to certified groups of Deaf people and to schools. Their showings become social occasions, as well as moviegoing events, the screening rooms providing a place to meet their friends. With the advent of captioned television and the increasing number of captioned videotapes, attendance at showings of captioned films has dropped, as was true for general moviegoing when television first became widely available.

THEATER

Deaf people created their own theater long before there were extensive written records. How long ago is indeterminate, since their homemade productions were not reviewed in the press and the plays themselves were given in sign language that did not have a written form. Prior to 1860, only occasional notes in publications of Deaf organizations would indicate that such and such a production had taken place. Once Gallaudet College came into being, in 1864, the situation changed. Almost from the beginning, the college students produced theatricals. Some were written by the students— fraternity skits and such—and others were signed adaptations of classics or of current theater: Shakespeare, Euripedes, and even Gilbert and Sullivan operettas.

By 1942, Gallaudet theatricals were of such a high level that Howard Lindsay and Russel Crouse, producers of the long-running

Broadway hit *Arsenic and Old Lace,* who happened to be in Washington on other business, came to the college to see the students' version of their play. Lindsay and Crouse were so impressed by the quality of the student production that they invited the entire cast to come to New York for one night and replace the Broadway company. It did and the reviews from the hard-bitten New York critics uniformly praised its work (see "The Press Sees Signs"). Not too long after, Gallaudet College established the first department of drama in higher education that was devoted to Deaf theater.

In 1966, David Hays and the Eugene O'Neill Foundation obtained a grant from the federal government to establish the National Theatre of the Deaf (NTD). Hays recruited Deaf actors, like Bernard Bragg, and normally hearing actors who knew sign, like Louis Fant, and sent them on tours that have nearly circled the globe over a two-decade span of time. NTD, like its Gallaudet College fore-

THE PRESS SEES SIGNS

In 1942, student actors from Gallaudet College gave one performance on Broadway of *Arsenic and Old Lace.* The tough New York critics were unstinting in their praise for the signed performance.

If one has never seen a performance in signs—which was your reporter's case—one thing will surprise him. Somehow the actor's hands convey differences of intonation. There are the gentle, conciliatory phrases of Miss Martha and Miss Abby. There are the staccato utterances of their brother Teddy, who imagines himself to be Teddy Roosevelt. When his fingers say, "Delighted," the word is bursting with energy. When he rushes up the stairs, one hand waving the signal "Charge," in memory of San Juan Hill, the gesture seems to shout, though there isn't a sound. When Jonathan Brewster, the arch-villain, makes his threats, his fingers are deliberate and menacing. (Helen Beebe, *The Herald Tribune*)

While the greater part of the audience was composed of Deaf people trained in the difficult art of reading sign language, many were present who were not Deaf. These persons of normal hearing were astounded at the lucidity of the play as presented and scarcely needed the aid of a reader who spoke the lines in a monotone while the Deaf actors made their speedy signs. (Burns Mantle, *The New York Times*)

runner, produces classics translated into sign, as well as plays written in sign. While Deaf actors sign, the script is read over
loudspeakers so the persons in the audience who do not know sign
can follow the play. Through its wide-ranging efforts, general audiences have become acquainted not only with sign language but also
with attractive, capable Deaf performers.

The Deaf community has been of two minds about NTD. The
normally hearing director, David Hays, sees NTD's function as
changing the attitudes of the general community toward Deaf people. He believes that NTD should demonstrate the capabilities of
Deaf actors and open places for them in the theatrical world, as well
as generally improving the employability of Deaf people. In those
ways, NTD has had success, with many of its alumni having had
impressive careers on television and Broadway. Phyllis Frelich won
a Tony award, in 1981, for her role in *Children of a Lesser God*. Linda
Bove has appeared regularly on "Sesame Street," and Ed Water-
street and Phyllis Frelich played the leads in the television movie
Love Is Never Silent. Other NTD cast members have gone on to television and local theater careers and to positions as drama teachers
and therapists in schools.

Others in the Deaf community want a national theater that
caters to their tastes, that aims to please them rather than general
audiences. They regard NTD as exploiting them, using their disability to raise funds for purposes not of their liking. In the meantime,
theater's popularity has not been diminished by captioned television. Gallaudet University's drama department has featured recently plays written by its Deaf director, Gilbert Eastman. His *Sign
Me Alice* and *Laurent Clerc* have had considerable popular and critical approval. Other Deaf playwrights have gained recognition—
Shanny Mow and Dorothy Miles, to name two—and their plays are
being seen by Deaf audiences. As more Deaf local and regional theatrical companies, like the Fairmount Theatre of the Deaf in Ohio,
are formed, the pressures on NTD to entertain Deaf people diminish, and Deaf people are more appreciative of its value to the Deaf
community.

What about opera? Interpreters' horizons have been broadened
recently by the New York City Opera. Productions of *Susannah*, *The
Merry Widow*, *Cunning Little Vixen*, *Sweeney Todd*, and *La Fanciulla del
West* were simultaneously interpreted in sign. At least two interpreters worked each performance, one doing the female and one
the male voices. They required extensive rehearsal to coordinate
their signs with the music, making the transitions from one sign to

another blend smoothly. The response from Deaf people has been excellent, with the eighty seats reserved for them often oversubscribed. The normally hearing audiences have not complained; in fact, many feel that the interpreters and the Deaf members of the audience enhanced the productions. In addition, New York City Opera now features captions for some of its performances. The captions are displayed on the proscenium, and they have found favor among both hearing and Deaf audiences, the former appreciating them when the operas are in a foreign language. These additions to the opera have demonstrated what can be done to open the resources of the general community to the Deaf community.

LITERATURE[29]

Because sign language has no widely accepted written form, the Deaf community's written records are in English. Each of the organizations of Deaf people publish some kind of periodical, with monthly newsletters being the most often chosen as the vehicle for circulating information about their members and opinions about issues of particular importance to Deaf people. The periodical literature has helped Deaf people to define their culture. The major associations of Deaf people have depended upon their publications to maintain contact with their constituents. As a result, these journals have assumed substantial influence in Deaf people's social and political affairs. They not only record the events of interest to the community, they also provide the forum for structuring future events. For example, the debate that led to reshaping the National Association of the Deaf's administration appeared in its periodical, *The Deaf American*, laying the groundwork for the reorganization that began in 1956, in Fulton, Missouri. Like NFSD's *The Frat*, *The Deaf American* is edited and largely written by Deaf people. The content reflects the breadth of the Deaf community, ranging from philosophical essays and scientific reports to news of beauty contests, social gatherings, and sporting events. Like similar periodicals of general circulation, periodicals in the Deaf community vary from gossipy to profound, from bare announcements to thoughtful articles. It is no wonder that there are presently over five hundred periodicals related to deafness being published today.

Residential schools' alumni usually circulate a periodical that is intently read by Deaf people to stay abreast of their alma maters and their former classmates. Most schools print a school newspaper or magazine, with the additional purposes of giving their students incentives to improve their English-language skills and tradeworthy experience. The first such paper was the North Carolina Institution for the Deaf and Blind's *The Deaf Mute*, in 1849. Similar publications soon appeared at other schools. Their periodicals fell into the habit of borrowing from each other, reprinting essays that had earlier appeared in another school's journal. At meetings of the Convention of American Instructors of the Deaf, the editors met in a loosely defined organization called "The Little Paper Family." One historian has characterized it as

> more than an artifact of the Deaf community. It was an institution that helped Deaf Americans forge and maintain their identity; it provided a training ground for leaders; and it led to employment for Deaf people. Today, it provides an important source of historical information.[30]

The Deaf community's literature is not limited to organization's periodicals. *The Silent News* is a privately published journal that circulates nationwide to three thousand subscribers in the Deaf community. Its publisher occupies a position in a distinguished line of Deaf publishers in the United States, dating back to Levi Backus, who, in 1837, is credited with being the first Deaf editor of a general-circulation newspaper, and Henry C. Rider, founder, in 1870, of the *Deaf-Mute's Journal*, the first weekly paper targeted for Deaf readers.

Several publishers specialize in books about deafness and Deaf people. Notable among these are Gallaudet University Press, founded in 1980. In 1966, the National Association of the Deaf began to market books about deafness through a mail-order catalogue. NAD later published materials such as Maxine Boatner's *A Dictionary of Idioms for the Deaf* and children's books in sign that other publishers would not attempt. A third major supplier of books on deafness is TJ Publishers, a commercial concern owned by Terrence J. O'Rourke, a former member of the NAD staff and a Gallaudet graduate. The Alexander Graham Bell Association for the Deaf publishes books on deafness that support its philosophy (support of oralism and opposition to sign language), so its publications are generally uncongenial to the Deaf community's readers. Deaf people have written poetry, novels, biographies, textbooks, and been war correspondents and playwrights. Among those writing today are poets Rex Lowman and Kathleen Schreiber, playwrights Gilbert Eastman, Dorothy Miles, Shanny Mow, and Bernard Bragg and Eugene Bergman, and novelist Douglas Bullard.[31]

As would be expected in the absence of a written form of ASL, Deaf culture has a tradition of passing stories from hand to hand. Visual poetry—playing with signs rather than words—is gaining appreciation not only by Deaf but also by normally hearing people. Deaf people now look upon signed poems with pride, whereas they once regarded them as something vaguely off-color. While sometimes written about as something new, poetic sign is probably as old as sign. Susan Rutherford writes, "The folkloristic tradition of Deaf America is over 175 years old and is replete with legends, naming practices, tall tales, folkspeech, jokes, sign play, games, folk poetry, customs, ritual and celebrations."[32] Earlier efforts to capture signing on film were expensive and required skill in lighting and developing, though the records that have survived are valuable sources of historical significance. Technology now provides a less expensive, easily mastered method for preserving this rich store of signed material—videotape.[33]

ART

Deafness has not prevented artistic talents from emerging. Among the widely acclaimed Deaf American artists, one finds sculptors, like Arnold Hillis and the incomparable Douglas Tilden; painters, like William Sparks and Morris Broderson; this country's foremost drypoint etcher, Cadwallader Washburn, and many more. These Deaf artists contributed greatly to the general community as well as to the Deaf community. The appeal of Tilden's magnificent *Bear Hunt* is not based on his deafness nor on the hearing status of its viewers. These artists have contributed substantially to society. Some, like Tilden, who became the first president of the California Association of the Deaf, have been leaders in the Deaf community. Some have filled their roles as artists and avoided the social-political affairs of the Deaf community. Have they contributed a "Deaf art," an identifiably different style of painting, sculpting, etching? No such claims have been made. What they have given their Deaf fellows is the pleasure of their work, which all humanity can share, and the pride of seeing another Deaf person succeed.

SPORTS

Athletics have a prominent place in the social life of the Deaf community. Casual observers might mistakenly conclude that, being aurally disabled, Deaf people endeavor to compensate by physical achievements. This Rankian view of their athletic participation, however, overlooks the fact that many Deaf adults are spectators, not participants. They attend sporting events to meet their Deaf friends, rather than to watch the athletes perform. A thousand spectators may come to a basketball game, but at any given moment, more of them are engaged in conversations than are watching the action on the floor. There are, of course, dedicated athletes, and the Deaf community has had a number who have become stellar performers: "Dummy" Hoy, in baseball; Bilbo Monaghan, in football; LeRoy Colombo, in swimming; Everett "Silent" Rattan, in wrestling; Eugene Hairston, in boxing. These athletes gained national attention.

The nation, however, generally does not understand the influence of the Deaf community on the way that some sporting events are conducted. The umpires' signals in baseball are signed because of the requests of Deaf players. They convinced the umpires to sign balls and strikes, fair and foul balls, safe and out, and the practice continues, even when there are no Deaf players in the game. Similarly, the huddle in football grew from the necessity of Deaf football teams to call plays in private. The first college to use a huddle was Gallaudet. Other teams adopted its practice and now do not accord the university credit for initiating it. Deaf culture, then, has added to general culture, as well as taken from it.

RELIGION

No religion is without Deaf members. The scant evidence available suggests that the Deaf population's religious preferences are similar to those for the general population. The proportions of Catholics, Jews, and Protestants in the Deaf community are much the same as in the population at large.[34]

DEAF CONGREGATIONS

The Episcopal Church was the first in the United States to have a congregation of Deaf worshippers. St. Ann's Church for the Deaf, in

New York City, was established by a normally hearing man, the oldest son of Thomas Hopkins Gallaudet. He became an Episcopal priest in 1851 and shortly thereafter founded St. Ann's. The second church for Deaf people was All Soul's Church, in Philadelphia, in association with St. Stephen's Church, which originally held special services for its Deaf members. All Soul's first religious leader was Rev. Henry W. Syle, the first Deaf person in the United States to be ordained as an Episcopal priest. Episcopal Deaf congregations subsequently have spread throughout the United States.[35]

The second religion in the United States to establish a church for Deaf worshippers was the Lutheran Church, which organized such a church in Chicago, in 1896. Our Saviour Lutheran Church for the Deaf was followed two years later by Emmanuel Lutheran Church for the Deaf, in Milwaukee. Many Lutheran congregations have been served by pastors who are assigned to more than one city, a circuit-riding minister. There are at least fourteen "missions to the Deaf" that supervise programs and provide for their maintenance.

The first Methodist church for Deaf people was formally established in Chicago, in 1894, when Philip J. Habenstab, a teacher at the Illinois School for the Deaf, became the first Deaf person ordained by the Methodist Church. The Chicago Mission for the Deaf was succeeded by the Christ Methodist Church, in Baltimore, in 1896, and Cameron Methodist Church in Cincinnati, in 1910.

Catholic Deaf people have had signed masses since eighteenth-century France, though they have usually not had separate congregations; that is, Deaf people have attended regular worship services in which the priest or an interpreter signs the vocal portions of the mass. In the United States, there are special services for Deaf congregants in a few cities (e.g., Denver, Omaha, New Orleans, Landover Hills, Maryland, and Warren, Michigan). The first prelingually Deaf priest in the United States, Thomas Coughlin, was ordained in 1977.

The Southern Baptist Ministry to the Deaf (SBMD), founded in 1906 by John W. Michaels, sought separate space in existing churches, in order to hold services for Deaf people. Michaels was not concerned whether the church was of the Baptist denomination, so he set up Sunday schools and congregations in Methodist and Presbyterian churches. SBMD also encouraged the publication of sign dictionaries, in recognition of the need for interpreters and manually proficient ministers. The Church of Latter-Day Saints (Mormon) authorized a separate congregation for its Deaf members in 1917.

Some religious groups have paid no specific attention to Deaf people. Orthodox Judaism did not accept Deaf coreligionists unless they could speak.[36] Jewish Deaf adults have tended to fend for themselves. In New York City, for instance, Deaf Jews maintain not one but three separate congregations.

Another example of Deaf adults striking out on their own is the Christian Deaf Fellowship. Begun in 1944 as a nondenominational group, it affiliated with the Central Bible Institute and Seminary (Springfield, Missouri) for purposes of preparing Deaf ministers. While the impetus for this movement came from a normally hearing minister whose parents were deaf, the fellowship is entirely managed by Deaf leaders.

Religious Schools

With respect to religious instruction for Deaf students, denominations differ again. The Catholic Church maintains nine schools for Deaf students. The Lutheran Church sponsors two schools for Deaf children, one in Detroit and the other on Long Island. There are no other denominational schools for Deaf children in the United States. Instead, most religions encourage the practice of giving public-school Deaf students released time for religious instruction.

At the postsecondary level, the major faiths support religious activities at Gallaudet University and the National Technical Institute for the Deaf. Some religions assign full-time clergy to work on campus with the students. Others send missionaries who pay occasional visits to students at the two institutions.

Deaf Ministers

In the United States, the Episcopal Church leads all denominations in the preparation of Deaf persons to serve as ministers, despite occasional opposition to them by nondeaf ministers. Forty-five Deaf Episcopal priests—all of whom lost their hearing before ordination—have served in various capacities throughout the country. Most have deaf-only congregations. Other religious groups have one or a few Deaf ministers: thirteen Baptists, six Lutherans, five Methodists, three Congregational, and one each Presbyterian, United Brethren, Evangelical Alliance, and Campbellite. There are two Deaf rabbis.[37] As noted earlier, Rev. Thomas Coughlin became the first American Deaf Catholic priest, in 1977.

RELIGIOUS ORGANIZATIONS

In keeping with their affiliative tendencies, Deaf people have formed or joined in forming organizations on the basis of their religious preferences. One of the oldest such groups is the Episcopal Church's Conference of Church Workers among the Deaf, which was founded in 1881. Its annual meetings bring together Deaf clergy with nondeaf clergy who serve Deaf congregants. Another long-established organization is the Ephphatha Conference of Workers among the Deaf, which started in 1903. The International Catholic Deaf Association, which has headquarters in Toronto, Ontario, Canada, has both hearing and Deaf members, although its principal membership is Deaf. The National Congress of the Jewish Deaf (NCJD), founded in 1956, limits its membership to Deaf persons.

THE ROLE OF RELIGION IN THE DEAF COMMUNITY

While every religion seems to have some policy with respect to Deaf coreligionists, the penetration of those policies to the local level cannot be taken for granted. One study conducted in a small town (Frederick, Maryland) and a large city (Baltimore) found many clerics unaware of Deaf persons in their purview. Of thirty-seven who did have Deaf congregants, only six were conscious of them.[38] Few ministers, regardless of their faith, can spend much time planning for or working with their Deaf parishioners. Their small numbers, their relative "invisibility," and the difficulties in communicating with most of them furnish substantial reasons for the lack of attention given by the average member of the clergy to Deaf people. Still, most of the major faiths have at least some clerics whose special assignment is to serve Deaf congregants.

As early as the sixteenth century, the clergy has been active in providing social services to deaf people, especially playing a leading role in their education. The first recorded efforts to educate deaf children were made by Catholic priests and monks.[39] Most famous among them have been Ponce de León, Pablo Bonet, Abbé de l'Epée, and Abbé Sicard. These pioneers changed society's views of deaf children as uneducable, pointing the way to piercing the veil of silence that engulfed them and, in so doing, altered the prevailing attitudes toward manual communication. However, while religious groups led the way to educating deaf children, their efforts tended to stop at the little red schoolhouse. One Deaf clergyman noted, "Prior to 1960 there was no chaplain on the [Gallaudet] campus, although there was a ministry to students on a part-time basis by parish clergy or missioners."[40]

Some ancient religious groups aimed to protect Deaf people from exploitation. Judaism's treatment of its Deaf members, which appears patronizing in modern times, was intended to prevent them from being abused by others.[41] Some easily misunderstood efforts by religious groups today can be cast in the same antiexploitative mold or as an attempt to compensate for the difficulties in communication between hearing clergy and Deaf congregants. After spending five years and $500,000, the World Bible Translation Center, in 1978, published a new Bible for Deaf people. The special edition of the New Testament provides the Scriptures in simplified English that avoids idioms, unusual words, and odd sentence structures that its translators think might confuse Deaf readers. To illustrate its approach, compare the two texts of 2 Corinthians 6:11–13, first the King James and second the new Deaf version:

> O ye Corinthians, our mouth is open unto you, our heart is enlarged. Ye are not straitened in us, but ye are straitened in your own bowels. Now for a recompense in the same, (I speak as unto my children) be ye also enlarged.

> We have spoken freely to you people in Corinth. We have opened our hearts to you. Our feelings of love for you have not stopped. It is you that has stopped your feelings of love for us. I speak to you like you are my children. Do the same as we have done—open your hearts also.[42]

Ministers of various faiths have championed family and child support, counseling services, recreation programs, and homes for elderly Deaf persons. The extent to which these activities for Deaf persons have been under religious sponsorship varies greatly from denomination to denomination and from place to place. Some wide-ranging examples include the Baptist ministry, which supports the Bill Rice Ranch, a national recreation program aimed at Deaf youth; the Lutheran church, in Minnesota, which has established a home for elderly Deaf people; and several branches of Catholic Charities that have rehabilitation programs for Deaf adults. Many denomina-

It's a Problem

The following story was sent to me by an interpreter, 28 February 1980. Identifying information has been changed.

We have a Catholic mission for the deaf here, and I have known the priest (Father Smith) for quite some time. He celebrates mass once a month for the deaf and hard of hearing. Although I am Catholic, I had not gone to the deaf mass for several months, and when I went last Sunday, I was overwhelmed. It was mostly hearing Baptists who sign! There were three hearing Catholics there, one of whom is the mother of a young deaf man who is Catholic. The rest of the room was filled with Baptists, and one of them got up and sang and signed three Baptist songs, which almost broke me up. Then her little kid closed the mass by singing and signing her Sunday School lesson or something. I thought things were getting weird when we began singing "America the Beautiful" at mass and "Ave Maria" was outlawed, but this scene was truly remarkable. Oh, yes, there were three other deaf people there, one young man I had never seen before, one who is nondenominational, and a Jewish woman.

The minute mass was over Father Smith took me aside and told me he had a problem. I wasn't going to mention it, but couldn't help but notice. He said he is happy to sign the mass for the deaf, but it had never been his intention to do this for hearing Baptists. . . . Anyhow, we were interrupted by the woman who interprets for the Baptist Church who came up to tell him he's signing "communion" wrong. I couldn't believe it. She showed him the "proper" sign which a deaf person wouldn't even be able to see from his seat. Father Smith is too kind for his own good, but I'm mouthy, so I asked her if she had any deafness in her family, and she said no, no, but she was an official interpreter. I pointed out to her that if the deaf don't recognize the sign, it's not much accomplished. Father Smith has worked with the deaf for twenty years, and he and I are from the same school of signing, ASL—communicate! We both learned from the deaf, so we're not great, but, boy, can we put the message across, because we understand the deaf.

tions sponsor volunteer efforts that bring special services to Deaf persons.

As for the attitudes of Deaf people toward their religions, such research as is available suggests that they are not more nor less religious than people in general. That judgment is based on avowed religious membership, which indicates that Deaf people state religious preferences that roughly approximate those of the general population.[43]

What about their religious *beliefs*, as distinct from *affiliations*? Deaf religious beliefs have had scant research, possibly because of the imputed difficulties in translating religious concepts into sign. One Catholic educator conducted a survey contrasting the beliefs of Deaf and normally hearing adolescents, and he found nearly equal proportions—about one-fourth of each group—either denied the existence of God or had serious doubts; conversely, nearly equal proportions were believers in the existence of God. He endeavored to introduce these Deaf adolescents to the mysteries of Catholicism and concluded that a deep level of religious instruction could be achieved, though only with considerable effort.[44] His conclusion is consistent with that reached by the Abbé de l'Epée in the eighteenth century, a belief on which he staked his reputation, and it would accord with the views of other religious workers, who are convinced that deafness is not an insuperable barrier to religious education.[45]

With regard to participation in church affairs, Deaf congregants tend to limit their participation, except in those instances in which they are members of all-Deaf congregations.[46] In other respects, church attendance by Deaf people appears to be like their attendance at other events; that is, an occasion to meet with their friends. That this can be annoying to the clergy is attested to by the incident reported in "It's a Problem." How widespread is attendance of Deaf members of one religious group at services of another has not been established. Personal observations support its occurrence at a fairly high rate in sparsely populated areas. In the metropolitan centers, there are sufficient numbers of Deaf members of the major religious groups to make such practices unnecessary to satisfy the desires of Deaf people to get together.

TRAVEL

Deaf people as a group are not stay-at-homes. They travel a great deal—not only within the United States but also internationally, but Deaf people on tour need special arrangements. Finding English-speaking local guides to foreign facilities is difficult enough, but locating one who knows ASL is often impossible. The answer is to bring one along. It creates an additional expense that is usually factored into the price of the tour. There are travel agencies that specialize in making travel arrangements for Deaf people. The Gallaudet University Alumni Association sponsors tours arranged by Charles Yeager, a faculty member. Travel arrangements made by specialists not only assure qualified interpreters but also congenial companionship, since all, or almost all, of the other members of the tour will be deaf. There are general travel agencies that will efficiently handle Deaf tourists, and some have agents who can communicate manually, but they are often unaware of the problems Deaf people encounter, such as not hearing announcements over airport public address systems, being unable to negotiate with hotels about inadequate accommodations, and encountering harried customs agents who become hostile when a Deaf traveler cannot promptly answer their inquiries. Judging from attendance at national and international meetings of Deaf people, these hazards do not inhibit them.

ARCHITECTURE

Deaf people seldom complain that most gathering places are designed to facilitate hearing, but they should, since the architecture of these places often makes it difficult for them to see and, if they use hearing aids, to hear. Our society builds *audi*toriums rather than *visu*toriums. Even residential schools for Deaf children are designed to fulfill specifications based on majority experience. There are some pleasant exceptions. The classrooms of the National Technical Institute for the Deaf have built-in slide projectors and other visual aids, and most have no windows, because staring into a glaring background inhibits sight in the same way that noisy surroundings interfere with hearing. Another example of a space designed for Deaf viewers is the Elstad Auditorium on the Gallaudet University campus. Its lack of pillars and the extreme pitch of its floor afford unobstructed views from any seat in the 850-seat room. As you enter this visutorium, you are instantly struck by how much closer you seem to be to the stage than in an auditorium of comparable size. You may also be startled by the acoustics. (See "Seeing Is Hearing?") This architectural example clearly has a message that

SEEING IS HEARING?

When he was Gallaudet College's dean of faculties, George Detmold struggled with the architects over the design of the Elstad Auditorium. His concentration on making the auditorium suitable for Deaf students led to an ironic outcome. In 1962, when the building was being readied for its inaugural use, engineers were startled to find that no provisions had been made for a sound system. The architects, so impressed by the need for perfect sightlines, forgot that hearing people might also be in attendance. Too late for alterations in the theater, the ceremonies proceeded without a sound-amplification system, and it was immediately apparent that even words spoken from the back of the stage could be heard easily in the last row of the upper balcony. The theater designed for seeing also had ideal acoustics!

applies to any auditorium: If it satisfies Deaf people's needs, it will likely satisfy everybody else's.

HOUSING

Ethnic groups tend to move into neighborhoods dominated by the presence of members of that group. Large cities have Chinatowns, Spanish sections, Italian neighborhoods, and so forth. Historically, immigrants to the United States clustered together to afford mutual aid. At the turn of the century, for example, the Lower East Side of New York City was home to waves of Jewish immigrants. Today, the same neighborhood has a largely Spanish-speaking population from the Caribbean Islands.

What about Deaf people? Paradoxically, Deaf people do not cluster geographically. What is paradoxical is that Deaf people so enjoy each other's company that, once together, they prolong the occasion. One minister finds that his Deaf congregation remains together for four or more hours after a one-hour service on Sunday. In fact, many Deaf congregants stay for the light supper on Sunday evenings even though their services end at 2:00 P.M.

Given that demonstrated eagerness to communicate with each other, and given the difficulties Deaf people have with telecommunications, it might be assumed that they would try to find homes in "Deaf neighborhoods." Yet, the opposite is the case. Deaf people seem to avoid choosing a residence near other Deaf people. Why?

Two explanations have been offered by Deaf people I have interviewed. For one, they wish to protect their privacy. They worry that Deaf neighbors would closely monitor their comings and goings. Awkward moments might arise if a Deaf friend visited them but not their neighbor, who also regarded that person as a friend. In a social gathering away from home, Deaf participants can cut off the contacts whenever they like; but if they reside next to a Deaf neighbor, they would find it difficult to control the relationship.

Another reason provides an interesting insight into the thinking of some Deaf people: "I would not want to live around too many Deaf people, lest I be judged by their actions." This respondent also said, "If they are boorish people, the hearing neighbors would probably judge me to be boorish, too. I want people to relate to me, not to some stereotype." Admittedly, that reason comes from a highly educated Deaf person, but it seems to have some currency in the Deaf community.

There are exceptions, of course. Several cities (for examples, Los Angeles, New York, and Columbus, Ohio) have built group quarters for elderly Deaf people. These apartments are usually much sought after. However, these arrangements include other advantages than Deaf neighbors: convenience, low cost, and special arrangements for communication and safety. At the other end of the age spectrum, newly formed Deaf families tend to avoid neighborhoods already populated by Deaf people.

HUMOR AMONG THE DEAF[47]

Perhaps the picture given so far of Deaf culture paints it in too somber tones. That inference leans far from the actuality. By and large, Deaf people have a fine sense of humor—perhaps more so than normally hearing people, but certainly no less so. Unfortunately for the general community, the language barrier prevents most normally hearing people from appreciating it. As with most ethnic humor, simply substituting words in one language for similar words in the other does not properly reveal the underlying humor.

Context and experience give special twists to words in one language that often take paragraphs to explain in another.

Mark Twain once noted, "Studying humor is like dissecting a frog. You might learn a lot about it, but you end up with a dead frog." Investigating what makes Deaf people laugh risks losing the funniness, yet learning what makes a people laugh can tell a great deal about that people. What is more, studies show episodes of laughter promote good health "because they restore homeostasis, stabilize blood pressure, oxygenate the blood, massage the vital organs, stimulate circulation, facilitate digestion, relax the system and produce a feeling of well-being."[48]

While some of the giggle is lost in the search for a joke's meaning, the explanatory process can be heuristically beneficial. Take, for instance, the story about an elderly gentleman, wealthy and very deaf, who purchased a new hearing aid. Two weeks later, he returned to the shop where he bought the aid to report that he could now hear and understand conversations even when they occurred in an adjoining room.

"Your relatives must be very happy that you can hear so much better," the dealer noted.

"Oh, I haven't told them yet," the old gent chuckled. "I've been sitting around listening, and do you know what? I've already changed my will twice!"

That people sometimes take advantage of the Deaf person's inability to hear is reflected in this tale of revenge. It also has an element of wish fulfillment: the deaf man gains hearing ability. Deaf people have many wish-fulfilling fantasies. Regaining the ability to hear can be dealt with humorously better than realistically.

That point is well-illustrated in the following anecdote told by a graduate student:

> I became friendly with a group of Deaf people from all walks of life. We met every weekend at the beach. Among the controversial topics we discussed was the story about the Deaf man caught in a rainstorm whose hearing was restored when he was struck by lightning. Many of my friends greeted this story with derision; others were more thoughtful. Suddenly my friend Jewel, while standing in the center of a circle of Deaf people all in bathing suits, looked up, held out her cupped palm, and gazed questioningly at the brilliant blue sky. Everyone laughed and quite a few followed her lead and walked around for a moment or two with a cupped palm waiting for rain. Then the laughter subsided. They shrugged and the joke and interest in the story disappeared.

Much of the humor in that anecdote depends upon Jewel's spontaneous, mocking response to the whole idea of lightning restoring hearing. But not far below the surface lurks a poignant streak of longing. It should not be misconstrued, however, to mean that Deaf people spend much of their time hoping to hear. It is a bit like a member of an oppressed minority group idly wondering what it would be like to be in the majority.

Jokes can relieve anxieties by overstating genuine concerns, as is demonstrated in this popular joke among Deaf people.

A deaf bank robber is captured, and the sheriff engages a signing interpreter to inquire where the stolen money is hidden.

The deaf man signs something, and the interpreter translates: "He does not know what you are talking about."

After half an hour of continual denials, the exasperated sheriff places a gun against the robber's head and says, "If you don't tell me where the money is hidden, I will kill you."

The interpreter signs this threat, and the terrified deaf man responds, "Okay, I hid it under the back stairs in my house."

The sheriff, aware that the robber has deviated from his persistent denials, eagerly asks, "What did he say?"

Quickly, the interpreter answers, "He says he's not afraid to die!"

The story exposes a fear of being misrepresented, a fear that many Deaf people realistically experience. It also betrays a wary attitude toward interpreters. Like gallows humor in any culture, such stories desensitize. They may also be a socially acceptable way of conveying a cautionary message: Watch out for interpreters. Deaf people are frequently dependent upon interpreters, hence they are vulnerable to any interpreter incompetence or ill will. The ambivalence created by this dependence/hostility can be sociably expressed in the guise of a joke.

Some humor, like the following, makes fun of the majority, its ignorance of deafness, and when its hearing becomes a liability. The variations on this theme in Deaf culture seem endless. In all of them, the fun comes from Deaf people confronting the arrogant members of the majority and turning the tables.

The beggar, flaunting his "Please Help the Blind" sign, looked so forlorn that the lady fished in her bag and gave him a two-dollar bill.

"Sorry, lady," he said, "two-dollar bills is bad luck. Ain't you got two singles?"

"How did you know it was a two-dollar bill if you're blind?"

"I ain't blind, lady. My partner's blind. It's his day off, so he's gone to the movies and I'm pinch-hittin' for him. Me, I'm a deaf-mute."

A deaf couple is staying at a motel. The wife wakes in the middle of the night and asks her husband to get some ice. Sleepily, he leaves the room and goes down the hall to fetch it. Returning, he cannot remember his room number. What to do? Without hesitation he goes to his car and begins honking the horn until every room light goes on—except one. Noting its location, he confidently heads for the one dark room.

The embarrassments that can occur because of deafness can be desensitized by making jokes about them, which can serve to overcome a sense of inferiority. Since deafness is supposed to make learning English difficult, word play is, for some Deaf intellectuals, all the more delightful. It is a way for a Deaf person to proclaim, I can overcome! Take the following puns: What are two of the greatest modern miracles? The deaf-mute who picked up a wheel and spoke, and the blind man who picked up a hammer and saw!

Deaf culture is certainly not humorless. No less than others, Deaf people laugh, sometimes at themselves, sometimes at others. To them, being deaf is not tragic. While their jokes may differ, their uses of humor are much like those of any other group.

VALUES

What is good and bad in Deaf lives? What are appropriate and inappropriate ways of behaving? What things are important and what unimportant to Deaf people? These questions bear upon the cultural values of Deaf people and their sense of how they would like the world to be at the same time as they adapt to the world in which they live.

School ties are important. Thus, when asked where they are from, Deaf people will often reply with the name of the residential school they attended. It provides more information to another Deaf person than the name of the city in which one resides, although that, too, will usually be disclosed early in the conversation. The

Deaf community being relatively small, it is important to reveal one's group ties early on.

Deafness is valued, not as the loss of hearing, but as group identification. When asked, the question "Are you deaf?" does not refer to degree of hearing. One responds, "I am Deaf," meaning that one belongs to the social group. As discussed earlier, Deaf people include many who have a substantial degree of hearing ability. Those who still say "I am Deaf," therefore, mean what coreligionists or natives from a particular country mean when they identify each other. They may differ in many other regards, but they have critical similarities that their identification reveals. For a minority group, that identification is crucial. A study of twenty-one randomly selected Deaf students entering Gallaudet University yielded some valuable information about how Deaf students regard potential interlopers. The investigators concluded,

> Excluding potential intruders in any community is a mechanism by which the community seeks to protect its group identity. The Deaf community, being surrounded by a larger and dominant Hearing community, allows intimate interaction with its members only if the individual exhibits appropriate behavior and language skills. This experimental group of students experienced exclusion at the time of their arrival at Gallaudet. If the subjects, in order to gain entrance to the Deaf community, must abandon behavior they previously considered crucial to survival, we can describe that behavior as incompatible with existing values of the community. Ethnocentric attitudes and behavior often present serious conflicts when an unaware individual seeks to interact with members of the Deaf community, as evidenced by the conflicts our subjects are experiencing. The process of making adjustments to these conflicts is a long and difficult one. The subjects' anxieties about changing their familiar behavior to accommodate newer, more acceptable behavior must be understood as a reaction to conflicts arising from two cultures in contact.[49]

Does the foregoing mean that the Deaf community remains closed to late-deafened people? No, hard-of-hearing and late-deafened people do gain places in the Deaf community. But not often. Mostly, they do not try to get in. Having spent the major share of their lives with friends and acquaintances who hear and do not sign, these deaf people do not easily shift allegiances. They remain "tweenies," in between two cultures, not able to enjoy their own and not willing to shift to another one. At the suggestion that she join a sign language class, a bright, middle-aged woman who had just lost her hearing responded, "Sign language? But that's for deaf people. Do you do this in public; it's so undignified, isn't it?"[50] Such an attitude will not qualify a person for membership in the Deaf community. Those who become members respond like the hearing-impaired young man who went through public high schools "faking it." He chose to enter Gallaudet, where his values completely changed.

> As I made my way through many educational and enjoyable se-
> mesters, learning a "new" way of communicating, I was en-
> thralled. I was able to understand a person 100 percent of the time
> without having to lipread or depend on notes. It is a special feeling
> to relax and listen when in the past you have had to pay so much
> attention to the person you were speaking with that you could
> never really relax.[51]

In the gadget-conscious United States, Deaf people, too, have attached value to devices that ease their daily living; for example, caption decoders, TDDs, and varieties of flashing signal lamps to advise that someone is at the door, the telephone is ringing, the alarm clock has gone off. The ingenuity of Deaf people is not new, nor are they apt to cease to find ways to improve their lives.[52]

Of greatest value are those things associated with sign language, as well as the language itself. Hands have heightened significance for Deaf people. They are not only the principal means of communication, they also embody beauty. Carol Padden points out, "Deaf people believe firmly hand gestures must convey some kind of visual meaning and have strongly resisted what appear to be 'nonsense' use of hands—one such example is Cued Speech."[53] An expressive face is good; a "stone face" is bad. By analogy, the face provides much of the communicative richness that vocal qualities carry for speech. Thus, a signer who has an unexpressive face is like someone who speaks in a monotone. Deaf people unabashedly speak of their beloved language, and they regard those who attempt to denigrate it as "the enemy."[54] By simple extension, then, those who are fluent in sign enjoy high status in the Deaf community.

SUMMARY

Deaf people have demonstrated their talents for adaptation, for finding ways to work with and move around barriers. These adaptations and the accompanying folkways and values form Deaf culture. It reflects the differences from the majority culture that enable Deaf people to adjust to a world that frustrates them, not out of malevolence, but because the majority has naturally structured the environment for their convenience. Spoken communication is a disaster for persons who cannot hear. Deaf people, therefore, have developed their own visual language and, being visual, it does not conform to the syntax of the majority language. Those in the majority who are discomfited by differences, especially language differences, have attempted to suppress ASL and signing. Over the last two centuries, Deaf people have had to fight for their right to communicate in sign. The battleground has been the classroom, but the residue from those battles has spilled over into Deaf culture, as reflected in its values.

In many other ways, Deaf people have had to adjust to a world that is designed for people who can hear. Much of everyday twentieth-century life in the United States involves the great advances that have enabled us to overcome spatial limits by swiftly transmitting messages over great distances. The introduction of telecommunications—television, radio, telephone—placed Deaf people at a disadvantage. While the disadvantages remain, steps have been taken to reduce them. In the meantime, Deaf culture reflects the inward-driving nature of those disadvantages, the tendency to look within the Deaf community for pleasures, knowledge, and emotional support. One woman who was born deaf was asked if she wanted to hear. "No way!" she replied, explaining that being able to hear would mean the loss of her identity and her place in the Deaf community. To her, not hearing was the preferred way of life.[55]

After the emphases on ways the majority and Deaf culture differ, we must state that nothing written so far should be construed to imply that an individual cannot participate in both cultures. Like bilingualism, biculturalism is a viable choice for many people. It might even be contended that those who limit themselves to a single language and one culture are undereducated and less well-prepared for optimizing their lives.

If it is possible to summarize Deaf culture in a few words, then a Deaf person can do it. The following poem by Mrs. Kathleen B. Schreiber expresses the view of someone who has resided on both sides of whatever lines divide Deaf and nondeaf people.

How We Are

You hear the sound of laughter,
I see a smiling face,
You hear the rapid footsteps,
I see the stride and grace,
You hear a joyous greeting,
I see a friendly hand:
Yours is a word that's spoken,
Mine is an act as planned.

You hear a shrieking siren,
I see a flashing light,
You hear the blare of traffic,
I see its glare at night,
You hear the lilting music,
I feel the catchy beat:
Yours is the sound of motion,
Mine is the mute repeat.

You hear a tree that rustles,
I see the swaying leaves,
You hear a wind that whistles,
I feel a steady breeze,
You hear a songbird calling,
I see its graceful flight:
Yours is the sound of nature,
Mine is the gift of sight.

You hear the preacher praying,
I see the way he stands,
You hear the people singing,
I see it signed by hands,
You hear the final Amen,
I see the bow above:
Yours is a vocal worship,
Mine is an act of love.

NOTE. © 1987 by Kathleen B. Schreiber. Reprinted with permission of the author.

NOTES

1. The reader is reminded that, when capitalized, "Deaf" refers to the social definition of deafness and when not capitalized to the audiological-medical definition. Thus, "Deaf culture" refers to the culture of those who accept their deafness and seek the company of other Deaf people.
2. As noted in chapter 1, I eschew use of "subculture" in reference to the Deaf community. Among anthropologists, that term means no more than that the subculture is embedded in a larger culture.
3. For more history, consult Atwood, 1964; Bender, 1981; Best, 1943; Boatner, 1959; Braddock, 1975; Brill, 1984; DeGering, 1964; Gallaudet, 1983; Gannon, 1981; Garnett, 1968; Lane, 1984; Schein, 1981 and 1984a, Scouten, 1984; Winzer, 1986; Woods, W. H., Sr., n.d.
4. Malouf, 1987, 8.
5. Lane, 1984, 271–72.
6. Gannon, 1981, 59.
7. Winzer, 1986.
8. Lane, 1984, 274–75.
9. The so-called Milan Manifesto refers to the first two of eight resolutions passed at the Second International Congress on the Education of the Deaf, held in Milan in 1880. The resolutions read, "The Convention, considering the incontestable superiority of speech over signs, (a) for restoring deaf-mutes to social life, and (b) for giving them greater facility of language, declares that the method of articulation should have the preference over that of signs in instruction in education of the Deaf and dumb. Considering that the simultaneous use of signs and speech has the disadvantage of injuring speech and lipreading and precision of ideas, the Convention declares that the oral method ought to be preferred" (cited in Brill, 1984, 20).
10. The leading proponent of the eugenics movement in the United States was A. G. Bell. His most forthright statement in opposition to marriages among Deaf people appeared in Bell, 1883.
11. Much of this section is based on Schein, 1984a.
12. Stokoe, 1960; Stokoe, Casterline, and Croneberg, 1965. How was this pioneering idea received? Badly, at first. Linguists could accept the basic idea, but they had limited interest in this language backwater. Deaf people, on the other hand, saw the claim that ASL and English were not the same as a disguised insult: they resented the idea! In time, these attitudes changed. Linguists in country after country confirmed Stokoe's observations. They found that the sign language used by their Deaf compatriots had a grammar that differed from the native spoken

language. The scientists also noted that sign languages differed from country to country, though they had some basic features in common. The notion of an international sign language proved as fallacious as that of an international spoken language. As for Deaf people, they eventually realized that the idea of linguistic independence complemented, rather than denigrated, their culture (Eastman, 1980). For a detailed discussion and a recent bibliography of publications on sign, see Schein, 1984a.

13. Nash and Nash (1981) would argue that manual communication is the sine qua non of the Deaf community, while Higgins (1980) sees it as one of several factors. Deaf people themselves might conclude that they have gathered together because of the ease of communication and the sympathy that they derive from their Deaf colleagues. However, satisfactory communication does not alone lead to the elaborate structure that, in the United States, is the Deaf community.

14. Stokoe, 1987.

15. The Walloons and the Flemings in Belgium are one notorious example. Canada has become peacefully bilingual.

16. Woodward, 1982.

17. Shroyer and Shroyer, 1984.

18. Padden, 1980, 96.

19. Padden, 1980, 97.

20. Kannapell, 1980, 111–13.

21. Kannapell, 1980, 107, 113.

22. Glickman, 1986, 2.

23. Much of the following is based on Schein and Hamilton, 1980.

24. *GA-SK Newsletter*, Spring, 1988.

25. Bellefleur, 1976.

26. Schein, 1980.

27. For further information about programming for Deaf viewers, see Bangs, 1987.

28. The quotation and much of what follows in this paragraph is taken from Schuchman, 1987, 279. See also Schuchman, 1988.

29. For delightful histories of Deaf periodicals and authors, see Gannon, 1981, Panara, 1987, and Van Cleve, 1987.

30. Van Cleve, 1987, 195.

31. Panara, 1987.

32. Rutherford, 1988, page 137.

33. Frishberg, 1988.

34. Schein, 1986b.

35. Berg (1984) has prepared a fascinating account of the Episcopal ministry in the United States, from 1850 to 1980. Anyone interested in religion and deafness will find this resource invaluable. Those less interested in religion will still be impressed with this chronicle for its stories of personal struggles and triumphs.

36. Schein and Waldman, 1986.
37. A third young Deaf man, a graduate of Gallaudet University, Alton Silver, studied for the rabbinate at Hebrew Union College, Cincinnati, but he died suddenly during minor surgery. There is one hearing-impaired rabbi. (Adele Shuart, personal communication, April 19, 1989)
38. Furfey and Harte, 1968.
39. Bender, 1981; Schein, 1984a.
40. Berg, 1968, 891.
41. A Deaf Jew could not be held responsible for a contract nor could their property be sold without the intervention of the government to assure that they were being fairly treated (Schein and Waldman, 1986). See also Ohsberg, 1982, and Yount, 1976.
42. Bishop and Dibell, 1978. Details are from a news account in the *Dallas Times Herald*, 8 July 1978.
43. Schein, 1968.
44. Russo, 1975.
45. Gawlik, 1969; Hourihan, 1979; Walters, 1979.
46. Schein, 1968.
47. "Humor among the Deaf" is the name of a column that ran regularly in *The Deaf American* and was presided over by Toivo Lindholm. Many of the examples in this section are taken from that excellent source.
48. Patricia Keith-Spiegel, quoted in *The New York Times*, 15 July 1973.
49. Padden and Markowitz, 1975.
50. Emmy Hammond, "A View of my Own," *The Glad News*, Spring, 1985, 25.
51. Mentkowski, 1983, 1.
52. Rutherford (1988, 135) notes, "In fact the Smithsonian has a collection which includes artifacts from before the advent of electricity, such as door knockers made from a cannonball attached to a rope. A visitor would pull on the rope outside the door, which would cause the cannonball to bounce repeatedly on the floor inside. The vibrations would call the attention of the Deaf person to the door. (Maybe such a device is best called a floor knocker.)"
53. Padden, 1980, 96.
54. The phrase is from a speech by a former National Association of the Deaf president, George Veditz, in 1913, when he proposed to establish a project to capture master signers on film (Frishberg, 1988).
55. Johnstone, 1984.

3

STRUCTURAL UNDERPINNINGS OF THE DEAF COMMUNITY

The Deaf community is highly organized. A Deaf person desiring to affiliate with other Deaf people can choose from among 14 national, 179 state and regional, and several hundred local organizations. Wherever Deaf people gather, they form groups with other Deaf people. In the size and diversity of organizations Deaf people have founded, they are unusual. Consider the following:

- No other physical disability has either the number or diversity of organizations made up entirely of persons who share their disability.
- The Deaf population numbers less than 500,000 persons of all ages, scattered across the fifty states, which hardly seems large enough to support so many organizations.
- Deaf people in the United States have a greater number and variety of organizations than have Deaf people of any other nation.[1]

What has led Deaf people to establish such an elaborate and extensive array of formal organizations?[2] Why have they evolved as they have? What will the Deaf community's organizational structure be like in the next century? These questions occupy all of this book, but this chapter focuses on describing the Deaf community's richly varied infrastructure. In addition to organizations of Deaf people, it includes government agencies and voluntary groups that devote part or all of their attention to deafness and those that endeavor to bring together normally hearing and Deaf people.

ORGANIZATIONS OF DEAF PEOPLE

Deaf people are noted for seeking ways of remaining together—staying with other Deaf guests late into the night and early morning, carrying on conversations oblivious to the restaurant closing its doors, and remaining together long after the theatrical or sporting event has ended. In these and countless other ways, they indicate their desire to stay in communicative contact with each other. They seem to have a nearly unquenchable desire for signing. And no wonder, most have no Deaf coworkers; their nuclear families have no Deaf members; their neighbors and the community at large do not sign. By contrast, when they are with other Deaf people, they enjoy relaxed conversation unfettered by concerns over how those they are conversing with may feel about sign. Being Deaf, they *know* their attitudes toward sign. So being together with other Deaf people is like being at home.

The organizations described in this chapter were not established solely to give Deaf people an opportunity to sign. They were founded and managed by Deaf people to meet their own self-determined needs. Those needs, of course, extend beyond the purely sociable and include mutual assistance to attain and to hold social and economic gains. Only those organizations that have survived to the time of this writing are discussed in this section, and they are treated separately by their purviews—national, state, and regional.

NATIONAL ORGANIZATIONS OF DEAF PEOPLE

The fourteen national organizations span over a hundred years in age, and they range from general to specific in purpose. To be included here, they must be national in scope, founded by Deaf people for Deaf people, and have memberships largely, though not exclusively, of Deaf people. They are grouped together in Table 2 to provide an overview based on their establishment dates and membership sizes. An interpretation of the data in the table appears

Table 2   Founding Dates and Estimated Membership of National
Organizations of Deaf People

Organization	Date Founded	Size of Membership
American Athletic Association of the Deaf (AAAD)	1945	6,000
American Professional Society of the Deaf (APSD)	1966	50
Friends of Libraries for Deaf Action (FOLDA)	1986	?
Gallaudet University Alumni Association (GUAA)	1889	4,000
International Catholic Deaf Association (ICDA)	1949	1,000
National Association of the Deaf (NAD)	1880	15,000
Junior National Association of the Deaf (JNAD)	1969	1,200
National Association of Hearing Impaired College Students (NAHICS)	1980	500
National Black Deaf Advocates (NBDA)	1981	500
National Congress of the Jewish Deaf (NCJD)	1956	1,000
National Fraternal Society of the Deaf (NFSD)	1901	13,000
Oral Deaf Adults Section, Alexander Graham Bell Association (ODAS)	1964	500
Rainbow Alliance of the Deaf (RAD)	1977	1,250
Telecommunications for the Deaf, Inc. (TDI)	1968	3,000

later in this chapter. Here, only a sketch of each organization is
presented, ordered chronologically rather than alphabetically to
provide a sense of their development over time.

National Association of the Deaf (NAD)[3]

The call for the First National Convention of Deaf-Mutes proclaimed, "We have interests peculiar to ourselves *which can be taken
care of by ourselves.*" Those "peculiar interests" revolved about the
attacks on sign language mounted in Berlin in 1876, which culmi-
nated in Milan in 1880 with a manifesto declaring that only oral

means should be used in educating Deaf children. Deaf people correctly saw in this action more than an attack on their adult use of sign; it threatened their positions as educators and administrators of schools for Deaf children. NAD's founders sought to defend the rights of Deaf people by joining forces. They made that clear in its charter, which states that NAD was "to bring the deaf of the different sections of the United States in close contact and to deliberate on the needs of the deaf as a class."

NAD was not only the first Deaf self-help group in the United States, it was also the first organization of disabled people. NAD's members come from a broad cross-section of the Deaf population. Early deafened people committed to oralism may join, but they do not usually participate actively in NAD. It is an organization committed to ASL, and those who oppose its use find NAD an uncongenial environment. The active core of NAD members often have steady employment, yet they still have time to devote their energies to organizational affairs. Until 1964, NAD accepted only Deaf people as members. In that year, the biennial convention voted to admit normally hearing persons, provided that they supported NAD's objectives. Despite that modification in the membership criteria, NAD remains *of* the Deaf: fewer than one hundred of its fifteen thousand members are nondeaf.

NAD altered its structure in 1960 to become a federation of state associations governed by a thirteen-member board. Its day-by-day affairs are managed by a full-time executive director and a staff of clerical and professional employees. Its headquarters building, since 1971, is located in Silver Spring, Maryland, a suburb on the northern edge of the District of Columbia, an area heavily frequented by national organizations desiring the ears of Congress and the federal administrators. NAD leases excess space in its three-story building mostly to deaf-oriented associations and businesses—an excellent way to call attention to its position as the foremost organization of Deaf people.

Through its early years, NAD remained fiercely independent. NAD did not try to raise funds from the public at large. Instead, it contributed to the general welfare by mounting successful fundraising drives in both world wars to purchase ambulances and other equipment for the Red Cross. NAD raised the money and gave the commission to Daniel Chester French to sculpt the statue of Thomas Hopkins Gallaudet and Alice Cogswell that commemorates the first public school for Deaf students in the United States. That statue is now listed as one of this country's national treasures.

At its centennial convention, in 1980, NAD adopted a budget of $2 million, a far cry from its 1964 budget of $25,000. Much of the increase in its funds came about from earnings on government grants and other activities. In 1969, it obtained a federal grant to conduct the National Census of the Deaf Population, the first study of its type ever conducted. It held contracts for nearly twenty years to evaluate movies for the U.S. Office of Education's Captioned Films for the Deaf. NAD has been a publisher of books on deafness and related topics since 1966. Its sales of books and equipment used by Deaf people have grown at times to over $500,000. Until recently, NAD owned and operated Deaf Community Analysts, a wholly owned subsidiary that conducted survey research. It jointly owned DEAF, in Boston, a rehabilitation facility serving Deaf youth and adults in New England.

What does NAD do with its funds? In 1908, it fought for and won the right of Deaf workers to be employed in federal civil service. It fought similar battles on behalf of Deaf participation in the Civilian Conservation Corps, in the 1930s, and in the Job Corps, in the 1960s. It aids its affiliated state associations in their efforts on behalf of more Deaf teachers and against attempts to limit Deaf drivers' licenses. After NAD moved to the Washington, D.C., area, in 1965, and appointed a full-time executive secretary, in 1966, it greatly increased its efforts in education and rehabilitation. Its most fervent cause is the preservation of ASL and the promotion of its use. NAD sponsors two programs for that purpose—a Communication Skills Program that encourages the teaching of sign language, and the National Consortium of Programs for Training Sign Language Instructors that works to improve the quality of sign teaching—and publishes and distributes books about sign. NAD supported a legal defense fund and a free information and referral service, sometimes handling over a thousand inquiries about deafness in a single month, mostly from the general public. In these and numerous other ways, NAD helps hearing-impaired people throughout the nation, not just its own membership.

This picture of NAD as a vigorous, courageous battler for Deaf people's rights has not always been true. Periodically, NAD has drifted, acting more like a social club run for entertainment than a national self-help group. Mervin D. Garretson (1962) offered this analysis:

> For many years the NAD has limited itself to a single *idée fixe*, that of preserving the continued status quo of the Deaf in matters of

legislation, employment, freedom of communication and other fundamental liberties, which misguided people sometimes challenge. Many of the Deaf casually assume these as unquestioned rights, quite unaware of the many battles that have been pitched on their behalf to insure these prerogatives for all of the Deaf of America, regardless of membership. In other words, from the beginning of its inception, the NAD has conceived its principal function as that of watchdog for the basic and equal rights of the Deaf. That our group must be eternally vigilant in matters of legislation has been proved again and again through a perusal of the case records of the NAD. In recent years, however, the national organization has been gradually broadening its fundamental working base and extending its contacts. The NAD has participated actively with the Office of Vocational Rehabilitation in several important projects of which we are aware. Now a liaison committee has been established to work with the American Hearing Society, and undoubtedly more of this sort of cooperative activity will emerge from this workshop, and from the new quota system and the establishment of a full-time executive officer as provided at the Dallas convention last July.[4]

The major change that led NAD to its finest hours was the election of Frederick C. Schreiber as secretary-treasurer, in 1964, and executive secretary, in 1966. Fred, as he was known to everyone, led NAD out of the doldrums into a whirlwind of productive activities that gave prominence to NAD and forwarded the causes of interest to Deaf people in all stages and positions of life. Since his death in 1979, NAD has experienced mismanagement that has led to financial difficulties that have forced it to retrench, drastically halting publication of its major journal, reducing staff, and generally constricting its activities. By 1988, the publications have returned to their established schedules, and activities have rebounded, though not to their pre-1980 levels. Those familiar with its history remain optimistic that NAD will regain its leadership role in the Deaf community and again exert influence on the federal government for the welfare of its constituency.

Gallaudet University Alumni Association (GUAA)[5]

Compared to other alumni groups in higher education, GUAA exerts unusual influence. Its four thousand members represent almost half of all graduates from its parent institution. Recalling that Gallaudet University's birth year is 1864 and that GUAA was founded in 1889, one realizes that the number of former students who remain in contact with it is very high, probably as high as, or higher than, alumni of any other institution of higher education. GUAA estimates that the bulletin it publishes and distributes eight times per year is read by about thirty-five thousand people. Traditionally, GUAA raises money largely to promote Deaf culture and to support the higher education of Deaf students. It has supported the publication of five books on deafness and given over $200,000 in scholarships from funds largely contributed by Deaf people. One of its scholarships was awarded to I. King Jordan to enable him to pursue a doctorate. In 1988, he became the first Deaf president of Gallaudet University—excellent validation of the scholarship fund's purposes and management. GUAA, having celebrated its centennial in June 1989, will undoubtedly chart an ambitious course for its future.

National Fraternal Society of the Deaf (NFSD)[6]

The Frat, as NFSD is also known, grew from somewhat different soil than NAD, though negative discrimination motivated the founders of both. NAD reacted to the economic and social threats posed by the opposition to sign language; NFSD responded to insurance companies' overcharges and arbitrary denials of coverage. In 1901, some graduates from the Michigan School for the Deaf met in Chicago to vent their anger over those abuses, and from that meeting emerged the Frat.

Initially a mutual-benefit insurance company, the Frat changed in 1907 to a fraternal society whose charter states that its purposes are:

> To unite fraternally all Deaf men and women, relatives of members and others involved in the field of deafness, all of whom are not more than sixty years of age at the time of becoming members and are possessed of good bodily and mental health, and are of good moral character and industrious habits; to give moral aid and support to its members in time of need; to establish and disburse endowments, annuities, cash surrender, loan values, paid-insurance and income options; and, on the demise of its members, to pay death benefits to those who have been named as beneficiaries in accordance with the laws of the Society. The Society shall also aim to uphold honor, fraternity and good citizenship, to encourage in-

dustry, ambition, honesty and perseverance; to prevent, if possible, members from being wronged, swindled or imposed upon, or ill-treated in any manner deemed unfair or disgraceful.

NFSD's affairs are managed by a nine-member board, a large professional and clerical staff, and a full-time, paid grand president, who oversees its 106 divisions in all of the states and parts of Canada. During the eighty-five years from its founding to 1986, only twelve men have held the post of grand president.

NFSD's basic character, as an insurance company, fosters a businesslike attitude among the members; it has a job to do—insuring them against their uncertain futures. It appears to do that job well. In 1986, its assets reached $9 million, and its assets-to-liabilities ratio was excellent. Its management has been praised by the insurance industry for its wise stewardship, and its membership has gained economically through low premiums and assured protection.

For the social functions noted in its charter, the Frat has relatively less appeal to its membership, though by no means does its social side fail to satisfy a large proportion of its members. While the divisions' monthly meetings handle much routine business, they also have a large social component that attracts members' attendance.

NFSD gives awards for excellence to Deaf athletes, grants scholarships, advocates for legislation, and has from time to time donated funds to purchase ambulances, as it did in World War II, and to refurbish the Statue of Liberty, as it did in 1986. The Frat's social-business mix may be expected to alter somewhat under the leadership changes since the retirement of Frank B. Sullivan, its grand president from 1964 to 1984. However, radical shifts in policies and activities do not seem likely. In the Frat, the word that goes with "change," is "gradual."

American Athletic Association of the Deaf (AAAD)[7]

The premier sports organization in the Deaf community is the American Athletic Association of the Deaf (AAAD). It sets uniform rules for athletic competition, fosters interclub competitions, offers a social outlet for Deaf people, and sponsors national championships in basketball, softball, and volleyball. It also supports the United States teams that participate in the World Games for the

Deaf (managed internationally by the Comité International des Sports des Sourds). AAAD holds a five-day annual meeting that combines athletics and socializing. It also maintains a Hall of Fame, honoring Deaf athletes, and publishes a quarterly journal. Its governance covers eight regional associations that represent over 150 Deaf clubs. AAAD insists that its activities be "without interference or assistance from persons with normal hearing." Its first president avers, "AAAD can be viewed as an inspiration to all Deaf organizations, for it is the one with the greatest number of participants on all levels."

Bowling has brought into being a large number of organizations, dating back to the 1930s, when the Chicago Club established a bowling league. Several states have bowling organizations. Regionally, there are ten bowling organizations. The Great Lakes Deaf Bowling Association (GLDBA) refers to itself as the "American Bowling Congress of the Deaf." Its annual tournaments enroll as many as 130 teams and 650 bowlers. It recently celebrated its fiftieth anniversary. The American Deaf Women's Bowling Association is its female counterpart, holding its tournaments concurrently with the GLDBA and attracting like numbers of participants. Since 1963, a nationwide organization, the National Deaf Bowling Association, has held a World's Deaf Bowling Championship and publishes a quarterly newsletter, *The Deaf Bowler.*

International Catholic Deaf Association (ICDA)

The "international" in ICDA's name marks its Canadian origin. The organization rapidly spread across the border to the United States, which now has the majority of its membership. ICDA promotes social activities among its members. Oddly enough, some of them are not Catholics, having joined because their spouses were or simply to enjoy the fellowship that it affords. It publishes a newsletter, contributes to charitable causes, and holds conventions that bring together its widely scattered members. While ICDA receives considerable guidance from the church, it qualifies as principally an organization of Deaf people.

National Congress of the Jewish Deaf (NCJD)[8]

Motivated by their concerns about limited opportunities for Deaf Jews to practice their religion, indeed to even learn about it, a conference was convened in 1956 which led to the formation of NCJD. It bring together eighteen local affiliates and individual members. While it does not forbid membership to nondeaf people nor to members of other religions, NCJD's membership is overwhelmingly Deaf and Jewish. Among its activities, NCJD has set up an endowment fund to support the education of a rabbinical student willing to learn sign and serve the Jewish Deaf community after ordination. NCJD publishes a quarterly newsletter and has published a book to counter the use of signs it considers offensive and to broadcast those that are needed to interpret Jewish ritual. NCJD has also been an influence in the World Congress of Jewish Deaf, which was founded in 1977.

Oral Deaf Adults Section (ODAS)[9]

Established in 1964 as a section of the Alexander Graham Bell Association for the Deaf, ODAS's purposes are "to encourage, help, and inspire all concerned with hearing impairment so that hearing impaired children and adults may improve their educational, vocational, and social opportunities in the hearing environment through cultivation of their speech, speechreading, and residual hearing." ODAS publishes a newsletter and membership directory, sponsors social events for parents of hearing-impaired children, and raises funds to provide scholarships for qualified deaf students.

American Professional Society of the Deaf (APSD)[10]

Desiring to refute the notion that Deaf people are not capable of high-level intellectual achievements and to encourage other Deaf people to enter the professions, nine Deaf men met in New York in 1966 and founded APSD. It established a scholarship fund to further its second major purpose and, for a time, published a newsletter. In 1979, it amended its charter to enable states to establish chapters, which New York and New Jersey did. However, APSD has not grown beyond seventy members and so is presently inactive.

Telecommunications for the Deaf, Inc. (TDI)[11]

TDI's parents were better known for quarreling than cooperation. In 1968, the Alexander Graham Bell Association for the Deaf and NAD joined forces to promote a common good—the distribution of equipment that would enable Deaf people to use the telephone. Originally a service agency named Teletypewriters for the Deaf, Inc., it became a membership organization in 1979. It has since had a rapid growth, bringing it to fourth place in size of membership among the organizations of Deaf people. A part of its growth can be attributed to its changing the meaning of the *T* in its name from *Teletypewriters* to *Telecommunications*. That nominal alteration signaled the advent of captioned television, in which TDI has played a role as a distributor of the decoders required to view the closed captions. It also has meant that TDI promotes the use of other electronic means of improving communication for Deaf people. TDI communicates with its members in traditional style, through a newsletter and conventions. It also publishes the *International Telephone Directory for TDD Users,* and it is experimenting with a computer network ("electronic mailboxes"). TDI has agents in thirty-eight states who distribute and service telecommunications equipment, and it has twenty-four state chapters. As often happens with children, TDI may grow taller than its parents.

Junior National Association of the Deaf (JNAD)

To accommodate different interests within NAD and to attract more members, NAD encouraged the development of the Junior NAD, in 1969. Directed at high school students, JNAD operates largely independently from NAD, while taking advantage of its staff and facilities. JNAD sponsors a summer camp in Pengilly, Minnesota, to provide Deaf youth with leadership training. During the year, newsletters and local activities maintain a sense of fellowship among the members. The recent movement to install a deaf president at Gallaudet University attests to the success of the program, since many of the Gallaudet student leaders had been members of JNAD.

Rainbow Alliance of the Deaf (RAD)[12]

During the AAAD tournament, in 1977, a group of Deaf homosexual men and women met to form RAD. They recognized their mutual interests and concerns and felt that they could not gain favorable recognition from any of the existing organizations of Deaf people. Within a relatively brief span of time, RAD has fostered eighteen chapters, with two in Canada, and attracted between one thousand and fifteen hundred members. (As with some other Deaf organizations, RAD has difficulty counting its members because they may join either the national group, a state chapter, or both.) RAD's activities are much like those of other Deaf social groups, largely facilitating the interactions of its members and exchanging information. A recent issue of RAD's *Tattler* carried the usual stories about members' comings and goings, organizational matters, and announcements of coming events. But it also contained two stories about AIDS and a review of a book about homosexual couples, detailing patterns in their long-term relationships. Until recently, RAD pursued a policy of maintaining a low profile, even refusing to permit publication of its members' pictures. That policy has changed, along with somewhat more favorable reactions to its activities than its leadership originally expected.

National Black Deaf Advocates (NBDA)[13]

Originally called simply Black Deaf Advocates, NBDA grew out of the First Black Deaf Conference, held at Howard University, in 1981. The participants at the follow-up conference the following year elected an executive secretary to manage the coalition of representatives from local organizations and unaffiliated individuals. NBDA's principal goal is "to prepare Black Deaf people for leadership roles . . . and to provide them with the opportunity to function as leaders or to interact with role models." Unfortunately, NBDA emerged at a time of federal retrenchment in funding of rehabilitation and social work and a climate hostile to the civil rights movement. NBDA suffered another blow when one of its brilliant young leaders, Linwood Smith, was accidentally killed. NBDA explicitly opposed black Deaf people joining existing Deaf groups. Ernest Hairston and Linwood Smith explain:

> . . . It would be the same old story—token Black person joins the organization and is a good fellow, outmaneuvered by sophisticated white members, smiling all the while. It is time for a different approach. It is past the time for a change. This is the time for Black Deaf people to pick up and wave their own flag and to feel good about themselves.[14]

National Association of Hearing-Impaired College Students (NAHICS)[15]

Founded in 1980 by students from Gallaudet College and the National Technical Institute for the Deaf, NAHICS held its first national meeting in 1983. Its purpose is to represent an estimated five thousand to six thousand Deaf students enrolled in more than fifty institutions of higher education in the United States. NAHICS is affiliated with NAD, but has established an independent headquarters in Rochester, New York. Its first president, David Nelson, is a former president of JNAD. He represents the new generation of Deaf students who fought for, and won, a Deaf president for Gallaudet University. His earliest efforts have been directed at winning equality for Deaf people.

Friends of Libraries for Deaf Action (FOLDA)[16]

The announcement of FOLDA's birth states its hopes "to improve library and information services for the Deaf community; to promote access for members of the Deaf community to the profession of library science and other learned professions; to improve the awareness of the Deaf community concerning their rights and potential while at the same time improving the awareness of the public concerning the strengths and needs of their Deaf fellow citizens." The author of that charge, Alice Hagemeyer, is a librarian in the District of Columbia public library system and the author of the *Red Notebook*, a looseleaf collection of periodical literature on deafness that is supplemented by lectures and consultations. It is too early to ask whether FOLDA can survive as a membership organization—it presently numbers fewer than a hundred members—but if it succeeds as well as the notebooks, it has a bright future.

REGIONAL AND STATE ORGANIZATIONS OF DEAF PEOPLE

Thirty-three years after the opening of the first state-supported school for Deaf children, in 1817, a gathering of Deaf people took place in Hartford, Connecticut, that attracted two hundred Deaf people from Maine to Virginia. The swiftness with which the meeting was brought together and the smoothness with which it was carried out illustrate that some organizations of Deaf people were already in place.[17] Three years later, in 1853, much the same group established the New England Gallaudet Association of the Deaf. Immediately after the Civil War, in 1865, New York and Ohio set up state associations. Others followed as their Deaf populations grew, until Wyoming was the last state to establish an association, in 1979. The District of Columbia, Puerto Rico, and Guam also have associations of Deaf people.

Today, every state has an association of Deaf people, most of which are affiliated with NAD. In addition, AAAD has 8 regional affiliates, NCJD has 18 affiliates, and NFSD has 103 divisions. These state and regional organizations form a large potential network, which as yet lacks regular interconnections between its strands. These associations hold annual or biennial conventions. During the interim between conventions, they remain in contact with their members through periodicals. For purposes of affecting legislative and administrative actions within their states, the associations usually can muster their memberships on fairly short notice. However, almost none of the states have full-time executives to manage the organization. Usually, management is in the hands of the elected officials, who must devote most of their time to their regular employment.

LOCAL ORGANIZATIONS OF DEAF PEOPLE: THE CLUBS

Most Deaf organizations have been formed principally to enable their members to enjoy each other's company, so they provide a meeting place and an occasion for them to get together. The number of Deaf clubs is at least equal to the number of major cities in the United States. Some cities, like New York, Los Angeles, Philadelphia, and Chicago, have more than one Deaf club. Small towns frequently have none since their Deaf populations are too small to meet the financial demands.

To illustrate the diversity of their structures, purposes, and management, two actual examples of local organizations and one composite of many appear in the following section. Both clubs are long-established—the Union League of the Deaf, in New York City, started in 1886; and the National Literary Society of the Deaf, in Washington, D.C., started in 1887. For the "typical club," I have drawn on my visits over the last quarter century to many clubs and on the descriptions given to me by others. The composite aims to capture the essence of an average club.

Union League of the Deaf (UL)[18]

Four graduates of what is now Lexington School for the Deaf met 3 January 1886 to draw up a constitution and bylaws for the Deaf Mutes' Union League (UL). The need for a social organization that would satisfy their interests impelled their actions. They wanted to develop the "intellectual faculties of its members, this to be accomplished by lectures given in turn by each member." The Union League's first major social event, a ball held in December 1888, brought out another feature of the organization, charitableness: a share of the proceeds were donated to the Gallaudet Home for the Deaf. The ball's success impressed the Deaf community. Despite the fact that it had only fourteen members, it attracted to this event over a hundred people, including Alexander Graham Bell and Rev. Thomas Gallaudet. UL reached its peak in 1972 with five hundred resident and one hundred nonresident members. By its centennial, UL's membership had declined to about 150 active members (largely because the younger Deaf people have found other associations more attractive). Its fiscal affairs, however, continue to flourish, due mainly to the fact that some of its members have Wall Street connections. Today, UL boasts that it is "the nation's oldest and wealthiest club for Deaf." As if to affirm that appellation, UL held its hundredth birthday party at the Waldorf-Astoria's grand ballroom, which was packed with a black-tie crowd who had paid $100 per plate. UL no longer strives to develop its members' "intellectual faculties." Most of its meetings are dominated by card playing, leaving political and educational pursuits to the many other clubs in New York City.

National Literary Society of the Deaf (NLSD)[19]

Like UL, NLSD began with the purpose of improving its members' educations. In 1887, a small group started to meet on the Gallaudet campus and in the homes of members to discuss literature. Most of the members were associated with the college. Over the years, NLSD's membership has waxed and waned, though it has never been large. Its appeal is to the intellectually inclined Deaf person. It meets once a month during the academic year on the Gallaudet University campus. Those attending hear guest speakers address them on a wide range of topics; occasionally, there may be a debate or a poetry reading. Though called "national," it is actually a local organization. However, being in the nation's capital, its founders felt its name was appropriate. Ambiguous appellation notwithstanding, NLSD illustrates the viability of an organization of Deaf people that exists to provide intellectual stimulation of a high order.

Typical Club of the Deaf (TCD)

Entering the building housing the TCD, we must climb a steep staircase. At the top of the stairs we turn into a long, narrow room, furnished in a style we might call "early Goodwill." Tables covered with oilcloth tacked to their tops are surrounded by plain wooden chairs and, against one wall, sits a worn sofa that has probably been donated. Across the room from the entrance is a bar, the money spent at the bar pays TCD's rent. Next to the bar stands a television set. At the far end of the room is a small platform. It serves as the stage for lectures, plays, or other entertainments.

The small, often difficult-to-collect dues barely cover the other maintenance costs, so TCD can only be open Tuesday, Friday, Saturday, and Sunday nights. When we arrive at 5:00 P.M. on a weeknight, we find the clubroom nearly deserted, except for the bartender, who is also TCD's treasurer. Two hours later, the room has filled and the level of activity is dazzling. Everyone appears in conversation with someone, except for a lone male intently watching a captioned television program. We can identify at least half a dozen separate, loosely formed groups. Each can be characterized by age and sex. The groups continually dissipate and re-form until a bit past eight o'clock, when the president attempts to bring the meeting to order. For a brief moment, as the lights are turned on and off to attract attention, the crowd turns to the podium. Half or more turn back to their companions and continue their conversations. Throughout the meeting, members' attention drifts. It is a virtue of the "silent language" that these competing conversations do not unduly interrupt the proceedings, though it makes conducting club business difficult. When the meeting adjourns, the crush around the bar increases and then subsides as people leave for home. By eleven o'clock, TCD has nearly emptied. Half an hour later, the bartender shoos out the last customers, still deeply involved in their discussion, which they continue as they descend the stairs and head into the night.

What is the crowd like? Mostly middle-aged, mostly Deaf (occasionally normally hearing children of Deaf parents put in a brief appearance), more male than female, displaying no great wealth, but not appearing "tacky." Economically, they fall at the lower end of the middle-class scale. In spirit, they are at the upper end of a mood scale, not boisterous but in a persistently good humor. All in all, TCD provides a comfortable, unimposing setting for a pleasant evening, validating the description of the club as "the Deaf adults' second home."

Returning to the general atmosphere, different views of Deaf clubs prevail. Lou Ann Walker, the hearing daughter of Deaf parents, a professional interpreter and writer, says that "as a child, one of the reasons I hated going to Deaf social events was that they were held in seedy, decrepit buildings. The Indianapolis Deaf Club was above a porno peep show. The Deaf community just didn't have enough money to support anything else."[20]

What she found demeaning, others easily overlook. Ernest Hairston and Linwood Smith, two distinguished Deaf authors, see the clubs in terms of their functions, not their locations or physical appearance.

> It is often said that the club is the Deaf person's second home. It has also been said that the club is the heart of the Deaf community. It is at the club for the Deaf where ideas are exchanged, friendships formed, dances held, the latest happenings in the community shared, and where certain members merge as leaders. For many Black Deaf people it is the only opportunity to get together with other Deaf people on a regular basis.[21]

ORGANIZATIONS FOR DEAF PEOPLE

Organizations *for* deaf people also have impact on the Deaf community. Unquestionably the greatest influences on Deaf lives come from the governmental agencies. Those agencies will be discussed in chapter 5, which takes up education and rehabilitation. This section will focus on voluntary and membership groups, mostly at the national level, though some local groups and quasi-governmental groups, like the state commissions, are also considered.

MEMBERSHIP ASSOCIATIONS

General membership groups interested in deafness are few in number. Nationally, only two qualify—one embraces professionals, parents, lay persons, and deaf people; and another represents parents of deaf children.

Alexander Graham Bell Association for the Deaf (AGBAD)[22]

AGBAD exerts its influence on Deaf people through its advocacy of oral-communication policies. Originally called the Association to Promote the Teaching of Speech to the Deaf, it was founded by Alexander Graham Bell, in 1890. From its inception, AGBAD has been devoted to encouraging the use of speech, speechreading, and residual hearing by deaf people. Members include "all who [are] interested in oral instruction, including the parents and friends of deaf pupils who have been taught to speak." Its present membership hovers between four thousand and five thousand lay and professional people from the United States and thirty-eight foreign countries. The Oral Deaf Adults Section has already been reviewed in this chapter as a separate organization of deaf people, though AGBAD views it as a subdivision. Another division provides parents with information and encouragement to follow AGBAD's philosophy. AGBAD's location in Washington, D.C., provides it with a base from which to lobby Congress and interact with federal administrators. Except for ODAS, AGBAD seldom has had Deaf representation on its governing boards, so its views are those typical of normally hearing persons who have a professional or friendly interest in deafness. Because it is seen by most Deaf people as opposed to ASL, AGBAD often conflicts with NAD on policy matters.

American Society for Deaf Children (ASDC)[23]

Started in 1965, ASDC was originally called the International Association of Parents of the Deaf. During its early years, it had active support from NAD, which saw the organization as a counterbalance to AGBAD's parent section. ASDC promotes Total Communication, which means that it supports speech *and* the use of sign in the instruction of Deaf students. It is, therefore, generally looked upon as an ally by Deaf people. In its role as an advocate for Deaf causes, the largely parental makeup of ASDC gives its claims for legislators' attention great validity. However, as discussed in chapter 4, parents of Deaf children are often so beset with problems they have little time to devote to organizational activity, which limits their political influence.

PROFESSIONAL ASSOCIATIONS

While pediatricians, otologists, speech and language pathologists, and audiologists appear significantly in the lives of most deaf children, their professional associations do not have special sections devoted to the social lives of Deaf people. The three professional organizations devoted solely to Deaf people are sketched below.

American Deafness and Rehabilitation Association (ADARA)

Formerly Professional Rehabilitation Workers among the Adult Deaf, ADARA was established in 1966 during the federal government's "war to eliminate the ravages of disease, poverty and disability." In that climate, a group committed to deafness rehabilitation formed ADARA. Its largely professional membership has not found much sympathy from colleagues in the American Psychological Association, American Speech-Language-Hearing Association, American Association of Social Workers, and even in the National Rehabilitation Association. The primary function served by members of ADARA is rehabilitation, whether as counselors, therapists, psychologists, etc., and its purposes are consistent with that function. Within a relatively brief period, ADARA's numbers grew to almost two thousand members, then it declined as the federal climate changed and that peak has not been recovered. ADARA's Deaf members are a minority, and they have a proportionally small say in its governance. As is true of professional organizations generally, ADARA espouses its members' views, which are not necessarily the views of Deaf people.

Conference of Educational Administrators Serving the Deaf (CEASD) and Convention of American Instructors of the Deaf (CAID)

These two closely related organizations represent the education of deaf children in the United States, along with AGBAD, which joins them on the Council on Education of the Deaf (CED), a certifying body. CAID began in 1850 and CEASD in 1869. Membership in the two organizations overlaps, with many administrators also joining CAID. Both are devoted to educating deaf children; both provide similar support—mutual education through meetings and a journal, certification of programs, and advocacy on behalf of relevant issues. Until 1974, when Robert Davila became president of CAID, no Deaf person had been elected to that office. What is more, few Deaf educators had served on any of the CAID's governing committees. However, since Davila's election, other Deaf persons have been elected to the presidency and taken other authoritative positions. Davila went on to become president of CEASD. With the decline of residential and day schools for Deaf children, CAID-CEASD's dominant position in education has declined. Teachers and administrators who have only part-time relations with Deaf children are less apt to join these organizations.

STATE COMMISSIONS ON DEAFNESS[24]

The state commission on deafness is a recent innovation. Since 1971, when the Texas legislature established the first commission for the Deaf in the United States, sixteen states have followed its lead. Despite their potential importance, these agencies have had a lukewarm reception from the Deaf community. The National Association of the Deaf sponsored the First National Conference for State Commissions on Deafness in 1977, when only ten states had commissions, but NAD has not sponsored a similar conference since that time. Subsequent meetings between agency representatives were informal and largely unpublicized until 1988, when they formed an association. Average Deaf citizens do not seem impressed by the commissions' potential influence on economic, social, and vocational conditions in their states. Nor have most of the professionals who devote all or a major part of their practices to Deaf people paid much attention to the commissions.

To date, seventeen commissions have been established, and all but one are still functioning (see Table 3). The discrepancy between those established and those remaining is due to the abolition of Maryland's commission. The entries in Table 3 are arranged by the year the state adopted a commission. The commissions' dates of enactment are scattered: 1977 and 1979 are the banner years, with three new commissions in each of the two years. Otherwise, none or only one or two per year have been established in the other years, leaving no discernible trend.

The scope of the commissions varies widely from state to state. Some commissions have fairly narrow charges, others very broad. Advocacy is the most frequently mentioned purpose. Most states

Table 3   State Commissions on Deafness, by Year of Establishment

Name of Commission	Year Established
Texas Commission for the Deaf	1971
Oklahoma Commission on Deaf and Hearing Impaired	1972
Virginia Council for the Deaf	1972
Connecticut Commission on Deaf and Hard of Hearing	1974
Massachusetts Office of Deafness	1974
Deaf Services of Iowa	1975
Maryland Commission for the Hearing Impaired[a]	1976[a]
Arizona Council for the Deaf	1977
New Jersey Division of the Deaf	1977
North Carolina Council for Hearing Impaired	1977
Tennessee Council for the Hearing Impaired	1978
Michigan Division of Deaf and Deafened	1979
Nebraska Commission for the Hearing Impaired	1979
Wisconsin Bureau for the Hearing Impaired	1979
Louisiana Commission for the Hearing Impaired	1981
Kansas Commission for the Hearing Impaired	1982
Kentucky Commission on the Deaf and Hearing Impaired	1982

Source: Jerome D. Schein, "State Commissions on Deafness," *The Deaf American* 36, no. 5 (1984): 16–19.

[a]Decommissioned in 1981.

want their commissions to coordinate services, to eliminate duplication, and to assure that essential services are not being overlooked. All commissions have some involvement in the provision of interpreting services, though only a few have that function spelled out in their enabling acts.

State commissions personify the changing fortunes of Deaf people in our society. Since the turn of the century, most states have had commissions on blindness. Blind people, however, have not considered these commissions an unmixed blessing. They have sometimes complained that their views have not been adequately presented because they have not had adequate representation on the commissions. All commissions have Deaf people on their boards. The proportions of the memberships that must be Deaf range from none to 75 percent. But simply having a large proportion of the policymaking body be Deaf does not assure that the representation will be satisfactory. For example, members might be selected who, though deaf, have no roots in the Deaf community.

Deaf people should also beware of *token* commissions, of bodies that have the title but not the funding nor the authority to do what Deaf people would like to have done. A commission that lacks authority to develop services and funds with which to conduct its business can, in the long run, do more harm than good. Legislators are apt to point to the paper entity as proof that they are adequately serving the Deaf community. Thus relieved of further obligations, the legislators can deny reasonable requests from the Deaf community with the argument that they have already done enough. An ineffectual commission can become merely an excuse for *not* providing services. Another reason for the Deaf community's lack of support for state commissions may be the feeling of its leaders that the commissions represent competition—competition for funding, for authority, and for the attention of the Deaf community. As a relatively recent innovation in the Deaf community, it is too early to declare that state commissions will not contribute positively and thus gain acceptance of its constituency. They could overcome the doubts about governance, effectiveness, and possible conflicts with established Deaf groups, and they could demonstrate their ability to benefit the Deaf community and become better known in it. They could, and they might.

Advocacy Organizations

While NAD, NFSD, AGBAD, and the professional organizations like ADARA and CEASD engage in lobbying on behalf of issues involved with deafness, none have that as their sole purpose. As will be discussed in the section on coordinating bodies, having so many organizations claiming to represent Deaf people has the obvious danger of confusing legislators and government administrators. Deciding which groups speaks for Deaf people places bureaucrats in a position most would prefer to avoid. Of all the national organizations, only Deafpride has the sole aim of advocacy on behalf of Deaf people.

Deafpride[25]

In 1972, some Deaf and normally hearing people jointly created Deafpride "to work for the human rights of Deaf persons, especially their right to equal educational opportunity." This group of about 150 individuals and a sizable number of corporate members has sponsored conferences, published papers, issued a newsletter, and lobbied in Congress. Most of the normally hearing members are parents of Deaf children; the Deaf members have been drawn most frequently from the faculty of Gallaudet University. However, Deafpride has members in at least twenty-three states, the District of Columbia, and Puerto Rico. Interestingly, Deafpride has affiliated with United Black Fund for fund-raising, though many of its members and officers are not Black. As an advocacy organization, Deafpride has focused its efforts on public and governmental relations, and in these endeavors it has enjoyed some success. It has not, however, merged its programs with those of other national groups to achieve goals of mutual interest.

COORDINATING BODIES

The survey of organizations of and for Deaf people confirms the initial impression of large numbers and diversity. Add to it the church groups discussed in chapter 2 and the governmental agencies to be discussed in chapter 5 and it is apparent that the Deaf community could suffer from organizational confusion, with groups offering conflicting opinions while all claim, "We speak for the deaf." Deaf leaders also have seen the overlapping services, authorities, and interests, and they have sought means for coordinating the activities of these organizations.

SCHISMS

It is easy to idealize the Deaf community, to see it as a superior arrangement of people without rancor, with total acceptance of others, especially others like themselves, and with widespread cooperation among its members. That is simply not the case. Like the larger society in which it is embedded, the Deaf community has many factions.

Age creates a major distinction within the Deaf community, as it does generally. For example, NAD's companion organizations, JNAD and NAHICS, stress the interests of youth, while a separate Senior Citizens Section addresses the problems of older members. Deaf women encounter discrimination on the basis of their sex as do their colleagues in the general community.[26]

Education creates another division in the Deaf community. APSD, GUAA, and NLSD may be considered elitist groups, since almost all members of each have attended college, usually Gallaudet University. AAAD, on the other hand, draws more broadly across the educational–economic spectrum for its membership.

The Oral Deaf Adults Section represents yet another schism— signers versus oralists. Deaf people who depend solely upon speech and speechreading for communication are a minority within the Deaf community. They tend to be less well organized, largely because their numbers are small. At the local level, an active group of speech-oriented Deaf people in New York City, the Merry Go-Rounders, has persisted for nearly half a century as a social group dedicated to providing opportunities for social interaction among Deaf people who prefer to communicate orally. Though it is currently in decline, it once numbered its membership in the hundreds. Those who join it frequently belong to other groups, like the Union League and ODAS or NAD.

Occasionally, practical issues divide the Deaf community. In 1947, Byron B. Burnes, then NAD president, testified before Congress in opposition to an extra tax exemption for Deaf people. Despite the passage of over four decades, the correctness of his decision still stirs debates.

Organizations of Deaf people have not responded uniformly to racial discrimination. Almost from its inception, AAAD insisted on accepting all racial and ethnic backgrounds. NAD dropped its racial bars in 1965. NFSD did not accept black members until 1967. Gallaudet University admitted its first black Deaf student in 1954, but did not admit another for four years. Hispanic Deaf people encountered similar discrimination.[27] Today, when racial bars are exposed, the emotion associated with the revelations tends more often to be resignation than indignation. In 1983, Hairston and Smith said, "Two Washington, D.C. area clubs, MWAD (predominantly white) and CCAD (predominantly Black) are housed 12 blocks apart and are open to all races. Although members from each club intermingle, there is no great effort to integrate on a widespread scale."[28]

To say that the Deaf community does not outdo the general population in its humaneness and social justice does not mean that it is desperately flawed. Deaf people act much like their nondeaf peers in the general population, and their society reflects their fallibility.

COORDINATION IN THE DEAF COMMUNITY

Schisms build barriers to cooperation. Yet, for a group as relatively small as the Deaf community, cooperation in dealing with its problems is proportionally less than would be expected. Conflicting voices within the Deaf community can, and frequently do, provide the excuse for inaction by legislators and administrators. The rhetorical question, How can we agree to do what your group asks when other Deaf people do not want us to do that? will not be answered satisfactorily by pointing out that the "other Deaf people" are a tiny minority within the minority; the officials do not want to act, and that splinter group provides the rationale for inaction. This scenario was among those that led Deaf leaders who attended the Fort Monroe, Virginia, conference in 1961 to recommend a national organization of organizations to provide a forum from which current issues could be debated and consensus achieved. Where no consensus could be reached, the cooperating groups would be forewarned against approaching the government for those specific actions.

Council of Organizations Serving the Deaf (COSD)[29]

From a meeting of Deaf leaders in 1961 came the recommendation for an organization that would bring together groups promoting the welfare of Deaf people. Deaf people had no consensus on priorities nor a unified strategy for attaining any objectives, and they needed a forum in which to discuss and resolve disputes within and between those whose principal interests focused on deafness. A federal grant was given to start COSD, and, in 1966, its bylaws were ratified by AGBAD, AAAD, Board for Missions to the Deaf, the Lutheran Church (Missouri Synod), Canadian Association of the Deaf, Conference of Church Workers among the Deaf (later, Episcopal Conference of the Deaf), CEASD, CAID, GUAA, ICDA, NAD,

National Association of Hearing and Speech Agencies (later, the National Association for Hearing and Speech Action, now a part of the American Speech-Language-Hearing Association), NCJD, NFSD, ADARA, Registry of Interpreters for the Deaf, and, as associate members, the Board of Missions of the United Methodist Church, the Deafness Research Foundation, and the Ephphatha Mission for the Deaf and Blind. Eight of the nineteen members and associates were organizations *of* Deaf people; the remaining eleven provided services *to* Deaf people or advocated *for* Deaf people. Not all were members at the start of the organization, and as time progressed, some of the original member organizations withdrew from COSD.

Throughout its few years of existence, COSD had a Deaf person directing its activities. It had two means of achieving a unified voice on issues of interest to Deaf people. The first was to hold meetings of the council at which representatives of the constituent organizations debated the issues brought before it. The second was to hold national and regional forums at which a particular topic would be covered in depth. COSD conducted seven forums.

When federal funding was about to be withdrawn, COSD sought income by inviting memberships from individuals. It also began to apply for other government grants. COSD's member organizations suddenly saw it as a competitor, as another agency trying to do what they themselves were trying to do. Several more withdrew. When the federal funds ceased, COSD soon after disbanded.

While the organization collapsed nationally, it left a strong legacy. Several states have adopted the COSD model. Connecticut, for example, still has a Connecticut Council of Organizations Serving the Deaf. Even at the local level, there are remnants of the council's philosophy; New York City continues to have a Council of Organizations Serving the Deaf, as does Baltimore. Though these state and local organizations may lack the prestige of a national body and the legal authority of the state commissions, they can, nonetheless, add importantly to coordination among those agencies that stay with them.

Greater Los Angeles Council on Deafness (GLAD)[30]

GLAD, as this relatively new local organization prefers to be known, brings together forty-five agencies and fifteen hundred members in the Los Angeles area. It is affiliated with NAD. The stimulus for its inception was a paper by Henry Klopping, superintendent of the California School for the Deaf, who was a graduate student at the time he wrote it. He pointed out the sorry state of services for Deaf people in the Los Angeles area and recommended an organization to coordinate activities on their behalf. Thus, in 1969, a small group from the California Association of the Deaf and California State University at Northridge met and established GLAD. Under the direction of an Assembly of Delegates, its executive director, Marcella Meyer, manages an enterprise that exceeds the sum of its parts. GLAD did not begin to provide direct services until 1974, when it offered an information service. Shortly after that modest beginning, it received support from California's Department of Rehabilitation to provide interpreting services. GLAD has since expanded its services to include counseling, advocacy, and vending books and products made for Deaf consumers. Its offices at 616 South Westmoreland Avenue resemble the headquarters of a major corporation. In addition, GLAD maintains offices at five other locations in the Los Angeles area. GLAD is committed to Deaf self-determination in an organization that is of, by, and for Deaf people.

Mutual Alliance Plan (MAP)

Speculation about why COSD failed nationally should not be regarded as idle, since the idea of an organization that would coordinate efforts on behalf of Deaf people remains active. Soon after COSD's demise, NAD took steps to replace it. MAP began to take shape in 1976, and by 1979, it had been considered by many of the same organizations that had formerly belonged to COSD. The essence of the plan was to promote active discussions among the participating organizations. To avoid COSD's mistake, MAP would have no elaborate staff, no expensive headquarters, no other goals than promoting cooperative action among its members. It would seek no grants or individual memberships. The author of MAP, NAD Executive Director, Fred Schreiber, recognized that he would have to be patient, but he also knew that without great persistence the concept would not come to fruition. He worked assiduously to convince the leaders of other organizations to join in MAP, but, unfortunately, he died in 1979 before he could bring it into being. His devotion to MAP was not immediately shared by his successors in the organizations that serve Deaf people. The idea of agency coordination at the national level, however, has not passed into obscurity. A new coordinating group has come into being, encompassing some of the former agencies and, significantly, including the relatively new organization, Self Help for Hard of Hearing People. The broadening of its base to include hard-of-hearing people strengthens the political potential of the combined forces, but may weaken the common interests that initially united COSD. It remains to be seen how effectively these various groups can function in tandem when addressing issues of mutual, national concern.

ANALYSIS OF THE ORGANIZATIONAL STRUCTURE OF THE DEAF COMMUNITY

Other than providing a sense of the complexity of the organizational underpinning of the Deaf community, the preceding descriptions should yield some generalizations about it. The following analysis attempts to reveal some of the principles governing the nature of the Deaf community's organizations.

TRENDS AMONG ORGANIZATIONS OF DEAF PEOPLE

Referring back to Table 2 two trends appear. First, national organizations did not emerge until the last fifth of the nineteenth century, and following an initial growth spurt, none was formed for almost the first half of the twentieth century. Since 1950, the total number of national organizations has more than trebled, from four to fourteen. Second, the organizations founded after NAD tended to be more specialized, either in purpose or membership. GUAA, of course, limited its membership to those who had attended the university. NFSD initially had a narrow purpose, to provide insurance for Deaf people. Thereafter, limitations on membership (APSD, ICDA, JNAD, NBDA, NAHICS, NCJD, ODAS, and RAD) and specific purposes (AAAD, TDI, and FOLDA) characterize the organizations.

Much of the organizational growth spurt in this century might be attributed to the civil rights movement. Yet, aside from NBDA, the organizations dating from that period—APSD, FOLDA, JNAD, NAHICS, ODAS, and TDI—seem motivated more by inward-looking Deaf interests than by the demands upon the majority for equal employment opportunity and community participation.

Among the Deaf leadership, the civil rights movement had a substantial impact, particularly on NAD, which joined with other disabled groups to bring to public attention injustices, inequalities, and discriminations imposed on the Deaf community.

Membership Size

The estimated memberships for each of the national organizations in Table 2 cannot be added to get an estimate of the numbers of Deaf people who belong to national organizations for two reasons. One is that NAD is a confederation, which means that members of the affiliated state associations may or may not be members of NAD, depending on the state association's policies; conversely, some NAD members do not join state associations. The other reason is that a segment of the Deaf population belongs to more than one of these organizations.[31] Considering that the Deaf population of the United States is only about half a million, NAD's fifteen thousand members represent a sizable proportion—a comparable organization representing *all* persons in this country would have almost seven million members.

Tools of Organization

Organizations of Deaf people make use of all of the tools that other organizations use—conventions and meetings, newsletters and magazines, planning and budgeting, networking with other organizations of and for Deaf people. Deaf organizations hold elections and they struggle with finances, membership apathy, and internal divisiveness. None of the organizations appears to have uncovered new solutions to these old problems. With respect to management techniques, organizations of Deaf people are run very much like other group organizations.

Participation

To what extent do Deaf people participate in their organization's decision-making? What means are provided by the organization to ensure that their members' opinions are given weight in whatever decisions are made? Here, too, Deaf organizations do not seem unique, neither in the difficulties in motivating participation nor in the methods used to improve it. Of course, there is the ubiquitous matter of communication in the Deaf community. But aside from the modes of communicating—sign language, lipreading, etc.—deaf organizations appear no better and no worse than other groups. The fact that the Deaf community has so many organizations, and that so many have survived for so long, supports the conclusion that Deaf leaders communicate effectively with their constituents.

SETTING PRIORITIES

Service providers and those who finance their efforts often face the difficult task of setting priorities because the resources available to them cannot deal with all of the problems confronting their agencies. The Deaf community has benefited from a number of landmark meetings that have set the directions for years that followed their convening. One such important meeting was the previously mentioned Fort Monroe conference in 1961, which led to a great number of important developments in rehabilitation. It focused on techniques and strategies Deaf people could use to increase control of their own destinies and gain more input to government programs that aimed to assist them.

Ten years later, in 1971, a small group of experts on deafness rehabilitation met in Tarrytown, New York, for a meeting called "Current Priorities in the Rehabilitation of Deaf People." Seven of the thirteen participants were Deaf leaders, the remaining six were involved in deafness rehabilitation as administrators of service delivery programs or educators of personnel. Their deliberations resulted in fifty-two recommendations on administration, organization, staffing, facilities, job development, communication, and research, and a fairly large portion were implemented in one way or another. For example, the conferees noted the lack of uniform services provided to Deaf clients by state rehabilitation agencies, and it suggested that a prototypical service plan be circulated to assist states in upgrading their programs. In 1973, the first of several model state plans for serving Deaf clients was published and, importantly, accepted to some degree by all of the states.[32] The Tarrytown conference also urged the use of manual communication throughout the educational programs for deaf students, a proposal that has been fulfilled, to some extent.

As the decade was coming to a close, the New York University Deafness Research and Training Center, which had hosted the

Tarrytown Conference, called a meeting to prepare an agenda for the 1980s. The meeting brought together twenty-three participants, of whom seventeen were deaf. They represented major factions in the Deaf community, educators and rehabilitators, advocates, and service providers. Priorities were established for communication, education, employment, mental health, physical health, and community relations. The group's report was simultaneously published by AGBAD's *The Volta Review* and NAD's *The Deaf American*, two organizations usually holding opposing views about deafness. With that broad-based support, the majority of the priorities established at this meeting have been implemented. For example, the plea for more and better-qualified interpreters has been answered by federally funded interpreter-training programs; better TDDs have been marketed by private industry; captioned television has expanded with federal support; and more postsecondary education for Deaf students is now available than ever before. While mental-health services have not improved as rapidly as would be desirable, the recommendations remain as guideposts in mapping future action.

In 1988, two national meetings pointed the way to the future. In El Paso, Texas, a large number of professionals and Deaf leaders met to face the last decade of this century. Their deliberations can be expected to exert further influence on the directions that government and voluntary agencies will pursue in the near future. Earlier in 1988, after an eighteen-month study, the congressionally appointed Commission on Education of the Deaf delivered its report, containing fifty-two recommendations and the following summary:

> Among the recommendations concerning deaf children and youth, we emphasize those dealing with appropriate education and the least restrictive environment concept. Of our postsecondary education recommendations, we stress establishment of comprehensive services centers, a new role for the federally supported Regional Postsecondary Education Programs for the Deaf, and competitively available research funding. We also regard our recommendations on professional standards for educators, interpreters, and rehabilitation specialists, as well as new requirements for captioned TV services, as among the most important.[33]

Because of the successes of earlier efforts, these most recently promulgated sets of priorities can be expected to have a positive impact on Deaf people. Those successes will encourage future gatherings to prepare national objectives for Deaf people, some sponsored by the government and others by groups of organizations serving deaf and hard-of-hearing people. Though not a conscious intent of those who plan these meetings, they have the interesting side effect of bolstering the cohesiveness of the Deaf community by emphasizing the common interests of the diverse social elements of which it is made.

ORGANIZATIONAL EFFECTIVENESS

How effectively do organizations of Deaf people succeed? Applying two measures of organizational effectiveness—survival and relative membership size—several organizations of Deaf people score well. NAD and NFSD have persisted from their founding to this date. Relative to the size of the Deaf population, both memberships encompass a sizable proportion of the Deaf population. Others, like APSD and ODAS, have done poorly, being relatively new and remaining small in size. Thus, it would appear that those organizations of Deaf people that appealed to a broad segment of the population have succeeded better than those that give the appearance of being more elitist in their membership appeals. The future, however, may favor those groups that serve specialized interests of the Deaf community and attract narrower segments of the Deaf population; organizations like TDI, which aims to improve telecommunications, and NBDA and RAD, which are established for minority groups within the Deaf community.

Of course, survival and growth are indirect measures of the extent to which an organization serves its members' purposes. If the organization provides members what they want, they will see that it survives. If the organization provides what many potential members desire, they will join it and it will grow. Over time, the organization's adaptability to changes will determine its fate. Thus, even the most successful organizations must remain alert to shifts in their members' interests and to alterations in their growth rates. To do otherwise is to court extinction.[34]

NOTES

1. Systematic comparisons between different nation's Deaf communities fall outside this book's scope, though such studies should prove exciting and enlightening. The differences between United States and Swedish Deaf communities are discussed in chapter 8.
2. While this chapter's focus remains on formal groups—those with stated purposes, written bylaws, specific meeting dates and places, and prescribed officers—the role of informal groupings cannot be overlooked. It is, however, the subject for another study.
3. This segment is based on material in Schein, 1981, and Schreiber, 1979.
4. Garretson, 1962, 2.
5. Most of the data in this segment are from Gannon, 1987. Gallaudet College became Gallaudet University in October 1986, at which time the Alumni Association appropriately changed its name.
6. Material on the Frat comes from the article by its recently retired grand president Frank Sullivan (1987) and from a personal interview that he graciously gave me.
7. All of the quotations and most of the information in this paragraph are from Kruger, 1987, 17–19.
8. This section is based on Fleischman, 1986–1987.
9. For further details, see Conlon, 1987.
10. Rowley (1987) provided the basis for this segment.
11. Schein, 1987c.
12. This information is based on interviews with Mary Anne Pugin and Ernest E. Hoffman, to whom I am deeply grateful.
13. The information is from Hairston and Smith, 1983, supplemented by personal interviews with some NBDA members.
14. Hairston and Smith, 1983, 48.
15. "Student Founds National Program for College Peers," 1984.
16. The pamphlet from which this sketch was drawn was prepared by Alice Hagemeyer.
17. A teacher at the American School describes the affair's inception: "The deaf and dumb were entirely self-moved in this matter. The idea originated with Mr. Thomas Brown, of New Hampshire, one of the earliest and most intelligent of the pupils of the Asylum. . . . a committee was chosen to procure the necessary funds, and in a very short time, the handsome sum of six hundred dollars was obtained; wholly, let it be understood, from the deaf and dumb themselves. The entire credit of the transaction belongs to them" (Rae, 1851, 42). If his tone sounds condescending, recall that he was writing a few years after the found-

ing of the first school for Deaf children in this country, a period in which many lay persons and quite a few professionals did not believe Deaf people could be educated.

18. Lerner, 1986, 3. This delightful pamphlet and a news release prepared by Michael A. Schwartz supplied most of the remaining information.
19. Information in this paragraph is from Higgins, 1983.
20. Walker, 1986, 149.
21. Hairston and Smith, 1983.
22. Conlon, 1987.
23. Mendelsohn, 1987.
24. Schein, 1984.
25. Deafpride, 1976.
26. Wax and Danek, 1984.
27. Delgado, 1984.
28. Hairston and Smith, 1983.
29. Schein, 1987a.
30. This section is based on the essay by Meyer, 1987.
31. Schein (1968) found almost half of Deaf people in Washington, D.C., belonged to an organization of Deaf people and about one-third joined more than one organization.
32. Schein, 1973, 1977b, 1980. For a study of implementation of the plan, see Schein, Delk, and Gentile, 1977.
33. Commission on Education of the Deaf, 1988, xiv.
34. Paul Higgins, in a personal communication, pointed out that an organization can shape its members' interests; it need not only be a reactor to them.

4

Family Life

Most deaf children have hearing parents. When they grow up, they marry deaf spouses. When these deaf couples have children, those children most often will have normal hearing. These three facts dominate any discussion of family life in the Deaf community. Their rates of occurrence appear so regularly in the research literature that I refer to them as the "90-percent rule" of deaf family life because

- 90 percent of deaf children have hearing parents,
- 90 percent of deaf adults marry another deaf person,
- 90 percent of children born to deaf couples have *normal* hearing.

The coincidence of the one quantity—90 percent—for three facets of deaf family life is easily remembered. It is based on numerous studies, whose results have been averaged to exploit their similarity.[1] The 90-percent rule has profound implications for the Deaf community. In its capsulized form, it highlights the isolation that deafness imposes—isolation from normally hearing people. It plays a significant role in the theory of Deaf community development, contributing both explanatory and illustrative features. It also signals *the three-generational impact of deafness.*[2] Deafness affects three living generations—parents, their deaf children, and the deaf children's children. These three generations feel the impact of deafness.

Sociologists regard the family as the fundamental unit in Western civilization. Aside from providing basic nurturance for the young, the family transmits the culture, the mores, the folkways, and the language that identify a particular group. That is not the case for deaf children. Their parents, at least 90 percent of them, know nothing about Deaf culture, ASL, and the Deaf community. They will seldom become involved with the Deaf community until they reach adolescence or adulthood. For the children's socialization, this situation proves awkward because the parents' own experiences do not provide much of the information that would be most relevant to raising their deaf children.

Parental hearing ability is not usually a direct cause of deafness. The four possible parental combinations account for the following percentages of the deaf population: (a) two normally hearing parents—92 percent; (b) hearing-impaired mother, normally hearing father—2 percent; (c) normally hearing mother, hearing-impaired father—1.5 percent; and two hearing-impaired parents—4.5 percent. The ensuing discussion examines the different kinds of families into which deaf children are born and the effect of parental hearing ability on raising a deaf child.

THE DEAF CHILD IN THE HEARING FAMILY

The most common family into which deaf children are born is headed by two normally hearing parents. They have no preparation for raising a deaf child. They know little or nothing about deafness and less about Deaf people. They cannot rely on their own experience for guidance. They lack empathy for their deaf child's behavior. They feel cut off from the child; they have difficulty understanding the child and greater difficulty making the child understand them. Their emotional reaction to the deaf child affects their judgments and, worst of all, is often communicated to the child. Society, represented by professionals the parents meet, family members, and neighbors, reinforces the parents' feelings of anger, sorrow, frustration, and bitterness.

THE DIAGNOSIS OF DEAFNESS

At the outset, parents enter what may seem like a conspiracy designed to postpone the diagnosis of deafness. Deafness occurs in less than 1 of 1,000 live births. Unless there is a family history of deafness or the mother contracts some illness in pregnancy, such as rubella, the birth of a deaf infant will shock all concerned. The improbability of deafness at birth, along with the natural inclination to avoid bad news, both on the part of the parents and their physician, prolongs the period of uncertainty before a definitive diagnosis is made. Consider one parent's account:

> All these clues should have alerted me to Charlie's hearing loss. My list of excuses for why they did not is impressive for its length, but the fact refuses to be altered. I did not see Charlie's problem. Suspected? Yes. Ignored? Possibly. Feared? Most definitely. Even later, when the clues were more evident, I could hardly say that I sought an answer to the question of whether Charlie could hear. More correctly, I inhibited the process.[3]

Another mother, who had rubella during pregnancy, gave the following description of the moment when all previous assurances that the baby had escaped any consequences of the maternal infection were swept away. Standing by the baby's crib, this mother put her suspicions, built of numerous hints, to the test.

> Finally I called her name as loud as I could and when she didn't look, I went to her crib. Right away she turned to look at me! She smiled and waved her arms—it was almost like she had been playing a game with me. When I walked out of there I had the strangest feeling in the pit of my stomach, like something dreadful was about to happen and I couldn't stop it. I think she may be *deaf!*[4]

The same mother returned to her pediatrician with her suspicions confirmed and seeking help. Her husband recounted the physician's all-too-common reaction.

> Louise finally returned to Dr. Bales with additional evidence about Lynn's lack of hearing. She arrived home in tears. "I don't think he takes me seriously," she began as her mood turned into anger. "He says Lynn is just too young to tell anything for sure. Tom, I wish *you* had gone with me. Maybe he would listen to you." Then she broke into tears again.[5]

Long delays between parental suspicions and official confirmations of deafness are the norm. One study found an average of nine months elapsed between parental suspicions of profound deafness and the correct diagnosis, and in cases of severe hearing impairment the delay averaged sixteen months.[6] Delayed diagnoses cannot always be attributed to the professionals. Some parents engage in what two researchers term "doctor chase," going from specialist after specialist in hopes of finding that the initial diagnosis of deafness was in error.[7]

When the diagnosis of deafness is made, the professional's behavior often reinforces the parents' feelings that a tragedy has befallen them. According to a candid audiologist in a large hospital, "Telling parents their child is deaf is the toughest part of my work." Several times parents have said that when the professional finally used the word *deaf*, they thought he or she said *dead!* And the professional's manner suited the latter expression. Recent studies led a team of researchers to report that

> deafness is an invisible handicap, and the behavioral changes associated with it may easily be attributed to poor motivation, slow development, maternal overanxiety, etc. Most physicians have little experience with deafness, but lots of experience with worried parents who are suspecting all sorts of problems. Physicians probably tend to trust their own brief observations more than the countless ones made by parents. . . . One major recommendation from this study, then, is that medical schools and medical organizations seek to do a better job of impressing upon physicians the need to take parental concerns seriously, especially in the area of deafness. The long delay which so often occurs not only prevents the enrollment of the child into a much-needed program, but may also convince the mother that there is something wrong with her judgment, it may stimulate marital disharmony, and finally when the truth is realized the parents' confidence in professionals may be severely impaired.[8]

Testing the hearing of infants requires considerable skill. Sometimes the search for a diagnosis is complicated by conditions other than deafness that might explain some or all of the child's abnormal behavior (e.g., autism, cerebral palsy, or mental retardation). In trying to determine the cause for his young child's aberrant behavior, one father summed up his frustration with the professional personnel after picking up his four-year-old daughter from a university preschool on a day when she had obviously not been well tended.

> I felt as though there wasn't competence anywhere. Audiologists couldn't decide if Jennifer was deaf; orthopedic doctors couldn't get to appointments on time; preschool teachers for the deaf were scaring little children on their first day of class; and now they couldn't change diapers.[9]

Often, parents state their feelings about learning their child was deaf in general terms because they believe most parents have similar responses.

> At that time, parents can experience feelings of guilt, "What have I done?" or feelings of sadness, "Why me?" These are emotional, uninhibited "gut" feelings, no doubt serving some emotional purpose. The parent is confused and disoriented. The initial shock, disbelief, and profound depression may render the parents incapable of positive activity.[10]

The saddest instances are those in which intellectually normal deaf children are placed in institutions for mentally retarded children, where their potential for normal development is destroyed by the staff's lack of awareness of the child's deafness. The symptoms—slow or no language development, inattention to parents' and professionals' speech, temper tantrums—might easily be mistaken for mental retardation, but prolonged observation should eliminate that diagnosis and others, like mental illness. Misdiagnoses should seldom occur in this enlightened era of psychological practice, yet they too often do.[11]

AFTER THE DIAGNOSIS: THE EARLY YEARS

As the preceding discussion asserts, once correctly diagnosed, 90 percent of deaf children are not welcome additions to their families—though it is the deafness, not the child, that is unwelcome. Intentionally or not, many professionals support those feelings of rejection by delivering a clear message to the family, *You have a flawed child.* Seldom do the parents have the wherewithal to respond, *Nonsense! With or without hearing, this child is ours and we are pleased to be the parents.* Instead, the family has an extended period of mourning, with more confusion and discomfort to come as new situations arise.[12]

A common response to problems that accompany the deaf child is overprotectiveness. This "smothering" reaction offsets parents' guilt aroused by their anger toward their deaf child; for other parents, overprotectiveness may be seen as compensating the child for the loss of hearing.[13] A related reaction is overcontrol, the parents' attempts to minutely direct their deaf child. Overcontrol often accompanies the efforts to make the child as normally hearing as possible. To this end, parents make sure the child attends regular schools, has only normally hearing playmates, and communicates exclusively through speech and speechreading.

The shift from infancy to childhood brings questions about schooling. Quite naturally, parents turn to professionals for counsel. What they often hear or read are conflicting opinions—be firm/ be permissive; insist on powerful hearing aids in infancy/do not put hearing aids on the child until after three years of age; use sign language/never use sign language; do/don't put your child in a classroom with other deaf children. Contradictions abound, yet parents should not consider that state of affairs odd. It is true in many fields of human endeavor that experts view the same problems from different perspectives. Few practitioners tell parents to examine all the options, think about the child, and then do what they believe is best. Fewer still will tell the parents that opinions are so varied because research is sparse and not definitive and, therefore, the parents should not feel anxious about making decisions. A notable exception is the team of Freeman, Carbin, and Boese, whose textbook counsels parents to "visit different programs and listen to different points of view, even if they are confusing at first . . . meet with deaf adults and children . . . meet with other parents."[14] Nor should they later feel guilty if their child does not progress as fast and achieve as much as they had hoped. Parents would understand that if their child were normally hearing like themselves, but the fact that the child is deaf destroys their self-confidence and deprives them of a major guide to child-rearing—their empathetic reactions.

Parents usually get advice from nonprofessionals, too. Relatives, friends, neighbors, and even casual passersby seem ready to provide instructions about where to go and what to do, and how to handle a crying fit or a mild tantrum—until they realize the child is deaf. Then come the unanticipated reactions: friends visit less often or stop coming altogether; relatives gently or abruptly suggest that the parents not bring *that* child to the next family gathering; neighbors sometimes refuse to let their physically normal children play with the deaf child, as if the deafness might rub off! These are common complaints heard by counselors who work with parents of deaf children. These reactions cast another shadow on the deaf child.

School Days

In our society, the family shares with schools the responsibility for preparing children for adulthood. Parents feel at a great disadvantage in deciding about schooling for their deaf child. They cannot rely upon their own experience, and discussions with neighbors about the community's schools usually are not helpful, because they, too, have no experience with deafness. A noted authority on the education of deaf children, who is deaf himself, has observed that:

> an education is so many things that to presuppose a single, rigid route towards its attainment is ridiculous, especially for a child with no hearing. It is a mistake to assume that all Deaf children are similar in personality and intelligence. Nothing could be more naive. Except for his physical disability, the Deaf child is as diverse, positively and negatively, as his hearing counterpart; and too frequently, it is the emphasis on the disability that blots out his individuality.[15]

Unless they can communicate fluently with their deaf child, something few normally hearing parents can do, they find great difficulty in transmitting their values and their ways to the child. Children in general learn many rules of behavior from overhearing conversations between parents. The deaf child does not. Children develop restraints on their actions through verbal corrections uttered by one or the other parent. The deaf child seldom does.

Some parents find relief in sending their child to a residential school, thus relieving them of day-to-day frustrations. Others prefer to have their child close to home. Putting a deaf child in a neighborhood school makes a declaration of normalcy: see, Dick/Jane goes to the same school with all the other children in the neighborhood. In the latter cases, parents frequently find that the school personnel know as little as they do about deaf children and that many teachers have never met a deaf child before. The school placement issue forces parents to make yet another decision, and as with earlier ones, authorities do not agree on what is best for the deaf child.

Regardless of the setting parents choose for their deaf child's education, they should expect to cooperate with the instructional personnel. Parent participation is mandated by federal law, which means that, at the least, a parent must sign the child's Individualized Education Program annually. No matter how pro forma this requirement may seem, it serves to remind parents that their deaf child is different from their other children, if they have other children, and from themselves, because such formalized procedures are not demanded for regular school students.[16]

ADOLESCENCE

The difficulties of parenting a deaf child markedly increase when the child enters adolescence. In their teens, children desire nothing so much as peer acceptance. Let one come to school with torn jeans and next day they all will. Being part of the group often means more than gaining parental acceptance. In their teens, many physically normal children will not go out in public with their parents; and oh how they wish their parents were like everybody else's parents.

The deaf child, however, cannot be like everybody else in a group whose members have normal hearing. Hence, many deaf teenagers in regular schools find adolescence a far more difficult time than do their normally hearing peers. This is not to say that deaf adolescents in schools with other deaf adolescents find the transition from childhood to adulthood easy. They simply find it easier.[17]

An intellectually above-average, seventeen-year-old deaf girl attending a regular high school found herself lonely. She expressed in a poem her frustration at being rejected by students who in earlier grades had been friendly toward her. A few lines convey her feelings:

I walk in the crowded hall filled with students
to see if I could make friends; no one notices me
Students who I know in the past years said
"Hi" to me as I thought they want to make me happy
Why a single word sounds making me happy?
One word? Everyday—they continue to say the same word
I'm tired of it.

She concludes her ratiocinations with a poignant outburst, "But everything except learning in school ruins my life!"[18]

As for parental relations, deaf teenagers find it difficult to identify with their normally hearing parents. They cannot emulate Mother and Father in at least one important regard—they cannot hear. The deaf daughter of a famous opera singer cannot aspire to her mother's career. The deaf son of a famous movie actor will not follow in his father's footsteps. For role models, deaf teenagers must look outside their families and into the Deaf community, if they are even aware of it. As noted in the previous chapter, they may not

HATE

An exceptionally articulate mother describes her reactions to her son's deafness.

I still carry some pain around that occasionally surfaces. With each major change in Jeffrey's development, I have found myself going through the same emotional adjustments I did in the very beginning. Such adjustments come in differing degrees, and I have learned to recognize them and know that the pain will pass. I still cry, too. The only difference is that now I cry mostly because I'm so proud of Jeffrey and what he has become. At 14, he's okay; he's going to make it. I still hate the deafness, but we've all learned to live with it.[19]

come home until they pass out of their adolescence into adulthood. The imminent move from adolescence to adulthood brings questions about career choice. As was true at earlier junctures, normally hearing parents cannot depend solely on their own backgrounds to advise their deaf children, to empathize with their agonies and triumphs, to guide their children's futures from an inside position. Though not easily done, many parents do come to accept their children's deafness as they mature into young adults, thus bringing the parent–offspring relationships to a more satisfying level of mutual respect and affection.

YOUNG ADULTHOOD

Alienation from parents usually peaks when the deaf child matures and takes a spouse. As the statistics indicate, the spouse will also be deaf 9 out of 10 times. The normally hearing parents then meet bride and groom with whom they usually cannot communicate easily and whose acceptance of a different culture they will have difficulty understanding. The happily anticipated birth of a grandchild can turn bitter when the grandparents betray their overwhelming desire for a normally hearing infant. That desire is understandable, but its expression recalls to the Deaf parents the earlier rejection they felt as children. So the normally hearing grandparents should not be surprised to find themselves rejected by their children as the children believe they were rejected. On the other hand, the new addition can provide the basis for a late rapprochement within the family. To achieve it, however, takes giving and forgiving by all parties concerned.

SIBLING RELATIONS

If there are other children in the deaf child's family, the usual sibling rivalries are exacerbated. Handicapped children require more attention from parents, and in the family economy, that means less time is available for the nonhandicapped children. Nor is this situation necessarily better when the parents are themselves in the helping professions (see "When the Doctor Gets Sick"). The normally hearing siblings' resentments can appear in numerous ways, sometimes overt. On the other hand, some deaf children are fortunate in having siblings who learn to communicate with them and who invite their companionship.[20]

Parents may be blissfully unaware of strains in sibling relations, until a crisis arises. They may depend on a normally hearing sibling for communication with the deaf child, an ironic role reversal. Many parents don't realize that this places an enormous burden on their hearing children (see "Try It Sometime").

STRAIN ON THE MARITAL RELATIONSHIP

That the birth of a deaf child to normally hearing parents stresses their marriage seems indisputable. But how that stress manifests itself differs considerably from family to family. The guilt and anxiety that often accompany parental reactions to deafness can stress the marriage past the breaking point. Many counselors find that the birth of a handicapped child leads to the eventual breakup of the family unit. One or the other parent cannot handle the situation. Sometimes husband and wife blame each other for the tragic event, dredging up old quarrels, raking over petty faults, and inventing weird theories to account for the child's disability. Yet one study challenges the "clinical lore" that preducts a higher divorce rate among parents of deaf children. Its authors recognize, however, that their results may not generalize outside Canada, where they did the research, and they add, "We are not asserting that the deaf-

When the Doctor Gets Sick

When a physician's wife bears a deaf child, the impact on their relationship is the same as for other parents. The mother of a child who was born deaf contrasts her two sons, one deaf and the other normally hearing. In reading her remarks, bear in mind that her husband is a practicing psychiatrist.

> I have a thirteen-year-old hearing son and an eleven-year-old profoundly deaf son. Looking back over the thirteen years I have been a parent, I realize how much I have learned. . . . Our first child made my husband and me feel very comfortable in our roles as parents. He was easy and quiet and self-contained. He kept himself busy by the hour with cars, trains, roads, and tracks. . . . And then, two and a half years later, Joshua was born. From the beginning he was different from his brother Aaron. He was overly active, never quiet, always wanted company, and demanded to be entertained. We began to doubt ourselves as individuals able to cope with the world.
>
> After three years of struggling to find the answers to all the questions we had about Joshua, he was finally diagnosed as deaf, and our lives changed radically. We were thrust into a new world of other parents—parents who were not sitting in a park proudly watching their young child at play, but parents who were dealing with grief, anger, and feelings of helplessness. For a period of time, our entire lives revolved around deafness and, of course, our deaf child. His "normal" brother was pushed aside in the frantic flurry to make up for three years of lost time, three years of deafness with no communication, three years of bitterness, anger, and inability to do something—anything for this child.[21]

ness produced no difficulties for the families—quite the contrary."[22] How the family reacts to such stresses will depend to a large extent on local mores and individual capabilities.

From the Deaf Child's Viewpoint

What does all of this look like from the deaf child's side? In most instances, the family cannot hide its disappointment. The adults are

TRY IT SOMETIME!

A father wrote a letter to me to enlist support for an idea he had to improve his deaf daughter's social life.

Possibly this is not a unique situation for a young deaf person: My daughter, Jane, 25, congenitally deaf (90 db binaurally) and doing well in her job with IBM, appears in need of wider socialization than she now limits herself to. Her speech has been improving very much due to her work with therapist Edith Kent, and Jane thinks that before long she will be able to operate effectively and exclusively among the hearing and continue to rule out contact with other young Deaf adults.

Realistically, however, the girl has a severe hearing loss to which I believe she should be giving a greater degree of acceptance. Of course, there is no reason to exclude herself from the hearing community nor should she be doing the same with respect to the Deaf. [He then describes an instructional program that he would like to offer.]

Jane's younger hearing sister, Maude, who, having grown up with Jane (she says, "Try it sometime") is a proficient and fluent signer and would be helping me with communication. I believe this could turn out to be an enjoyable and beneficial project for any of your NYU young Deaf people who might be interested. Obviously, I hope to cajole Jane into a state of compliance so that she will join in. Even if she doesn't, I think the idea would still be of value to all concerned.

not accustomed to adjusting their daily lives to accommodate in such fundamental ways as deafness demands. When parents rely on oral communication, the action-reaction connections between everyday happenings often remain complete mysteries to the deaf child. Is it unreasonable for the child to wonder if he or she is the cause of the argument between the mother and father? How is the deaf child to know? Too easily, parents forget that when they speak, the child does not hear. It annoys them to repeat, to be sure their faces are visible to the child when addressing him or her. Parents may be annoyed with themselves for their forgetfulness or their momentary loss of patience, but what the deaf child sees is rejection, unexplained and easily misunderstood. Of course, a deaf child's life

THOUGHTS OF A DEAF CHILD

My family knew that I was deaf
When I was only three,
And since then, fifteen years ago
Have never signed to me.
I know when I'm around my house,
I try and use my voice.
It makes them feel more comfortable;
For me, I have no choice.
I try, communicate their way—
Uncomfortable for me.
My parents wouldn't learn to sign—
Ashamed, or apathy?
I never cared about the sound of radios
    and bands;
What hurts me is, I never heard
My parents signing hands.
                    Stephen J. Bellitz
                    The Florida School Herald,
                    April 1983

is usually not one of unrelieved hostility. Most parents provide at least some moments of warm affection. For many of the children, however, their homes, instead of being warm and accepting, are unpredictable sources of displeasure—displeasure that the children believe they cause.

PARENT ORGANIZATIONS

Sociologists have noted the importance to families of neighborhood contacts—over-the-back-fence advice, the kaffeeklatsch, the gossiping in the supermarket checkout lines.[23] In such informal, daily situations, much social information passes and opinions on the widest range of topics are censured or affirmed. But the parents of a deaf child can learn little of value from most neighbors because most neighbors are like themselves, they have had little or no contact with deafness. Neighbors quickly tire of discussing deafness because they cannot meaningfully participate, yet these discussions are of the utmost importance to the parents of deaf children.

Self-help groups, bringing together parents with similar problems, would seem to be the answer to assisting normally hearing parents adjust to their deaf child. These types of groups provide comfort and guidance to parents, and in that way they have some impact upon the lives of deaf children. They have not enjoyed a significant role in Deaf community affairs. Organizations like the Alexander Graham Bell Association's Parent Section and the American Society for Deaf Children remain outside the Deaf community, the former especially having no contact with the major organizations of Deaf adults. Their leaders seldom invite Deaf adults to participate in their affairs. By and large, they focus on the early years of the deaf child's development. As the children mature, the parents tend to drift away from these organizations, leaving them a relatively weak force in most areas. On the national level, none of the parent organizations exert much influence on policies relevant to Deaf adults.

THE DEAF CHILD WITH ONE HEARING-IMPAIRED AND ONE NORMALLY HEARING PARENT

Deaf children with one hearing-impaired parent, whether mother or father, have received little formal study. Only 3.5 percent of deaf children have a hearing-impaired mother or father. Does it matter which? Chances are that it does, but no systematic evidence tells us in what ways. We can speculate in the hope of stirring empirical research, and we can point to famous individuals who had a deaf parent. One of the most outstanding is Edward Miner Gallaudet, a noted scholar, author, and educator, who brought to a pinnacle the work begun by his famous father, Thomas Hopkins Gallaudet, who established the first state-supported school for deaf children in the United States. Edward successfully lobbied the Congress to support the establishment of the first and only liberal arts college for deaf students in the world—in 1863–64, while the nation was torn by civil war. In doing so, he extended his father's work to higher education and brought honor to his Deaf mother, Sophia Fowler Gallaudet. How much Edward's mother contributed to his ambition to establish a college for deaf students can be inferred from this quotation from his memoir: "I entered the profession of deaf-mute instruction with enthusiasm and with a strong ambition to do more for the interesting class of persons, of which my mother was one, than merely to teach them or to become the principal of a school."[24]

Deaf men marry normally hearing women less frequently than deaf women marry normally hearing men.[25] The finding does not accord with the probabilities, since deafness occurs more frequently in males than females. Deaf males have statistically fewer opportunities to find a deaf female than deaf females have of finding a deaf male. Deaf males, therefore, should be forced to look outside the Deaf community for a wife. Deaf females, being relatively less numerous than males, should have less difficulty finding a deaf husband. Whatever meaning attaches to this asymmetry, it applies only to the less than 10 percent of deaf adults who do *not* marry another deaf person, a minority within a minority.

The effect of parental hearing impairment also depends upon whether or not the affected parent is the head of household and whether or not the parent is the same sex as the child. A deaf boy may empathize more readily with a deaf father than a deaf mother, and a deaf girl with a deaf mother than a deaf father. Unfortunately, not enough research has been done on this matter to enable even educated guesses to be made about these potential effects, if any do, indeed, occur. A stance of objective ignorance is recommended until more research is done.

Without more research evidence than is presently available, we can say little that is definitive about the families in which only one of the parents is deaf. The analysis of the differences between having a deaf mother and a deaf father on a deaf female or deaf male child might be particularly rewarding. Does it matter? If a deaf boy has a deaf mother and a hearing father, is he more likely to adjust better than if the sexes of the parents were reversed? Many more intriguing questions can be posed but, given the present evidence, not answered. Even when such studies are made, several cautions will impede easy interpretation of the evidence. There may be selective factors that tend to attract more or less adequate deaf individuals to marry someone who is normally hearing. Granting the difficulties that research of this kind presents, it would be valuable to have the results, even if somewhat flawed. Why? Because one study tends to beget another, and this aspect of deafness research needs that stimulation.

DEAF CHILDREN OF DEAF PARENTS

Deaf parents await the birth of their children much as other parents do, except that they do worry that their child may be born deaf. If the newborn is deaf, Deaf parents may be as disappointed as normally hearing parents. But they adjust rapidly, and they do not have the shock of deafness—it is familiar to them. They have experience in dealing with it. They do not hesitate to set their priorities. Consider the case of the Deaf educator who has both hearing and deaf children. His remarks about his deaf child in "Cherry Blossoms Bloom" provide an appealing illustration of the ready acceptance the deaf child can receive from Deaf parents and, equally important, how the deaf parents' behavior provides an atmosphere conducive to the child's full, secure development.

Most research has found that deaf children of Deaf parents tend to outperform deaf children of normally hearing parents academically and socially.[27] With respect to social development, some recent studies indicate deaf children of Deaf parents develop at about the same rate as normally hearing children with normally hearing parents; the deaf children are neither precocious nor delayed in their development. Other studies have found that deaf children of Deaf parents mature more rapidly.[28] Does this mean that Deaf parents are superior to parents in general? Perhaps they are—for deaf children. This research contrasts sharply with a much-criticized study by Galenson and her colleagues that pronounced Deaf mothers as unfit parents. The conclusion was based on observations of ten Deaf mothers who were in psychotherapy, hardly typical of Deaf parents. Probably the most devastating criticism of the research is that the interviewers did not use sign language, casting doubt on the data from which the study's conclusions were drawn. The publication of those views aroused a storm of protest not only in the Deaf community, but also in the professional community.[29]

The attitudes of people in the Deaf community toward their own abilities varies. Rachel Harris, a third-generation Deaf parent, has described the attitudes of Deaf people of her parents' and grandparents' generations as follows:

> Some Deaf parents depend on hearing people or their hearing children for many things. They think hearing people are smarter because they can hear. Many families have shared this common experience: "Do not sign in public or people will stare at us. They will think that we are some kind of weirdos." They sign at home with no problems, but when they are in public, sign language be-

CHERRY BLOSSOMS BLOOM

A Deaf educator talks about the early years raising his daughter, who was born deaf.

Since we had four hearing children, we did not expect a Deaf child, nor did we discover our daughter was Deaf until she was eight months old. Our immediate concern was to establish an effective line of communication with her, to reach and stir a mind that was a veritable tabula rasa. . . . Our primary concern was not to help our child talk and speechread, but to catalyze thought and language. Thought produces language; it fills the child with a need to express himself, and the freer he is to do so, the greater the chance for success. [Specific instances of instruction are given.]

As cherry blossoms come to bloom, so Carol's mind begins to flower, the best and most important part. When she was only a little over a year and a half she wanted a book which her brother was sitting on. He would not get up, so she threw a ball to divert his attention and thus grab the book. Because she was given an effective visual and expressive symbol system, she has been able to recall past events. . . . An internal language structure seems to be developing within her rather than being superimposed upon her by drills and imitation. She is able to invent and generate language when there is a pressing need to express something, such as her desire for a *milkshake, ketchup,* the opposite of the word *long.* She is able to manipulate her thoughts into expressions that make sense. She gave me a piece of gum and when I greedily asked for another, she said, "You pig, fat you pig." Coming from a hearing child, this would invite a spanking. Coming from a Deaf child it seems like a miracle, like a soul set free to communicate joyously.

Carol understands directions, asks and answers questions, relates experiences, peeps in and understands the conversations of others. She enjoys herself and takes pleasure in herself. (Our next door neighbor said she is the happiest baby he has ever seen.) She is free to use her hands or to use her voice. She will sign to the ocean waves, saying, "stay, stay," as they creep near her mudpies. She will talk to herself or to her dog, urging him to eat. She will yell at her Daddy with her hands, saying "bad, bad, bad," if he drives away without taking her. Because there was reciprocal communication, we could tease each other, and when she entered preschool her sense of humor showed.[26]

comes a taboo. I had this experience and it took me years to overcome this irrational behavior. "Once you become Deaf, you are Deaf in everything, and you will never be better than hearing people."[30]

She contrasts such attitudes with those of parents "who have shouted for the rights of their children and have become assertive."

Another member of a three-generation Deaf family, Leo Jacobs, became a highly successful educator and widely published author. His family's attitude sharply contrasts with Harris's.

> I was born Deaf of Deaf parents who had an older Deaf son. Therefore, my family was entirely Deaf, and we lived in a world of our own, where manual communication was the order of the day. I grew up in a loving atmosphere and never knew any deprivation of communication; my parents knew my wants, and I knew just how far I could go without bringing their wrath down on my head. The conversation was full and interesting at the dinner table. I learned all the facts of life at appropriate times. I attended a residential school as a day pupil. My only communication difficulties arose when I began doing business with the outside world, but I thought nothing about them because I had observed my parents' methods of overcoming these barriers. I merely followed the same road—that of employing a pad and pencil to convey my wishes, and attempting to read lips at first, then offering the pad and pencil to the other party if I failed to understand him.[31]

Perhaps that is the basis of the higher achievements of deaf children of Deaf parents over the deaf children of normally hearing parents—the former provide their children with directly applicable, immediately relevant coping skills. "Deaf Mother to Deaf Daughter" conveys that idea in the important area of self-image. Deaf children must soon be aware that most of the world does things she cannot. How wise the parents who help their children find their strengths rather than dwelling on their weaknesses. Hardly a new concept, but refreshing to see it in this context. Additionally, of course, the Deaf parent generally communicates more effectively with the deaf child than would a normally hearing parent. The deaf child can mix easily with the Deaf parents' friends, who will mostly be deaf, too. So the deaf child grows up in an environment in which there are ample successful adult role models, an atmosphere in which not hearing is often common and accepted. The "everydayness" of deafness for these children contrasts sharply with the "otherness" of deafness for deaf children of hearing parents.[32]

DEAF MOTHER TO DEAF DAUGHTER

A Deaf mother of a deaf daughter related an everyday encounter.

I would like to mention one experience I have encountered with my eldest daughter. It occurred several years ago when my daughter was about four years old. We went to a shopping mall to do our Christmas shopping and came upon a group of schoolage children, approximately 6 or 7 years old, standing in line waiting for a picture to be taken with Santa Claus. Raychelle, my daughter, begged me to let her have a picture taken. So we stood in line with the hearing children. The children were jabbering to each other and my girl asked me what they were saying. I could not understand a single word so I decided to explain to her that I could not understand anything that was being said. She asked me why not. I told her I could not hear them talking, but I quickly added that they also could not understand what we were signing because they were not Deaf. Therefore, we were even. You should have seen my girl with her wide eyes and open mouth as she began to giggle.[33]

The ease of communication and comfortableness Deaf parents have with their deaf children prompted a Deaf mother to say, "When our son Todd was born, he showed so much alertness with his eyes and was so unresponsive to normal sounds that we knew he was like us."[34] That phrase, "like us," tells a lot about the differences in parental reception for a deaf child of hearing versus Deaf parents. And yet, in the long run, both parents have similar anxieties. This Deaf mother has also said that her "main concern was not his inability to hear (he is nearly five now and I still don't even give it a thought), but was instead how well he could live within the hearing world." Typical Deaf parents, however, have the advantage over hearing parents of having practiced coping tactics and adaptive strategies, so they have experience with successfully dealing with many of the situations that their deaf children will face.

FAMILIES RAISED BY DEAF PARENTS

Do Deaf people make good parents? A very important question, since 9 out of 10 children born to Deaf parents have normal hearing. The question is also important because of court cases in which *the very right of Deaf people to be parents* has been challenged. These legal encounters will be described at length in chapter 7. This section focuses on the social-psychological aspects.

If their child is born with normal hearing, many Deaf parents have mixed feelings. They are pleased for the child, but wary about their own ability to cope with the alien. Some critics of Deaf parenthood of hearing children snidely intimate that Deaf parents' wishes for hearing children merely stem from their desire to have built-in interpreters. A second objection to Deaf parents raising a normally hearing child is that the child will not develop good speech and language. Research by a variety of scientists has allayed that worry.[35] When one thinks about the multitude of opportunities the normally hearing child has to learn language—from neighbors, relatives, radio, television, and in the schools—and when one adds to that the deeply rooted ability to learn language that resides in every individual, the fact that these children develop language and speech is no surprise. As one study of normally hearing youngsters and adults who had Deaf parents concluded, "No instance of the cessation of speech has come to light in the present study nor had anyone interviewed in the course of this survey heard of an example."[36]

What about personality development? Does having Deaf parents necessarily have a deleterious effect on a normally hearing child's growth into adulthood? The answer cannot be derived from research because there has been almost none. As one hearing child of Deaf parents has wryly noted, "Most of the literature concerns itself with deaf children of hearing and deaf parents; it is too bad that we hearing children did not anticipate this and maintain anecdotal records of our experiences."[37]

Deaf parents probably have the same run of luck as parents in general. They number among their offspring such highly achieving persons as former congressman and present federal judge Homer Thornberry, movie actors Lon Chaney and Louise Fletcher, author Lou Ann Walker, and numbers of college professors, successful business people, and just plain good citizens. Yet, again, having Deaf parents can have both advantages and disadvantages.

Normally hearing children sometimes do find themselves called upon to interpret for their Deaf parents, especially if they are the first-born. I recall a Deaf colleague's six-year-old son negotiating a lease over the telephone with a real estate agent. The boy did very well, of course coached by his father, who followed the negotiations via sign language. Experiences like that give these children an early

Two Views of Helping Out

Two highly successful, normally hearing sons of Deaf parents discuss their upbringing.

I learned Ameslan [ASL] as a child. I cannot recall not knowing it. My parents always communicated with me in Ameslan. . . . My English developed normally because I had relatives nearby. In school, reading and spelling were my best subjects. I did have a slight deficiency in vocabulary, but that was made up by the time I reached the third grade. I recall missing only one thing: sound. When I got my first radio I ran it day and night. . . . My parents rarely asked me to be their interpreter. I am grateful they didn't ask. I would discourage Deaf parents from using their hearing children too frequently as interpreters for anything other than phone calls and neighborhood small talk. For important transactions, an adult interpreter should be called in. I feel interpreting places a great deal of pressure on a child. He is required to understand adult language and translate it into appropriate Ameslan, and he will likely be too immature to do this. . . . My parents made me feel secure. I suppose that is another way of saying that there are good and bad parents, just as is the case with hearing people.[38]

I am an only child, a hearing child of low-verbal Deaf parents who communicated via what is now called Ameslan. My parents were painfully aware of their inadequate formal education, and as a result, they made every effort to insure that I was surrounded by books. . . . As I look back, two things were very painful to me. . . . First, I was the interpreter for my family, primarily at my mother's insistence. My father was much more independent. I interpreted everything from loan negotiations to simple grocery transactions, and I did this at a very young age. At the time, it was very painful, but I now realize that it taught me patience and diplomacy (for example, I did not always interpret what my parent was really saying about the insurance salesman). Most of all, it taught me a sense of responsibility and gave me an ability to do things that I did not particularly enjoy doing, a talent very useful in later life. Second, my mother, who loved me very much and who took great pride in my accomplishments, used to accuse me of being ashamed of my parents' deafness whenever I balked at doing something desired of me . . . it was a whip against me. I would recommend that they never accuse their children of being ashamed of their parents, even when they suspect it is true. An understanding parent can handle that problem in other ways.[39]

opportunity to mature. Some resent the imposition, others find it worthwhile (see "Two Views of Helping Out").

One study of children whose fathers were paraplegic or quadriplegic found few differences between the children and their matched controls.[40] Compared to the control children, children with paralyzed fathers reported they spent more time with their families, responded more rapidly to parental requests, did not resent helping their fathers, and more often felt protective toward both parents. The groups did not differ significantly on measures of personality disorders.

Would studies of hearing children with a Deaf parent show similar results? Interviews with normally hearing British children whose parents are deaf elicited comments like, "I was proud of being the only boy in the school with deaf parents;" "Father was well known and respected by all who knew him;" "We tried hard at school to show other children that we could 'beat' them despite our 'odd' parents."[41] Lacking a systematic study of children in this country, an anecdote told by a Deaf parent might serve, as it is "Out of the Mouths of Babes."

All is not sweetness and light in families raised by Deaf couples. Problems certainly arise; normally hearing children and Deaf parents conflict, as do children and parents generally. Some Deaf parents make poor judgments in raising their children, regardless of their hearing ability. Having said that, however, such evidence as we have indicates that, on the average, Deaf parents rear children as well as parents in general.[42] One investigator summarized his years of experience as a counselor and educator by saying that

OUT OF THE MOUTHS OF BABES

A Deaf adult proudly recounted to me an incident involving his normally hearing son, Bob, when he was ten years old. The family had recently moved to a new neighborhood. One day, Bob got into an argument with another neighborhood boy of his age.

"Your old man can't speak," taunted the boy.

To which Bob promptly replied, "Yeah, well your old man can't sign!"

deaf parents, on the whole, do an effective job in raising hearing children. They demonstrate genuine interest and concern for their early education and are inclined to sacrifice their own needs in order to make postsecondary education possible for their hearing children. As a result, hearing offspring of Deaf parents tend to make wholesome adjustments to life and are contributing members of their community. Many professions, such as education, rehabilitation, social service, and the religious ministry to the Deaf, owe much to the influence and contributions of hearing children of Deaf parents.[43]

Parents who have good children are probably not lucky, just good. It should not be necessary to elevate Deaf people to sainthood to counter the calumnies they have suffered from time to time and place to place. The tendency to set the record straight should not be misread as glossing over those Deaf individuals who fail or overpraising those who succeed as parents.

MARRIAGE AND DIVORCE

Research on the stability of families involving Deaf people has been sparse. As noted earlier, normally hearing parents' marriages are severely stressed by the advent of deaf children. The little research on the impact of deaf children on the marriage suggests that, at least in some societies, that stress does not sunder the marriage; divorces and separations seem no more frequent than among couples with normally hearing offspring.

Deaf-by-deaf marriages also seem comparatively stable. Deaf people have divorce rates close to the national average.[44] Marriages in which one partner is deaf and the other normally hearing seem a bit less stable. Since such marriages are the exception (recall the 9-in-10 rule) and since Deaf people are sparsely represented in the population, the actual number of such marriages is small, requiring intensive research to establish whether they are more or less stable than marriages between like-hearing partners.

FAMILY–DEAF COMMUNITY INTERACTIONS

How do these various family relationships affect the Deaf community? The 9-in-10 rule overwhelms other considerations. Families headed by normally hearing parents seldom have contact with the Deaf community. Their deaf children must "leave home" to affiliate with Deaf people. These families have a negligible effect on the Deaf community; that is, they have little or no influence on it.

Deaf children of Deaf parents provide the close cultural ties that enable traditions to pass through the generations. Yet the Deaf community recruits the major share of its members from families with hearing parents, simply because they are more numerous. For the new recruits, cultural identity and different social skills must be learned in or close to adulthood from Deaf contemporaries rather than from parents. The Deaf community's continuity depends upon this cultural exchange. New recruits accept the culture as a whole, recognizing the older and younger Deaf members as those with whom they can be comfortable, if it not convivial.

AGE AT ONSET

The Deaf community also deals with others who touch it but do not find themselves at home in it. "I am not a real member of the Deaf community," says a Gallaudet graduate and faculty member who lost his hearing in a motorcycle accident at the age of twenty-one. "I am a deafened hearing person."[45] Late-deafened people do not, as yet, feel the attraction to the Deaf community that early-deafened people do. They may learn sign, participate in some activities sponsored by Deaf organizations, and even work with Deaf people, as teachers, counselors, and so forth, but they remain aliens to intimate Deaf social life. They struggle to hold on to their previous relations with family and friends—a difficult, seldom satisfactory lifestyle. Powerful as age at onset is in predicting who will become a Deaf community member, it does not account for all of the variance. Systematic studies of age at onset and the tendency to affiliate with the Deaf community have yet to be done. They should be rewarding, providing further clues as to what induces some late-deafened individuals to join the Deaf community and some early-deafened not to.

HEARING FAMILY MEMBERS

What about those left behind? What about the parents and the normally hearing siblings? While they may remain fairly close to Deaf

CRIPPLED INSIDE

A press release from the Deafness Research Foundation, Fall 1987, quoted its thirty-five-year-old president Lawrence Meli, who is also the father of a profoundly deaf four-year-old son. About Deaf people, he said, "They are crippled inside. They lead isolated, lonely lives—with minimal opportunities to enter the mainstream of America."

The statement was, understandably enough, resented by the majority of Deaf adults who do not find themselves leading "isolated, lonely lives." Sixty-four members of the Northeast Ohio Senior Citizens of the Deaf signed the following reply:

It is truly sad that Mr. Meli is first of all the president of Deafness Research Foundation and most important has a 4-year-old son who is going to "suffer" needlessly. . . . We realize the importance of the Meli situation and hopefully information can be suggested to Mr. Meli as to how he could first of all alter his thinking regarding deafness and also to somehow receive the information to provide his son (the victim in this case) the opportunities and services he deserves as a human being! (*The NAD Broadcaster*, December 1987, 13)

family members, they seldom join the Deaf community. Parents rarely attend its functions or participate in its deliberations. Some parents' attitudes make it difficult, if not impossible, for them to relate amicably to the Deaf community. Deaf persons' lack of hearing blinds parents to their abilities. A reaction of pity, in particular, draws strong negative emotions from the Deaf community, and it makes negligible contributions to the Deaf community. Some normally hearing siblings find employment in or near the Deaf community, most often as teachers and interpreters. Still, they tend to limit their social contacts in the Deaf community to those solely associated with their employment.

IN LOCO PARENTIS

The theory of Deaf community development notes the *alienation* of the majority of deaf children from their own families. The *demographics* dictate that this group (the 90 percent with hearing parents) constitutes numerical dominance of the Deaf community. The influences of the *milieu* and *education* in shaping it can be seen in small measure in this discussion of family life. Finally, of course, *affiliation* remains a dominant factor underlying these discussions. Their interplay is seen as the mosaic unfolds. That 9-in-10 deaf children have normally hearing parents means that the parents' functions—as role models, as shapers of personality, as guides to behavior, as cultural transmitters—are diminished, if not eliminated altogether. Faced with children with whom they have difficulty communicating, parents naturally develop a sense of alienation toward them, a feeling the children most frequently reciprocate. The Deaf community stands *in loco parentis*. As substitute parent, it can fill a void in the lives of the majority of deaf children. It does so through contacts with Deaf houseparents in residential schools, with Deaf teachers, and with Deaf adults whom the children meet in planned or casual social encounters. Occasionally, introduction to the Deaf community does not occur until a deaf child is near maturity. Such relatively late associations with Deaf persons, nonetheless, appear to have a strong, lasting impact on newcomers to the Deaf community, one that reshapes their lives.

On the other hand, Deaf parents of deaf children fill the customary parental roles, and their deaf children have been shown to carry that benefit into school, tending to greater academic achievement than deaf children with normally hearing parents. They play key roles with respect to deaf children who do not have Deaf parents, teaching them American Sign Language, acquainting them with Deaf folklore, and providing peer models for them. They become substitute siblings to those deaf children whose family members are normally hearing.

Sooner or later, deaf children—some with Deaf and some without Deaf parents—enter the Deaf community that makes them feel at home.

NOTES

1. For example, Best, 1943; Rainer, Altshuler, and Kallman, 1963; and Schein and Delk, 1974. That the 90-percent figure is likely to be an underestimate is supported by data from the 1984–85 Annual Survey of Hearing Impaired Children and Youth. Jordan and Karchmer (1986, 137)

write, "Only about 4 percent of the Annual Survey population have two deaf parents; an even smaller percentage have one hearing impaired and one normally hearing parent."

2. Margaret Mead (1970) introduced this phrase to indicate that culture passes through three contiguous generations. In this context, it refers to the potential cultural disjunct between three living generations.
3. Forecki, 1985, 8.
4. Spradley and Spradley, 1978, 20.
5. Spradley and Spradley, 1978, 31.
6. Freeman, Carbin, and Boese, 1981. See also Freeman, Malkin, and Hastings, 1975, for Swedish data. Grandparents often are the first to raise the suspicion of deafness; having had child-rearing experience, they more readily detect deviations from normative behavior.
7. Carver and Rodda, 1987.
8. Freeman et al., 1975, 401.
9. George Harris, 1983, 52.
10. Allen and Allen, 1979, 283.
11. Two cases have recently appeared in New York State, both stemming from evaluations at the same state institution. Donald Snow and Joseph McNulty, both born deaf, were labeled "idiots" and committed to a New York State institution within six months of each other, in 1965–66. Snow's true intelligence (IQ greater than 100) was uncovered at age twelve. He was returned to his parents, who eventually sued the state for medical malpractice. Snow won a million-dollar judgment. McNulty's correct intelligence was not established until he was nearly seventeen years of age. Nine years later, though a court awarded him $1.5 million, he continues to live in a group home for retarded men while the state appeals the decision, continuing to claim he is mentally retarded.
12. Freeman et al. (1975) found that, unlike parents in several U.S. studies, parents in the two Canadian provinces they studied did not mourn the birth of a deaf child. The results might reflect psychiatric intervention at an early stage and/or it may be due to cultural differences in the populations studied so far. Whatever the explanation(s), the findings merit further attention from researchers.
13. Freeman et al., 1975; Carver & Rodda, 1987; Schlesinger and Meadow, 1972.
14. Freeman, Carbin, and Boese, 1981, 88–89. That parents of older deaf children have less satisfactory relations with professional personnel than parents of younger deaf children is not surprising. In the early stages, most normally hearing parents have no idea what to expect, so they depend heavily upon "expert" advice. Later, they learn that professionals all too often know little about deafness. Meadow-Orlans, 1985; Naiman and Schein, 1978.
15. Denis, 1974, 11.

16. Gjerdingen, 1979.
17. Rosen, 1981, and Scott, 1986. These two novels, both written by authors who lost their hearing in adolescence or young adulthood, have the same themes: the teenager's desire to belong to the group, to be like the others, and their tendency to perceive rejection by the group.
18. The anonymous poem is found in Naiman and Schein, 1978, 8–9.
19. Allen and Allen, 1979, 282.
20. Murphy, 1979a; Banta, 1979.
21. Mendelsohn, 1983, 2.
22. Freeman et al., 1981, 167.
23. Caplow et al., 1982; Nash and Nash, 1981.
24. Gallaudet, 1983, 4–5.
25. Best, 1943; Schein and Delk, 1974.
26. Newman, 1979, 170, 176–77.
27. Brasel and Quigley, 1977; Corson, 1973; Meadow, 1968; Stuckless and Birch, 1966; Vernon and Koh, 1970, show significant differences in academic achievement favoring the deaf children of Deaf parents. Two contrary studies, Conrad and Weiskrantz, 1981, and Parasnis, 1983, argue that deaf students of hearing parents who learn sign in childhood can make up the early achievement gap in adolescence and early adulthood.
28. Meadow, Greenberg, and Erting, 1984.
29. Galenson et al., 1979. A fellow psychiatrist wrote a blistering letter of protest to the journal that published the article. It reads, in part, "As a fellow of the Academy [of Child Psychiatry], I have always until now been proud of the high professional caliber of our Journal. I am distressed by the apparent change in editorial policy which has resulted in the publication of such unscientific, unethical material as the Galenson et al. article. . . . The four tables contain personal identifying information about each of the ten families, which is an unconscionable violation of their privacy. The references to 'Literature' consist of a biased sample, totally excluding contrary data contained in publications by such authoritative scientists as the psychologist McCay Vernon or the psychiatrist Luther Robinson, among others. The validity of the data is, at best, open to question, since it includes material obtained from Deaf parents by staff who could not communicate in the sign language used by many Deaf people! The parenting behavior that is ascribed to Deaf mothers (propping bottles, facing away from the baby, etc.) is certainly no different from that which is observed and reported in numerous hearing mothers. There is not even a pretense at an effort to prioritize the many variables which are noted in the 'study' population, nor any proof of causal relationship between specific parenting behavior and developmental assessment."
30. Rachel Harris, 1983, 6.
31. Jacobs, 1980, 13.

32. Like all generalizations, exceptions abound to this one: there are hearing parents who seek out Deaf playmates for their Deaf child and who arrange for the child to meet and be with Deaf adults. These parents are also apt to learn to sign and, hence, to develop fluent communication with their Deaf child, overcoming the usual barriers to easy exchange of ideas and emotions that enable them to have a strong influence on the child.
33. Rachel Harris, 1983.
34. Judith Williams, 1980, 181.
35. Ainoda and Suzuki, 1976; Bunde, 1979; Clifford, 1977; Corfmat, 1965; Critchley, 1967a and 1967b; Day, 1975; Jones and Quigley, 1979; Lenneberg, Rebelsky, and Nichols, 1965; Maestas y Moores, 1980; Mathis, 1975; Mayberry, 1976; Murphy and Slorach, 1983; Sachs, Bard, and Johnson, 1981; Schiff and Ventry, 1976; and Schiff-Meyers, 1982.
36. Critchley, 1967a, 52.
37. Schuchman, 1974, 229.
38. Fant, 1974, 225–26.
39. Schuchman, 1974, 228–29.
40. Buck, 1980; this doctoral dissertation is summarized in *Rehab Brief*, 1982, 5(1).
41. Critchley, 1967b, 56–57.
42. Vernon, 1974.
43. Mathis, 1975, 286.
44. Schein and Delk, 1974.
45. Benderly, 1980, 12–13.

5

EDUCATION AND REHABILITATION

Scientists have estimated that only a third or less of the average child's knowledge comes from the classroom. The remainder derives from incidental learning—from radio, television, overhearing conversations, talking with others. Deaf children, however, are cut off from some or all of those sources of information. Until they can read English, captions are useless. In daily contacts, they may observe, for example, an adult who is obviously angry with another child, but they do not learn a lesson from the incident because they do not hear the accompanying dialogue. Thus, deaf children learn by formal tuition, or not at all, many of the customs, taboos, and folkways that normally hearing children learn effortlessly.

Rehabilitation also exerts a strong influence on Deaf adults. Since only disabled people may avail themselves of rehabilitation, its process has no direct parallel for those who are nondisabled. The encounter with government bureaucracy at a relatively young age has a strong potential for shaping Deaf people's attitudes and modifying their behavior.

This chapter looks at education and rehabilitation from the Deaf side, in relation to Deaf culture. The focus is on how these agencies impact on the Deaf community rather than on how Deaf individuals respond to particular situations. The search is for generalizations that will have predictive value.

EDUCATION

Can the school be the seedbed for the Deaf community? In chapter 4, we observed that most Deaf people come from normally hearing families. These family members lack connections with the Deaf community and have little or no knowledge of Deaf culture. Bringing together deaf youngsters as they do, the schools often provide these children's first meeting with others like themselves. The school's place as a recruiter for the Deaf community or as a transmitter of Deaf culture is another matter.

Capsule History of Deaf Education[1]

Until the eighteenth century, most deaf children received no formal education. A mistranslation of a brief quotation from Aristotle legitimatized the deprivation of instruction to deaf children. The early translation read, "Those who are born deaf become senseless and incapable of reason." Scholars agree that a more accurate translation is "Those who become deaf from birth also become altogether speechless. Voice is certainly not lacking, but there is no speech."[2] Too bad for Deaf people that the second translation did not prevail.

In the fifteenth century, a scholar or two challenged the Aristotelian dictum, but the great breakthrough did not occur until the sixteenth century. Two Spanish monks, Pedro Ponce de León and Juan Pablo Bonet, working with deaf sons of the aristocracy, became the first teachers who also wrote of their successes with deaf students. Their results led to the seminal work of the Abbé Charles Michel de l'Epée, in France. He modified French sign language to suit spoken French grammar, demonstrated the capabilities of many deaf students, and established the first public school for deaf students, in Paris, in 1771.

The progress of Deaf education in the United States follows a direct line from the Abbé via a student of his school, Laurent Clerc, who was brought to America by Thomas Hopkins Gallaudet. Gallaudet was a normally hearing clergyman who had tried to teach a neighboring deaf child, Alice Cogswell. Her parents and parents of other deaf children raised funds to enable him to go to Europe to study Deaf education. He went first to England, but was rebuffed by the leading authorities; he then turned to France for the keys to educating deaf students. Gallaudet returned a few months later with Clerc to establish a school that continues to this day. The American Asylum for the Deaf and Dumb, in Hartford, Connecticut (later renamed the American School for the Deaf [ASD]) opened in April 1817, with funding from the Connecticut legislature.

Clerc, deaf and an experienced teacher, served ASD for forty years as the resident expert and as a model for what education of deaf children could accomplish. He wrote and signed gracefully, and his influence spread widely. Within a year after ASD was founded, New York opened a school for deaf students, and, shortly after, Pennsylvania, Kentucky, and Ohio followed. By 1850, the United States had thirteen public and parochial schools for deaf students. At first, Deaf adults shared in developing the education programs. Clerc not only set the curriculum at ASD, he trained teachers and taught courses. Other states invited Clerc to assist in setting up their schools, hired his students and former teachers, and made some of the latter administrators. Clerc retired in 1858.

In 1863, Thomas Hopkins Gallaudet's son, Edward, approached the Congress with an audacious request. He wanted to establish higher education for deaf students, and this at a time when some people regarded those who were deaf as ineducable, only a small portion of able-bodied Americans obtained any education past high school, and the United States was torn apart by a bloody civil war. Edward Miner Gallaudet persisted in lobbying for his dream of higher education for deaf people. In 1864, with Confederate troops a few miles south of the capital, the Congress issued the charter for Gallaudet University, the first institution of higher education for deaf students in the world—a great event in the history of Deaf education and a splendid example of national rectitude.

By 1900, most states had at least one school for deaf students. But the nature of Deaf education in this country began to radically change after the 1880 conference on the education of deaf students, in Milan, Italy.[3] By the end of the nineteenth century, the battle lines were firmly drawn: manualism versus oralism marked the poles of a debate that continues to this day.[4] Influenced by the oralist approach of Heinecke, in Germany, and the Braidwoods, in England, many educators rejected sign language as a means of educating deaf students. The Milan Manifesto signaled the imminent end of significant participation of Deaf adults in the education of deaf children. The premonition that led to the establishment of the National Association of the Deaf, in 1880, had come to pass: Deaf teachers and administrators ceased to hold a dominant position in Deaf education.

That state of affairs lasted through the first half of the twentieth century. The promises of Deaf education were proving empty, as study after study showed that deaf students left school after twelve or more years with educational achievement levels far below the national averages.[5] Influenced by the civil rights movement and encouraged by ASL's new status, Deaf leaders struggled to regain their places in Deaf education and to restore the use of sign in instructing deaf children.

In March 1988, the Deaf community reached a landmark—the selection of Gallaudet University's first Deaf president. The university occupies one of the most prestigious positions in the Deaf community. Its presence belies any fiction that Deaf people cannot profit to the fullest from education. As the only university in the world entirely for the higher education of Deaf students, it has great practical, as well as symbolic, value for Deaf people. Up until 1988, Gallaudet had had six presidents, none of whom had been deaf. When the sixth president announced his retirement in 1987, the Deaf community adopted the slogan "Deaf President Now." The 124-year wait had exhausted its patience. The university's board, however, miscalculated the strength of the Deaf community's desire and underestimated the political skills that the Deaf students had learned. The board chose a hearing, nonsigning person over two Deaf candidates. There followed a seven-day student strike that captured national and international attention. Support for the students poured in from many previously disinterested individuals and groups. Congressmen and presidential candidates took stands in favor of the Deaf President Now movement. Following unprecedented media coverage and the intransigence of the student protesters, the board succumbed, accepted the resignation of their selection, and voted to make I. King Jordan, one of the two Deaf finalists, the first Deaf president of Gallaudet University. A new era had begun.

DEAF PRESIDENT NOW

The Deaf revolution—the strike to force the Gallaudet Board of Trustees to select a Deaf president—did not begin on March 6, 1988. When Gallaudet University's sixth president, Jerry C. Lee, resigned in October 1987, Deaf organizations immediately declared themselves in favor of a Deaf president. The university, founded in 1864, had never had a Deaf president, and as Alan B. Crammatte wrote in the *Gallaudet Alumni Newsletter*, November 1987, "Isn't it about time that truly serious consideration be given to a deaf person as president of this educational institution for deaf students?" *The NAD Broadcaster* carried a position paper about the same time, urging "the

Board of Trustees to take this opportunity to continue its bold leadership and select a deaf president for Gallaudet University." The sentiments were not new; they had been expressed among Deaf people for many years. Hopes had been high that the fifth president, in 1983, would be deaf. The Deaf community's disappointment was expressed with restraint. Perhaps that is why the board gave little heed to the current request; perhaps it was stated with too little fervor. The board missed, however, the strong organization building in support of that idea. Letters were being circulated, group meetings held, and articles written with the same theme, "Deaf President Now!"

SUNDAY, MARCH 6   The board invites students and faculty to a meeting on campus at 8:30 P.M. to learn which of three finalists, two deaf and one nondeaf, will be president. Instead of a meeting, however, a mimeographed broadside is passed out: the board chooses Elisabeth Zinser. She is nondeaf, has no experience in Deaf education, and does not know ASL, but is willing to learn. The reaction from the campus is swift. A group, without a parade permit, marches on the Mayflower Hotel in downtown Washington, D.C., where the board is meeting. Board chair, Jane Spilman, meets with three student representatives and lights the spark that explodes into the student strike. She says, through an interpreter, "Deaf people are incapable of functioning in a hearing world." [She later denied having said it.] The students meet to plan their response.

MONDAY, MARCH 7   In the morning all entrances to the university are blocked. Students issue four demands: (1) replace Zinser with a Deaf president; (2) replace the board's chair; (3) increase Deaf representation on the board to a majority; (4) assure no reprisals against the protesters. Following an aborted meeting between students and trustees, students again march without a permit to the Capitol and the White House. Their moves are extensively reported in newspapers and on television. The alumni house on campus becomes the command post for the strike and, not incidentally, a communications center for the media and friends off campus.

TUESDAY, MARCH 8   Support from off campus begins. GUAA president, Gerald Burstein, arrives from California to encourage the students. He had earlier wired alumni displeasure to the board. GUAA contributes $1,000 to a Deaf President Now (DPN) fund. Newspaper and television reporters swarm on campus. The visually oriented students are a bonanza for television. The board maintains a low profile, letting it be known that their position is firm. Hearing a rumor the board expects the excitement to subside once students leave for the spring recess on Friday, DPN leaders urge students to cancel travel plans and remain on campus. Most agree to do so.

WEDNESDAY, MARCH 9   Congressmen and presidential candidates issue statements in support of DPN. The students scrupulously avoid doing any physical damage or being assaultive. They depend on logic and justice to win their demands. DPN leaders meet with congressmen and gain their support by expressing their arguments so well, whether directly voiced or through interpreters. Associated Press bulletins about the strike are printed in papers large and small nationwide, and the network news programs feature it. Greg Hlibok and Academy Award winner Marlee Matlin appear on "Nightline" in direct confrontation with Elisabeth Zinser. The nationally telecast program, masterfully moderated by Ted Koppel, displays the capabilities of the Deaf participants and the worthiness of their cause.

THURSDAY, MARCH 10   More off-campus support pours in from parents, other schools for Deaf students, labor unions, political candidates, and interested citizens. That evening, Zinser resigns.

FRIDAY, MARCH 11   Three thousand Deaf people and their friends march to the Capitol. They meet House and Senate members and argue for their cause.

SATURDAY, MARCH 12   The DPN fund collects over $20,000. Encouragement comes from all over the U.S. and from other nations as well.

SUNDAY, MARCH 13   At 7:30 P.M., a call comes in for Greg Hlibok from Philip Bravin, a Deaf leader, who announces that Spilman has resigned, he has replaced her as chairperson, and the board has selected I. King Jordan to be the eighth president of Gallaudet! Bravin reports he is convening a task force to prepare for an increase in Deaf representation on the board. Students will not be penalized for their week-long absence from classes. Each of the students' four demands are met.

An historical account of the March 1988 "revolution" would be misleading if it left the impression that it had no precursors. Earlier battles had been fought when states chose nondeaf over Deaf applicants for superintendents of Deaf schools. Ronald Nomeland sued the Minnesota School for the Deaf under the provisions of the Equal Employment Opportunity Act, when he was passed over as superintendent in favor of an allegedly less-qualified, normally hearing applicant, in 1973. He lost, but the lesson was learned—Deaf people could not expect to have their rights without a fight. The Deaf citizens of Louisiana succeeded in winning a Deaf superintendent, Harvey Corson, for their state school, in 1975. A similar struggle occurred in Oregon. In the meantime, some schools had already selected Deaf administrators. Victor Galloway recently headed state schools in Pennsylvania and Texas before becoming professor and director of the Center on Deafness, at California State University at Northridge (CSUN). Larry G. Stewart superintends the Illinois school, and Ralph White the Oklahoma school. Deaf administrators also fill lesser positions that should, in time, put them in line for superintendencies. Pointing to these antecedents to the Gallaudet appointment in no way diminishes its importance to the Deaf community. A Deaf administrator seated on the pinnacle of Deaf education evokes profound emotions in the Deaf communities throughout the world.

THE EDUCATIONAL SETTING

Four models cover the settings for the education of deaf students. The residential (or boarding) school provides overnight accommodations for its students—all of whom are deaf. All of the day school's pupils are deaf, but they live at home. The day class, consisting entirely of deaf students, is housed in a school that accommodates nondisabled students. Placement in a class with normally hearing students is the fourth arrangement, often called "mainstreaming." Deaf students in such a setting are usually provided with an interpreter to enable them to follow class proceedings.

Combinations of these placements can also occur (e.g., residential students who attend some classes with normally hearing students in neighboring schools).

Regardless of the setting, deaf students need a specialized physical environment in which to receive their education. Realizing they are visually dependent means that the sources and amount of illumination should be carefully controlled for their benefit. Lighting should be arranged so that glare is minimized and shadows, especially those falling on faces, reduced.[6] Hearing aids function best when the classroom's reverberation times are low, which means that harsh surfaces need to be softened, windows should be covered by curtains, acoustical tiles installed on ceilings, and carpets on floors. When only a small number of deaf students attend a school, it is unlikely that school administrators will spend the money to make the necessary modifications of their classrooms.

The shift away from residential and day schools, in which large numbers of deaf students are brought together, toward day classes and individual placement of deaf students in classes with normally hearing students concerns Deaf leaders, who believe that deaf students are being deprived of the opportunity to learn about deafness, if not in the curriculum, at least from other deaf students. Growing up as the only deaf person in a school does not make for an easy social life. Many deaf children in regular classes find themselves wholly set apart from other students during school and without playmates after school. What is more, the integration of deaf students into regular classes occurs far less often than educators claim. A deaf student who attends gym classes with normally hearing students three times a week may be referred to as "mainstreamed" by a school administration. One recent study suggests that such partial integration among mainstreamed students is more often the rule than the exception.[7]

Despite the new-sounding title, "mainstreaming," the idea of educating deaf students in classes with nondisabled children, is not a recent invention. German educators attempted to integrate deaf students in regular classrooms as early as 1821. The experiment failed, in part because parents of normally hearing children objected to having deaf students in the same classes with their children.[8] Only a few decades ago, some educators railed against "institutionalization," the term for children educated in residential schools. Another emotion-laden term applied to residential schools was "segregation." The lack of research directed at testing the criticisms makes the issue seem more political-economic than educational. When a well-designed study was done, residential placement was found to have no deleterious effect upon deaf students' educational achievements when compared with a relevant control group.[9]

Prior to the passage in 1975 by Congress of Public Law 94–142 (Education for All Handicapped Children Act), more than half of deaf students were educated with other deaf students in day and residential schools. Deaf students in primary grades were usually in schools with deaf secondary students, thus allowing for interaction in a Deaf environment. After 1974, the proportion of students in day and residential programs fell. Today, a majority of deaf students in the United States meet only handfuls of deaf students, if any at all, while they are in school. The odds that a deaf child will be the only deaf person in her or his school has grown substantially.[10]

Mainstreaming has economic implications. Opportunities for Deaf teachers to work with deaf students have been threatened. A Deaf teacher is more likely to be hired by a school that specializes in educating deaf children than by a school that has only occasional contact with disabled students and, perhaps, none with deaf students. Economic consequences aside, the absence of Deaf teachers

MAINSTREAMING

Mervin D. Garretson, former president of the National Association of the Deaf and a distinguished educator, believes that

> mainstreamed deaf children may find themselves cast adrift without much of a self-identity because they are compelled to settle for half a life in a hearing community that is only partially accessible to them. When they finally reach their late teens and leave school as young adults and are forced to wrestle with these realities, they will seek out the deaf community. But the process of enculturation and adaptation to a new language is not easy. All too frequently they wind up not fully accepted by either the deaf or the hearing community. That is a major concern we have with P.L. 94–142 (Education for All Handicapped Children Act) and its implications for both deaf children and a possibly fractured deaf community.[11]

in the education of deaf children can have the effect of depriving deaf children of appropriate role models. Some educators hold that if deaf students never see Deaf persons in positions of authority, their self-concepts will suffer and their achievement motivation will decline.

While the philosophy underlying this approach to educational placement has been discussed at great length, little attention has been given to the practical realities. One might assume that education depended solely on the setting in which it occurs, and that teachers, curriculum, instructional methods, and other issues had little or no place in the debate. Two recent surveys have shown that the classroom teacher who receives a deaf child, however, often feels differently. The United States survey concluded, "It would, of course, be desirable for regular classroom teachers to be knowledgeable about hearing impairments and related educational implications."[12] Many teachers knew little and seemed to care less about matters of importance to deaf students. The Canadian study, which covered two provinces, reached essentially the same conclusions— regular classroom teachers lacked important information about critical factors in the education of hearing-impaired children.[13] In the Canadian study, this situation prevailed even after an orientation program had been provided to those teachers who were to receive students with hearing impairments.

The separation that occurs between deaf and normally hearing students in a mainstream setting has been poignantly described by Christine Wixtrom.

> During the afternoon, there is a rally in the gym. The deaf student arrives early, choosing a seat on one of the lower bleachers, where he will be close enough to see the speakers and the interpreter. Students stream in through doors on both sides of the building. It isn't long before the bleachers are jam-packed with talking, laughing, cheering students. The building is fairly bursting with spirited shouting, dynamic energy, and animated conversations. But no one talks with the deaf student. Set apart by silence, he cannot enter the world of words around him. Only an observer, behind a quiet barrier, he is alone in the crowd.[14]

In fairness to its framers, P.L. 94–142 does not use the slogan "mainstreaming." It requires that all handicapped children have "a free, appropriate education in the least restrictive environment." Clearly, what is appropriate for one child may not be for another.

Similarly, what is least restrictive for one child—one who can hear—may be most restrictive for another—one who is deaf. The difficulties with educational placement for deaf children come from failing to look past catchphrases and seeing the individual student.

THE ANIMAL SCHOOL

This fable was a favorite of the late Professor Donald G. Paterson, University of Minnesota, a leader in the psychology of individual differences and the son of Deaf parents.

Once upon a time, the animals decided they must do something heroic to meet the problems of a "new world," so they organized a school. They adopted an activity curriculum consisting of running, climbing, swimming, and flying, and, to make it easier to administer, all the animals took all the subjects.

The duck was excellent in swimming, better, in fact, than his instructor, and made passing grades in flying, but he was very poor in running. He had to stay after school and also drop swimming to practice running. This was kept up until his web feet were badly worn and he was only average in swimming. But average was acceptable in school, so nobody worried about that, except the duck.

The rabbit started at the top of the class in running, but had a nervous breakdown because of so much makeup work in swimming.

The squirrel was excellent in climbing until he developed frustration in the flying class, where his teacher made him start from the ground up instead of from the treetop down. He also developed a Charley horse from overexertion in swimming and then got C in climbing and D in running.

The eagle was a problem child and was disciplined severely. In the climbing class, he beat all the others to the top of the tree but insisted on using his own way to get there.

At the end of the year, an abnormal eel that could swim exceedingly well and also run, climb, and fly a little had the highest average and was valedictorian.

The prairie dogs stayed out of school and fought the tax levy because the administration would not add digging and burrowing to the curriculum. They apprenticed their children to a badger and later joined the groundhogs and gophers to start a successful private school.

Does this fable have a moral?

Curriculum and Instruction

By the turn of the last century, the curriculum aimed at assisting deaf students to overcome their handicap and to adjust to the "hearing world." To a large extent, that remains the principal objective of Deaf education. Never mind that the "handicap" of deafness is imposed by the majority; the educational philosophy declares deafness as something that must be overcome, hence education must be remedial from the outset.

For minority groups in the United States, the home has the responsibility to maintain ethnic traditions. Most Deaf people, as noted in the preceding chapter, cannot look to their parents for their Deaf identity. Should not their schools provide the missing elements of Deaf life? Courses in Deaf history are rarely offered to deaf students. ASL is almost never taught to them in school, so it must be learned from fellow students and Deaf adults. Seldom do deaf students read about prominent, successful Deaf people. Nor will most deaf students have much contact with Deaf adults who can serve as role models. Their teachers, administrators, and supporting educational personnel will most often be normally hearing. Until the 1960s, the only Deaf employees students met in most schools were apt to work as janitors and houseparents. Deaf teachers, if the school employed any, were usually found only in the upper grades, where they would hold positions in vocational, not academic, departments. What it means to deaf children to have only nondeaf teachers is well illustrated in the following reminiscence by Ronald Sutcliffe, a Deaf professor at Gallaudet University.

> At those times, we seemed to be self-sufficient citizens. We were told we were limited in our career growth. I remember in one of our classes when our teacher asked us what we would like to be after leaving school. One pupil wanted to be a truck driver. Another wanted to be a school principal. The teacher responded, "Oh, you cannot be this because you are Deaf. You cannot be that because you cannot use the telephone." We took it seriously. We were dependent on hearing people's judgments and opinions. . . . [B]ecause of the "can't can't syndrome," I never thought I would stand here with an earned doctorate degree. What is happening today was almost unbelievable years ago.[15]

Barbara Kannapell, a sociolinguist, who is also deaf and who holds a doctorate, recollected almost the same experience of negative motivation, albeit in a different school at a different time.

To explain where I am today and who I am today, I need to go back to the past, when I accepted all those negative labels that hearing people placed on me directly or indirectly, such as "oral failure." There were other labels, all part of the well-known "can't" syndrome. I do not mean to include all hearing people in this group. I refer to those who were involved in educating deaf children like myself, and who affected our personal awareness and self-concept. None of these hearing professionals looked at me as a person or as a friend. Indirectly they communicated to me that if I wanted to succeed in a hearing world, I must talk well or at least write English well. I know that I was an "oral failure" in the eyes of those people. I did not feel good about my speech and my English skills, but I tried hard to communicate with hearing people on their terms. I limited my facial expressions and body movements, was worried about using correct English, tried to use my voice, and was anxious to end conversations with them. Hearing people in general were always interested in how well I talked or heard or wrote English. They didn't seem to be interested in making friends with me. The teachers always corrected the errors I made in writing or talking and the supervisors always said, "Don't do this," or "Don't do that." They never sat down for a moment to chat with me or other students as friends. This is why I socialized only with Deaf people for a long time.[16]

Who controls curricular decisions? Are Deaf adults invited to participate in the development of deaf students' curricula? These questions have predictable answers. The society that pays for the education calls the tune, and the tune most often played is "Adjust to the Majority." That position stands the test of reason, but not necessarily of justice. Societies seek to preserve themselves. In focusing on that goal, they may be shortsighted in overlooking educational programming that would acknowledge the reality of Deaf persons' adult lives and prepare them for that reality.[17] Until the 1960s, the Deaf community accepted the general community's view of deafness as a pathological condition. From that it followed that education should strive to make deaf children as much like nondeaf children as possible. The curriculum naturally reflected these views. However, Deaf leaders are beginning to object openly, and they are being joined by some hearing educators. Sherman Wilcox, a deaf educator, denounced such educational policies, claiming

the Deaf community is an oppressed, disempowered minority. One way that power has been withheld from deaf students is the systematic confounding of their linguistic situation. As a result the development of literacy is both a problem and a solution.[18]

His solution, proposed before the 1988 strike at Gallaudet University, is that "the culture of silence must be broken from within, and the first blow must come from the deaf student."[19]

HIGHER EDUCATION

Figure 2 portrays graphically what happened to higher education for deaf students in the United States from 1900 to 1970. The entries in the graph are the ratios of students entering college to the total number of all students in education for the particular year. The reason for choosing that base is that until recently, few states provided a high school education for a majority of deaf students, so taking college admissions as a function of high school graduations would be misleading.

At the start of this century, hearing and deaf students went on to college at about the same rate (see Figure 2), which proved the feasibility of Edward M. Gallaudet's idealistic thinking. But within a few years, college admissions for the general population rapidly accelerated, while those for the Deaf population remained nearly constant. By 1950, the ratio climbed to over 8.5 to 1—students in the general population attended college over 8 times more often than deaf students. By 1960, an increase in the capacity of Gallaudet University helped reduce the differential to 7.8 to 1. The differential has continued to decline. It fell to 2.88 in 1970, but this still leaves deaf students at a substantial disadvantage. The proportion of students in the general population who go on to college is almost three times greater than that for deaf students, but the nearly two-thirds drop in the rate differential indicates what can be done. The improvement is attributable to changes in methods, educational philosophy, and governmental actions, as well as to changes in the makeup of the Deaf population.[20]

THE COMMISSION ON EDUCATION OF THE DEAF, 1988

In 1986, Congress passed the Education of the Deaf Act, establishing a commission to study the education of Deaf persons in the United States. After a year of intensive study, the Commission on Education of the Deaf issued its report, which reached the straightforward conclusion that "the present status of education for persons who are deaf in the United States is unsatisfactory. Unacceptably

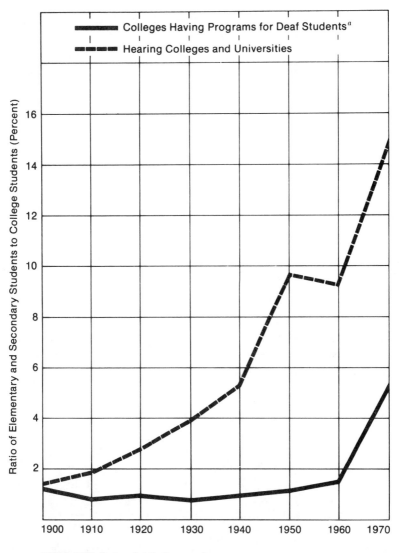

Figure 2. Ratio of college enrollments to elementary and secondary school enrollments for deaf and general population students: United States, 1900–1970.

NOTE: Reprinted by permission of the publisher, from Jerome D. Schein and Marcus T. Delk, Jr., *The Deaf Population of the United States* (Silver Spring, MD: National Association of the Deaf, 1974), 60.

[a]1900–1960 Gallaudet College only.

so. This is the primary and inescapable conclusion of the Commission on Education of the Deaf."[21]

The Deaf community might respond to that sad conclusion by saying, "Let us have a greater say in the education of deaf children and we will change conditions for the better." The Deaf community does not appear to want complete control of educational decisions affecting deaf children, but they do want—and reason would seem to argue that they should have—more participation in those decisions. Their perspective can add invaluably to the reshaping of a system that has inadequately served the majority of Deaf citizens.

REHABILITATION

No other social service agency has a closer relationship to Deaf people than the state department of vocational rehabilitation. These state agencies, in partnership with the federal government, have been the twentieth-century answer to the public response to disabled people. Though Congress dropped "vocational" from the title of the act authorizing this country's continued involvement in rehabilitation, the act's main thrust remains an effort to aid disabled individuals to obtain gainful employment.

A HIERARCHY OF ATTITUDES TOWARD DISABLED PEOPLE

Societies vary in their treatment of their disabled members. The attitudes underlying their actions range from total rejection to complete acceptance. Figure 3 depicts a hierarchy of attitudes expressed by various societies toward their disabled members. The categories represent attitudes within the United States, as well as other countries. At any given time, certain approaches to disabled people prevail over the others, but all five, and their variations, have some support in the general population.[22]

Total Rejection

Primitive tribes reacted to disabled people by destroying them. For a nomadic group, such rejection was deemed essential because slowing its progress jeopardized its safety. Leaving disabled persons on the wayside to die of neglect or killing them outright was also justified on primitive religious grounds. The disability was thought to be visited upon the individual for sins committed or as evidence of the presence of evil spirits. Whatever the explanation, the reaction had the explicit approval of many ancient societies on the grounds that disposing of the disabled person protected the entire community.

Some prehistoric groups may have taken a more compassionate attitude toward disabled members. Scientists have recently uncovered an instance of charitableness, or more, in a society that existed twelve thousand years ago (see "Primitive Compassion"). The acceptance of physically disabled members, then, may not have been the societal norm among primitive tribes, but it did occur, if only rarely.

Unfortunately, calling this reaction "primitive" masks the fact that it continues to this day. Hitler's eugenics policies encompassed the destruction of disabled people as well as of Jews, gypsies, and

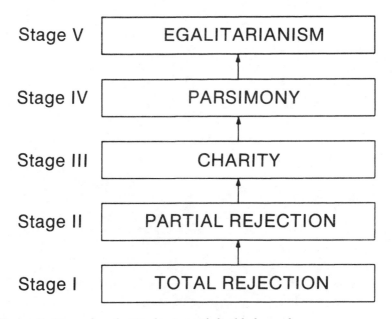

Figure 3. Hierarchy of attitudes toward disabled people.

SOURCE: Adapted from Jerome D. Schein, "Advocacy: A Dual Perspective," in *Hearing-Impaired Children and Youth with Developmental Disabilities* edited by E. Cherow, N. Matkin, and R. Trybus (Washington, DC: Gallaudet University Press, 1985), 347.

Primitive Compassion

This news story appeared in the *Sun-Sentinel* of Fort Lauderdale, Florida, 1 December 1987. It is reprinted by permission of United Press International.

In their prehistoric struggle for survival, cavemen still managed to care for members of their community too disabled to forage and hunt with the clan, according to evidence found in southern Italy. A researcher said the skeleton of a dwarf who died about 12,000 years ago indicates that cavemen had the time—and the compassion—to care for the physically disabled. The find also provides the first example of a clan caring for one of its members disabled from birth.

"These people were hunters and gatherers," David W. Frayer, a professor of anthropology at the University of Kansas at Lawrence, said in a telephone interview on Wednesday. The skeleton of the 3-foot-tall youth was discovered in 1963 in a cave in southern Italy but was lost to anthropologists until Frayer re-examined the remains and reported on his findings in the British science journal *Nature*.

"He couldn't have taken part in normal hunting of food or gathering activities, so he was obviously cared for by others," Frayer said. Archaeologists have found the remains of other handicapped individuals who lived during the same time period, but Frayer said their disabilities occurred when they were adults. The remains of one man found in Europe indicated he had a brain infection that would have disabled him for months, and another skeleton was of a man whose arm had been cut off below the elbow years before he died. "But this is the first time we've found someone who was disabled since birth, who was not a member of a community who suddenly became disabled," Frayer said.

There was no indication the dwarf, who was about 17 years old at the time of his death, had suffered from malnutrition or neglect, he said. Because of the nature of his dwarfism, which left him with extremely small arms, it is unlikely the youth could have fully supported himself in rough, mountainous region of Italy.

other "undesirable" ethnic-racial groups. More recently, widely publicized cases in the United States have led the federal government to promulgate regulations to prevent the deaths of disabled newborn babies. The Baby Doe rules forbid withholding life-preserving measures to disabled children. Federal authorities did not include regulations on murdering the infants because they felt this was already covered by the statutes. In England, however, a British jury—in a case that was tried in 1982—acquitted a physician who killed a mentally retarded infant with overdoses of morphine.

Partial Rejection

Rather than destroy the disabled individuals, some societies have put them out of sight. Lepers have been confined to leper colonies; mentally deranged persons have been housed in prisonlike institutions; and elderly, infirm persons have been moved into nursing homes. Once removed from public view, the society's conscience can be given some relief from the guilt that may arise from daily confrontations with those less fortunate than the ruling majority. Segregating disabled people prevents them from spreading infections, if they have any; from transmitting "evil" spirits; and from procreating. With respect to mentally ill people, the Supreme Court has ruled that such forced exclusion from society is unconstitutional, unless it is for the purposes of treatment. No doubt courts would hold the same views of the isolation of persons with acquired immune deficiency syndrome (AIDS). Nonetheless, many public actions have shown that partial rejection as a response to disability has not disappeared from our society.

Implied within the attitude that allows disabled individuals to be removed from society is the unspoken belief that they are subhuman, not worthy of citizenship and, hence, of the protection afforded citizens. Human experimentation is condoned. The Columbia-Greystone studies in the late 1940s, in which schizophrenic patients were submitted to mutilation of their frontal lobes, were reported in respected medical journals. Partial rejection, then, involves more than incarceration to separate disabled individuals from society; it devalues their lives just short of destroying them.[23]

Paternalism

A quantum leap in attitudes occurs when societies look upon the disabled person as someone who should be helped. Charity, however, is voluntary. One gives or withholds it as one sees fit. You can turn your face to the beggar cadging coins on a busy street corner;

you can ignore pleas for contributions to funds for disabled people. Giving to charities does not alter the status of the disabled recipients. The gifts provide momentary surcease, not rehabilitation.

Disabled individuals also see in this stage *paternalism*, the treatment by government agencies of disabled people as if they were children. It is not the provisions for funds and services to which disabled people react negatively, but the manner in which they are given. Instead of destroying or hiding disabled people, some government agencies treat them as incompetent, lacking the ability or the potential to attain independence. But, unlike children, disabled people cannot expect to outgrow their condition. The patronizing attitude does not allow for their growth. Instead, it stifles initiative and blocks, with regulations, efforts to attain independence.

Parsimony

This stage bears its peculiar name because the arguments supporting it are largely economic. Society is urged to rehabilitate disabled people in order to serve the community's interests. Once rehabilitated, the disabled person no longer needs charity and, indeed, can become a contributor to the general welfare. Following this argument, society is better off giving amputees artificial limbs (and the training in using them) than to provide them with a sum of money or some other charitable contribution. With respect to Deaf people, the argument makes excellent sense: provide education and rehabilitation, not handouts. Implicit in the argument remains society's choice, that is, rehabilitate only when it pays to do so. The parsimonious approach to rehabilitation does not include those treatments that merely make disabled individuals more comfortable, that relieve their pains, and that add to their independence but do not make them economically self-sustaining. Expenses for such programs could not be justified as returning the nation's investment in rehabilitation.

Egalitarianism

The egalitarian attitude tops the hierarchy, holding that, as citizens, disabled people are entitled to education and rehabilitation services and whatever accommodations are needed to enable them to exercise their citizenship. They have a right to any special accommodations that give them the same access and participation enjoyed by all citizens. Interpreters must be provided to Deaf people at public meetings, curbs cut and ramps made available to persons in wheelchairs, Braille codes marking floors posted in elevators for use by blind persons—all of these provisions are made as rights, not favors.

The egalitarian position is embraced in Title V of the Rehabilitation Act Amendments of 1973, sometimes referred to as "The Disabled Person's Bill of Rights." The federal law explicitly forbids discrimination in any facility or institution that receives federal funds. However, disabled people cannot become too sanguine about that legislative landmark. The other four attitudes remain active in this country in one or another form. Most insidious are the arguments now being made that our society cannot afford to give disabled people what they need to live on equal footing with other citizens. It is the economic argument used against disabled people, and they should be wary of its consequences. Particularly chilling are the exaggerations of what it would cost to accommodate all disabled people. Such gross misstatements of the expenses involved frighten legislators into drawing back from proceeding along previously adopted paths toward equality for disabled people. Worse yet may be moves to withdraw further support for education and rehabilitation on economic arguments that ignore inherent rights of citizenship.

In response to the Rehabilitation Act of 1973, rehabilitation professionals prepared a detailed outline of an exemplary program for Deaf clients. "The Model State Plan for Rehabilitation of Deaf Clients" appeared in 1974. It outlined how state rehabilitation agencies could provide adequate services, within existing statutes, to their Deaf clients. The model also stressed participation of the Deaf community in the rehabilitation process. Furthermore, it specified that some effort should be made by state agencies to bolster their state's Deaf organizations.[24]

In the spirit of goodwill prevailing at the time, the model plan was adopted, in principle, by all fifty states.[25] A decade later, the model faces disuse, as the political climate has changed. The Deaf community finds in rehabilitation, as in education, that its gains are never secure against attack. In reviewing current attitudes toward disabled and other minority groups, they and the general public should recall that societies identify themselves by their treatment of those least able to fend for themselves.

Discrimination defines us all.

A Brief History of Laws Affecting Rehabilitation in the United States

The National Defense Act of 1916, the Smith-Hughes Act of 1917, and the Soldier Rehabilitation Act of 1918 contained the first national provisions for care of disabled people. They limited their efforts to the vocational retraining of soldiers. In 1920, the Vocational Rehabilitation Act expanded the target population to include more disabled people and broadened the programs to cover prosthetics, counseling, and job placement, as well as training. The next major change occurred in 1935, when the Social Security Act established the first permanent base for vocational rehabilitation programs and opened federal participation to state programs for needy blind people. The following year, the Randolph-Sheppard Act encouraged blind people to operate vending stands in federal buildings. The Vocational Rehabilitation Act of 1943 authorized physical restoration services and the inclusion of mentally retarded and mentally ill persons in its programs. Changes in funding and other administrative matters were made by the acts between 1954 and 1973. The Rehabilitation Act of 1973 dropped "vocational" from its title. It set priorities for services, requiring that the most disabled be given precedence. Its many other landmark provisions have already been discussed.

Consumerism

Appearing as a leitmotif in the recent history of education and rehabilitation has been the theme of consumerism or, better, consumer participation. Rather than having policies being made *for* disabled people, more often policies are being made *by* them—or at least they are being made *with* them. This movement is the counter to paternalism, which implies that disabled people must be treated like children. There are several rationales for the newer strategy.

Disabled people, especially those whose disabilities leave them intellectually intact, as is true of deafness, can contribute a great deal to improving program efficiencies. They are expert on what is needed, what is wanted, and what is not wanted in the way of services.

The Rehabilitation Act Amendments require consumer participation in their state-federal rehabilitation programs. All persons in the rehabilitation process must approve in writing their individual rehabilitation plans. If they object, hearings must be held that can continue all the way up to the Commissioner of the Rehabilitation Services Administration, in Washington, D.C. Few such disputes arise. Perhaps sophisticated rehabilitation personnel confronted by largely unsophisticated clients make such use of due process highly unlikely. But even if such approvals are regarded as token gestures, they are important tokens, conveying to disabled persons the respect of the general public and granting them a measure of participation in matters vitally affecting them. States have also been urged to include members of the Deaf community in the planning and administration of their rehabilitation agencies. Many states have done so.

TRENDS

As would be expected, the trends over this rapidly concluding twentieth century have been mixed. Regressive tendencies in public attitudes remain. Progress is slow, and sometimes none is made. Viewed from a three-centuries perspective, the education and rehabilitation of Deaf people have tended in the egalitarian direction. Society has flirted with abandoning its hostile and paternalistic approaches to Deaf people, opting in favor of treating Deaf people as citizens with all the rights of citizenship, including the right to have such accommodations as will enable them to function as do nondisabled people.

Deaf people realize from their collective experiences that they cannot be overly optimistic. They have experienced numerous ups and downs in public attitudes toward them. Nonetheless, they have seen sufficient evidence of progress to be hopeful and to encourage them to continue to struggle for their just position in society.

NOTES

1. For fuller histories of deafness and the education of Deaf people, consult Atwood, 1964; Beggs, 1983; Bender, 1981; Best, 1943; Boatner, 1959; Braddock, 1975; Brill, 1984; Clarke and Winzer, 1983; DeGering, 1964;

Gallaudet, 1983; Gannon, 1981; Garnett, 1968; Lane, 1976, 1984; Schein, 1981; Scouten, 1984; Winzer, 1986; and Woods, n.d.

2. Bender, 1981, 20–21.

3. See the discussion in chapter 2 of the Milan Manifesto that led to the "outlawing" of sign language in the education of deaf children.

4. Since no educator seriously opposes teaching deaf children to speak, the usual dichotomy, oralism versus manualism, misleads those unfamiliar with the historical background of the debate and the practical classroom implications. In modern terms, the more accurate opponents would be posed as oralism versus Total Communication, the latter being an approach that combines all forms of communication and suits each to the occasion.

5. Commission on Education of the Deaf, 1988.

6. Schein, 1979a.

7. Moores and Kluwin, 1986.

8. Nix, 1981.

9. Quigley and Frisina, 1961.

10. Schildroth and Karchmer, 1986.

11. The quotation is from a speech by Mervin D. Garretson to a joint conference sponsored by the New Jersey Department of Education and the New Jersey Association of the Deaf, in Milburn, New Jersey, 10 September 1983. The entire speech warrants close reading.

12. Martin et al., 1988, 94.

13. French and MacDonnell, 1985.

14. Wixtrom, 1987, 15.

15. Sutcliffe, 1985, 1.

16. Kannapell, 1980, 106–7.

17. Carver and Rodda, 1987.

18. Wilcox, 1987, 164.

19. Wilcox, 1987, 173.

20. Among the significant government actions have been the opening of the National Technical Institute for the Deaf and the funding of several postsecondary programs, most notable of which are the "Triangle Schools." The federal support for higher education of Deaf students, however, can fluctuate as economic conditions and the political climate change. For a discussion of educational models in higher education, see Schein, 1986a.

21. Commission, 1988, viii.

22. Finkelstein (1980) stresses the environment's importance in determining societal attitudes toward Deaf people, dividing them into three phases: (a) in the primitive eras, disablement was associated with low status, blaming the individual or society's neglect for the occurrence of the disability; (b) during the Industrial Revolution, disabled people were seen as passive recipients of aid; (c) in these times of emerging technological developments, more disabled people are seen as being able to function independently.

23. Callous disregard for a racial minority is documented in Jones, 1981, which describes the Tuskegee syphilis experiment, in which four hundred black sharecroppers were never told they were infected. From 1932 until 1972, Public Health Service physicians deliberately withheld treatment, while pretending to give appropriate medical care. The purpose of the "experiment" was to learn about the natural course of the disease when untreated.
24. Schein, 1973.
25. Schein, Delk, and Gentile, 1977.

6

Economic Life

Deafness respects neither wealth nor social position. The raw facts of economic life intrude on the Deaf community as on any social group. Being Deaf provides no benefit, proves no asset, does not assist in the day-to-day business of earning a living and managing what goods are obtained from economic activities. To the contrary, deafness costs money. How and how much is the subject of this chapter because understanding the Deaf community demands an understanding of its economic position.

What is the economic status of families from which Deaf children come? When they are grown, how do they fare in the labor market? How do employers treat them? Where do they work? In what positions, in what industries do they succeed best? worst? How do their earnings compare to others? What trends have been discerned in the welter of available data about the earnings of Deaf people? Economic status involves more than earnings from wages and investments. What about purchasing power? How does deafness affect the ability to manage funds? In sum, then, what is the Deaf community's economic position?

ECONOMIC STATUS OF DEAF
CHILDREN'S FAMILIES

Deafness is associated inversely with family income. The National Center for Health Statistics consistently finds that the lower the income, the greater the probability of deafness. Its surveys have discovered that more than twice as many persons with severe hearing impairments (47 percent) reside in families with incomes under

$7,000 than do persons with normal hearing (21 percent).[1] Accidents, injuries, diseases—these more often afflict poorer than richer people. On the other hand, medical care, diets, and living conditions improve as income increases. So for the portions of deafness that arise from external causes, there is an economic relationship.

It follows, then, that proportionally more deaf children would come from poorer than from wealthier families. That is the finding of a study comparing the reported incomes of deaf schoolchildren's families in the United States with those of parents of schoolchildren in general. The proportions of the two groups in the middle-income category are equal, but deaf children's families are more frequently found in the lower than in the higher income categories (see Figure 4).

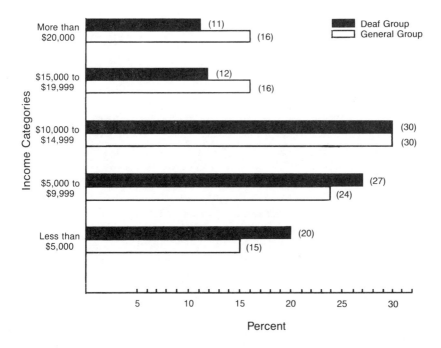

Figure 4. Parent's annual incomes in families of Deaf schoolchildren compared to families of all schoolchildren: United States, 1977.

SOURCE: Adapted from Rawlings and Jensema, 1977.

N.B.: Figures in parentheses show percentages in that category. Percents add up to slightly more than 100 percent due to rounding.

While the tendency for hearing impairment to be associated with low incomes prevails, the fact remains that wealthy people and royal families have deaf children.[2] For example, the mother of England's prince consort Philip was born deaf. The recessive genes that affected her can be traced back to the seventeenth-century Spanish throne. Even in genetic roulette, wealthier people have an advantage, since they travel more and, hence, have broader opportunities to choose their mates. Consanguinity (matings of individuals from the same gene pool) raises the probability of deafness in the offspring.[3]

THE COSTS OF RAISING A DEAF CHILD

Perhaps having deaf children so affects their families that their incomes decline. In that case, deafness would contribute to the families' lowered income rather than being the result of their inability to purchase proper care in the first place. Clearly, having a deaf child means increased expenses to meet the child's special needs. How much does deafness add to the cost of child-rearing?

Asking what are the extra costs of raising a deaf child is like asking how much a house costs; much depends upon choices the families make. Parents of a deaf child need a broad array of services and devices whose prices vary greatly from place to place and time to time. To illustrate the impact of having a deaf child on a family's budget, then, consider the *added* expenses of rearing a deaf child as shown in Table 4. The illustration comes from an actual case. It reflects costs in a particular region for a particular deaf child, so obviously it will deviate from those required by another deaf child. Since deafness does not save on the food, clothing, shelter, medical care, and so forth, that are needed for any child, these are excess costs.

Hearing aids will almost certainly be prescribed for a deaf child from an early age. Even though the aids cannot restore hearing for speech, they do enable the child to maintain auditory contact with the environment—to be aware of sounds as they occur—but not necessarily to be able to assign meaning to them. The benefit is largely psychological, reducing the isolating nature of the deafness and assisting the child in lipreading. For other children, the hearing aids may enable them to attain varying degrees of speech discrimination, a much-desired benefit.[4] In any event, the hearing aids (binaural or tactual) are expensive, requiring frequent maintenance and periodic replacement.

Table 4 Estimate of Additional Expenses Incurred by Family of a Deaf Child

A.	*Equipment*[a]	
	Binaural hearing aids	$800
	Pager/receiver tactual output	600
	Automatic answering machine	384
	TDD with printer and Baudot/ASCII capabilities	659
	Portable TDD with case, 2 @ $285 each	570
	Signal lamp for telephone	28
	Closed-caption decoder	265
	Fire-alarm system: wireless detectors, 6 @ $62.50 each	375
	Wake-up alarm	18
	Flashing doorbell assembly and installation	85
	SUBTOTAL	3,784
B.	*Cochlear Implant*[a]	
	Operation and postoperative rehabilitation	36,000
C.	*Hearing Ear Dog*[a]	
	Purchase of dog	200
	Travel to training center and per diem while in training	1,375
	Fee for dog/owner training	1,500
	SUBTOTAL	3,075
D.	*Additional Educational Expenses*[a]	
	Speech and language therapy: 3 hours per week for 36 weeks @ $60 per hour	6,480
	Special summer camp: Annual session, including travel costs	2,000
	SUBTOTAL	8,480
E.	*Supplies and Maintenance*[b]	
	Hearing aid batteries per year	360
	Replace and repair hearing aids (4 years)	200
	Batteries for other equipment	220
	Replace and repair other equipment (5 years)	1,380
	Cochlear implant (30 years)	1,200
	Upkeep of hearing ear dog (food, veterinary fees, etc.)	900
	Replacement of dog (6 years)	512
	SUBTOTAL	4,772
	TOTAL	56,111

[a]One-time costs. See E for upkeep and replacement costs for equipment.
[b]Annual costs. Life expectancy of equipment shown in parentheses.

N.B.: All prices and names of specific equipment are for illustrative purposes only. Prices change from time to time and place to place.

Other communication aids may be purchased. To receive captions on television requires a decoder. If parents wish their deaf child to have access to more than one television set, then they will need to buy decoders for each set. In order to use the telephone, Deaf people purchase a device that transmits typed messages over telephone lines to a companion machine that decodes the messages and displays them in print—a telecommunications device for the deaf, or TDD. Parents usually buy a fixed model for the home and a portable model the child can take to school or, later in life, on travels. Some families buy more than two; for example, buying a third one to give to an older, hearing sibling who is away at school and wishes to stay in touch with the deaf brother or sister.

Specially adapted equipment can be purchased to enable the deaf child to know when the doorbell or the telephone rings, when the smoke detectors are activated, or when the wake-up alarm goes off. The principle underlying these adaptations is to replace auditory signals with visual or tactual cues. Another system is available that enables a parent to keep in contact with a deaf child by means of a transmitter, which can be kept in the house or taken along on outings, and a receiver worn by the child. When the parent activates the device, the receiver provides a tactual signal that the child can learn to associate with various messages. Another approach to signaling children in and about the home is to purchase a trained dog (called a Hearing Ear Dog).

Deaf children are assured a free, appropriate public education under P.L. 94–142. Nonetheless, some parents opt for private schools because the local education authority might not agree with parents' requests for their deaf children or might be unable to afford the extra assistance. As examples, parents may wish their children to have extra language instruction or special training in some skill areas. Tuitions in private schools range up to $30,000 per year, not including travel expenses to and from the school. While similar expenses may be incurred with any child, they are more likely to be necessary for deaf children and the costs higher. Deaf postsecondary students usually receive support from their state vocational rehabilitation agencies. However, the strictures imposed by a state agency on choices of schools and programs may not satisfy the student and may necessitate further cash outlays to obtain the desired option.

A relatively new development in auditory rehabilitation is the cochlear implant. The first models did not produce great benefits for many of the adults on whom they were tried, but recent advances promise more substantial gains that may be extended to Deaf children. Cochlear implants do not restore hearing. They provide an electrical impulse that individuals can learn to use as they would auditory signals. The long-term effects of implanting these devices in the temporal bone are not known, so there are risks attached to accepting implantation. Still, some parents may elect this option for their child. Along with large initial costs they will incur additional expenses for maintaining the device, costs not shown in Table 4.

What the foregoing illustrates is the economic burden deafness imposes on a family. The amount of the additional expenses depends upon many different factors, but it is a significant burden— adding from $2,000 to $20,000 annually to the family budget plus a large one-time expenditure for items like a cochlear implant.[5]

ECONOMIC STATUS OF DEAF ADULTS

The added expenses of deafness continue into adulthood. Certain items, such as hearing aids and interpreter fees, remain as lifelong costs. Others, such as auditory training, usually are dropped as the individual becomes an adult. But the largest expenses of deafness are felt in their impact on earnings capacity. Deaf adults, on the average, earn less than their normally hearing peers.

LABOR FORCE STATUS

Over a hundred years of statistics on Deaf workers indicate that they are not lazy. They tend to enter the labor force at about the same rate as adults in general. Being in the labor force does not mean having a job. Unemployed persons are in the labor force, provided they are "ready, willing, and able to work." In short, they must also be seeking employment, if they are not already working.

Some recent national data on the labor-force participation of Deaf versus all workers show how rapidly the labor market can shift. In 1972, 80 percent of Deaf males and 50 percent of Deaf females were in the labor force. These rates are the same for males in general (80 percent) and slightly higher than those for females in general (44 percent).[6] However, five years later, the comparisons showed a decline of 5 percent in labor-force participation for Deaf men versus 1 percent for men in the general population, and a decrease of 2 percent for Deaf women, versus a *gain* of almost 5 percent for women in general. Clearly, during the period of "stagflation," Deaf workers suffered disproportionately. Historically, Deaf workers, like other physically disabled workers, tend to be more adversely affected than workers in general in periods of economic decline.

Distribution Among Industries and Occupations

Deaf people are employed in every industry. They hold positions that range from laborer to professional-managerial. Their positions most often are among those that do not appear to require a great deal of communication, but occasionally they hold those that typically do. For the most part, Deaf workers have tended to employment in blue-collar as opposed to white-collar jobs at greater rates than their peers in the general population, proportionally fewer Deaf persons work in sales and more work in drill-press operating.[7] As automation has reduced blue-collar positions, particularly in the machine-tending occupations, Deaf workers have drifted into positions in lower job classifications, rather than moving up into white-collar positions. There are indications that the trend may be reversed in the near future, but the historical position of Deaf workers has been toward the lower ends of the employment spectrum.[8]

In labor markets favoring employees, such as during World War II, Deaf people have been well received in industry and have established fine work records.[9] That Deaf people can perform in far

Silent Shears

Can you imagine a Deaf hairdresser? Karen Thompson works in J. C. Penney's styling salon, in Flint, Michigan. To accommodate its Deaf customers, Penney's has installed a TDD, so Karen can handle her own appointments. Deaf clients enjoy discussing their treatments in sign language, and they find Karen a talented practitioner. How does she feel about working in the salon? She enjoys it very much, especially because one of the other beauticians, Renee Coles, also uses sign language.[10]

more positions than employers usually believe they can has been amply demonstrated. (For example, see "Silent Shears.") But in labor markets favoring employers, they often refuse to make even simple adjustments that enable Deaf applicants to fill open positions for which they are qualified in all respects except hearing. For example, Deaf persons were refused employment as stockroom clerks in a naval station because the job specifications said normal hearing was essential. A team of job analysts showed it was desirable to have all stock requisitions in writing. When confronted with the superfluous requirement in the job specifications, management removed it, required all requisitions from the stockroom to be in writing, and hired a Deaf person as stock clerk.[11]

EMPLOYMENT AND UNEMPLOYMENT

In contrast to comparative labor-force participation rates, comparative unemployment rates show that Deaf people have greater difficulty gaining and holding employment than do their general-population peers. Within a single decade, drastic changes have occurred to Deaf workers. In 1972, Deaf men had an unemployment rate slightly over 5 percent and men in general, almost 5 percent. Deaf women did not fare as well, being unemployed at a rate of 16.5 percent versus 6.6 percent for women in general. Five years later, Deaf men faced unemployment at a rate of 10.2 percent compared to 6.2 percent for all men in the labor force. For Deaf women, the unemployment rate was 12.0 percent, while for all women in the labor force, the rate increased to 8.2 percent.[12] One explanation for the higher rate of unemployment among Deaf men and women is that traditional forms of employment have diminished, due to automation (as in automobile manufacturing) and to loss of operator positions (as in the garment industry) to other countries with lower wage rates.

UNDEREMPLOYMENT

A difficult concept to define is *underemployment*, employment at a level less than academic preparation and/or work experience would qualify an individual. Nonetheless, the term indicates an important reality for many disabled workers. While they hold jobs, these jobs are far below their experience, skill, and/or knowledge attainments. For Deaf workers, one measure of underemployment has been the differences between their levels of education and those of their normally hearing coworkers. The fact that for many categories of employment Deaf workers have higher levels of education than the averages for those positions suggests that they are indeed underemployed.[13]

Consider the too-common case of a Deaf chemist with fifteen years experience in industry who decides to teach. He applies to and is accepted by the local community college at its lowest academic rank, instructor. He notes others with only master's degrees who hold professorial ranks, and he protests to the dean. Following delays that extend over three years, he is promoted to assistant professor. Five years later, when he is refused promotion to associate professor, he leaves the college. He is replaced by a young hearing man who has a brand-new doctorate and no practical experience. The story, in general terms, is true; the specifics are invented to spare embarrassment all around.

EARNINGS AND INCOME

Family incomes of Deaf households averaged 16 percent below those for the general population, in 1972, the last year such data were available.[14] With the trend toward two-income families increasing, the full impact of deafness cannot be appreciated without looking at individual earnings. The reason is the familiar fact that 9 out of 10 Deaf persons marry Deaf persons, thereby compounding the economic burden.

Since the value of the dollar changes over time, average income for Deaf people is expressed as a percent of the average for the general population. In other words, the average dollars earned by Deaf people are divided by the average earnings for the appropriate general-population comparison group (see Table 5). In 1971, Deaf men and women each earned about three-fourths of the national rates for men and women. Five years later, like the labor-force participation and unemployment rates, the situation worsened. For men, the earnings rate dropped to 70.3 percent, and for women, to 59.5 percent. These declines are even more serious than they appear, due to upward educational changes in the compositions of the

Table 5 Median Personal Income from Wages and Salaries of Prevocationally Deaf Adults as a Percent of Median Income for the General Population, By Sex: United States, 1971 and 1976

	Percentage of Median Income for General Population	
Deaf Adults	1971	1976
Males	74.7	70.3
Females	75.4	59.5
Both sexes	74.6	64.2

SOURCE: Adapted from data in Schein, 1982.

1971 and 1976 samples. Even without consideration for these factors, the economic penalty attributable to deafness is very high.[15]

DEAF-OWNED BUSINESSES

What about Deaf entrepreneurs? Can Deaf people upset the economic predictions by entering businesses for themselves? A few have tried, and with notable success. Unfortunately, systematic studies of Deaf entrepreneurship have not been undertaken. What we are left with, then, are anecdotal accounts that may mislead more than they inform.

Capitalizing on their deafness, some Deaf attention has turned to publishing. Most book publishers are wary of materials targeted for Deaf audiences. Books *about* Deaf people, especially books about sign language, have done well commercially, but not books *for* Deaf people. The National Association of the Deaf (NAD) is the principal membership organization of Deaf people (see chapter 3); yet the bulk of its sales are not made to its membership but rather to professionals who deal with deafness and to the general public.

A cottage industry that supplies and services communication and other special equipment for Deaf consumers has emerged. Telecommunications for the Deaf, Inc. (TDI) is an organization that includes distributors of telephone attachments for Deaf users. TDI also vends caption decoders and other specialized communications equipment (see chapter 3 for more information about TDI). A number of small organizations market stationery, posters, and handscreened T-shirts that carry slogans and cartoons identifying them with various aspects of deafness. Some also distribute devices that Deaf people can use in their homes, such as the kits that convert doorbells to door lights. Wake-up alarms—alarm clocks that activate a vibrator placed under the pillow or turn on the bedroom lights—are some of the other specialized appliances sold to Deaf consumers. Typically, the companies making these sales are managed by Deaf people on a part-time basis, since the volume does not provide the proprietors with an adequate full-time income. Other purveyors of these specialty materials are organizations of Deaf people. Along with its book sales, NAD also markets devices for Deaf people. Some state associations use the sales of these articles to earn sufficient income to cover their convention costs, while simultaneously providing a service to their members. In any event, the potential volume limits the immediate future for businesses directed at Deaf consumers. For a further discussion of this point, see the section on demography in chapter 8.

Deaf Professionals

What about the upper end of the occupational hierarchy, the professionals? How do Deaf professionals fare in the labor market? That question and related questions were addressed by Alan B. Crammatte in research that he first did in the 1960s and repeated in the 1980s.[16] He documents the ability of Deaf adults to adjust to adverse working conditions—the professions usually demand high levels of communication—in two books published two decades apart. He shows that Deaf people do enter, and succeed in, the professions. That they are not compensated as well as their colleagues and that they have numerous problems associated with their deafness comes as no surprise. Of course, a disproportionate share of Deaf professionals find employment in the education of Deaf students. But Crammatte's data convincingly argue that they do succeed outside of such "sheltered" settings. Though not featured in the two texts, Deaf persons have established careers in medicine, the arts, and, most verbal of all, law.[17]

The message of these data is *Do not underestimate what a Deaf person can do*. Whether in business, the professions, or in other occupations, Deaf people have demonstrated their ability to compete. However, they still are not on equal footing because in most positions they are handicapped by lack of hearing and by widespread prejudices. Nor have they been compensated equally for their superior efforts. Still, they continue to make the effort, to accept the challenges that confront them. And they often as not succeed.

THE IMPACT OF DEAFNESS ON PURCHASING POWER[18]

A Deaf person given the same dollar as a normally hearing peer gets only about 90 cents in purchasing power. The reasons for this loss are not hard to demonstrate. For one thing, deafness cuts Deaf people off from sources of market information. Finding the best buys requires knowledge. That knowledge comes from newspapers, radio, television, and very importantly, from conversations with other consumers. Because of their poor reading levels, average Deaf people have difficulty understanding what they find in the newspapers. Advertisements often make use of colloquial speech; they are telegraphic in style. For anyone for whom English is a second language, advertisements muddle more than they enlighten. The same holds true for the stories about fraudulent practices, bad business practices, and other such information that leads informed consumers to avoid certain merchants. Deaf people cannot make use of the knowledge that normally hearing people derive from radio, both news accounts and advertisements. Since most advertisements and only a fraction of the programs on television are captioned, this source of market data is also of little benefit to the Deaf consumer.

What about word-of-mouth? Here Deaf people are at a great disadvantage. They depend on each other, with little input from normally hearing colleagues at work or in the neighborhood. Think about the flood of advice that is elicited when an ordinary person says to a group of friends, "I'm planning to buy a car." They promptly offer information about makes, models, prices, dealers, and much more. Within a few minutes, they reveal a wealth of data about market conditions in the immediate area. But the Deaf person learns mostly from other Deaf people who are as disadvantaged in gaining market information and evaluating the marketplaces.

At the point of purchase, deafness again intrudes, sometimes in small ways and often in large ways. Bargaining, to take a sizable factor in substantial purchases, becomes very difficult when the parties must exchange handwritten notes. No wonder that many Deaf people report that they often purchase new automobiles by reading the stickers and deciding whether or not to pay the printed

Realities

A noted Deaf leader muses aloud about the countless difficulties inability to hear causes in a world designed for hearing people.

Having to purchase with your new automobile an expensive sterophonic radio which you never hear anyway. Encountering car trouble on the expressway or autobahn and wondering whether you will be understood on the roadside emergency phone. Riding in an automobile with a foursome of hearing friends and wondering about the conversation going on in front or back and all around you. It would be naive to assume that the person sitting next to you is going to mouth everything for your special benefit. The reality is otherwise.

And some of the vicissitudes of air travel. Some airports do not post flight departure and arrival times on closed-circuit TV, and may even have several flights leaving from the same gate, so you have to be on the alert to ensure boarding the right plane at the right time. Even though you notify the desk of your hearing impairment, you continue to miss a flight now and then. Not hearing boarding announcements for the smoking or nonsmoking section—which group goes first? And even once airborne not everything is smooth sailing (or flying). Announcements from the captain go unheard, and generally you are not even aware they have been made. Ordering cocktails from the stewardess, trying to understand her questions about destination, magazines, or is she offering me a pillow?

Once on the road, we learn to forgo a number of conveniences that others may take for granted, such as calling room service at the hotel or requesting the desk clerk to wake you up at a certain time. Or notifying the bellhop to take your luggage when checking out. Or more alarming, how does the Deaf individual know when there is a fire warning? What if the hotel elevator balks midway between the twenty-ninth and thirtieth floor and you can't use the phone? Some Deaf persons simply refuse to step on an elevator unless there are other people on it.[19]

price. Inquiring about features, haggling about price and services, and determining the meaning of unfamiliar terms on the list of equipment (what does "Convenience Group A" include?) present great communication problems, not helped by the obvious impa-

It's YOUR Fault!

The director of a state agency describes what happened when she went to purchase a hearing aid. At the time she was a graduate student in a major university.

When I went to see the one last year who sold me the two aids, he tested my hearing in the office before selling me two new aids. They did improve my hearing . . . in his office. I should have realized that after I put on the new aids, he spoke louder and that his office was soundproofed. Anyway, when I went back two weeks later to complain that I was getting no benefit from the aids, he said he had to test my hearing again. It took him only a minute before he told me there was nothing wrong with the aids. My hearing had gotten a lot worse! Of course, I was despondent, and I left his office in tears, sure that I would soon lose the little bit of hearing I had left. Fortunately, I work with people who know better, and they quickly pointed out that I had been fooled.[20]

tience of a salesperson who eyes a busy showroom full of other potential customers. The tendency to "trust the establishment" exerts too much pressure for some Deaf people to resist, and they buy in haste and repent at leisure (see "It's YOUR Fault").

Does it seem strange that a Deaf person would trust a car salesperson? The experiences of most Deaf people teach them that normally hearing people are superior. They are the authority figures. Recall that many, if not all, of their teachers had normal hearing. Their parents, the school administrators, the figures on television and in the stories they have read—all have normal hearing.

In countless incidents, Deaf people find themselves in situations in which normally hearing persons have information they do not. For instance, they may have been in a class with normally hearing children who suddenly turned to look at the back of the room. The deaf children did not know why because they missed the auditory cue to which the others reacted. As these experiences pile up, deaf children come to believe that normally hearing people have an advantage, and they do. Deaf children are seldom taught that these same normally hearing people may take advantage of them. As pointed out earlier, deaf children are taught to trust those with normal hearing, sometimes to their sorrow.

What does the Deaf person do about small purchases? At the checkout counters of supermarkets, the clerk usually glances up and announces the total due—or so the Deaf person guesses they are saying that. Many Deaf people at that point simply hand the clerk the largest bill they have, then determine the amount of the purchase by counting the change that is returned. If the register is in view and the amount showing is $17.98, the clerk may still be waiting when handed a twenty-dollar bill. Why? Well, guess—is she asking for coupons? Or is she asking if there are other things wanted? The situation is an awkward one for a Deaf person, especially one with nonfunctional speech.

Deaf people also lose when items they have purchased are defective. Trying to explain the situation to a storekeeper can be so frustrating that they decide to forgo their rights to a refund or exchange. Unfortunately, some merchants exacerbate the already tenuous communication by shouting (a common response to the advice, "I am deaf"), making lipreading even more difficult and causing other customers and clerks to turn and stare, adding humiliation to the Deaf person's plight.[21]

The reduced access to market information, decreased bargaining power at the point of purchase, and difficulties in obtaining redress when purchases go awry diminish the value of whatever monies Deaf people have. A reasonable estimate of the reduction in purchasing power is 10 percent. Rather than viewing that sum as exorbitant, consider that it speaks highly for the adaptability and ingenuity of many Deaf persons to hold their losses at that point. Given the circumstances, an even more drastic reduction could be envisioned.

Adult Expenses of Deafness

Many of the childhood expenses of deafness—hearing aid costs, for example—continue into adulthood. But adult status brings with it additional expenses. When the Deaf person lives at home, some environmental modifications may seem necessary—wiring the doorbell so that it provides a visual signal, or attaching a light signal to the telephone to indicate an incoming call. A hearing mother can substitute for a special wake-up alarm to get a child out of bed. When Deaf adults travel, they find few motels that supply suitable alarms, TDDs, and other equipment that Deaf people need. For that

What's the Use?

Shanny Mow, a deaf writer, created a delightful character, Silent Sam, a kind of Deaf Everyman. In the following excerpt Sam buys a new car.

"But you can't see a thing from the driver's side," the Volkswagen dealer explains.

Sam reads the hurried scribbling and for a minute fingers his new driver's license. Under RESTRICTIONS, it reads, "Left and right rear view mirrors." Ten dollars goodbye for a right rear view mirror that doesn't give you the view you don't need. Since when did the bureaucrats at the Motor Vehicles decide deafness was a luxury? Be grateful that they let you drive at all?

Wearily, he takes the pad and writes, "Install it anyway. I'll be back."

reason, many Deaf people also purchase portable versions of these devices to carry with them on their travels.

An expensive item that is becoming increasingly common is the cost of interpreting. The greater availability of professional interpreters has increased Deaf adults' awareness of an interpreter's value when making a major purchase—buying a car or a home, for example. The disadvantages a Deaf person suffers in such transactions cannot be entirely eliminated by the interpreter, but the interpreter certainly reduces it.

A CASE HISTORY

One of the oldest continuous business ventures entered into by Deaf people is Columbus Colony, which the Ohio School for the Deaf Alumni Association (OSDAA) initiated at the turn of the century. OSDAA recognized the need for a home for aged and infirm Deaf people, so it acquired property vacated by a defunct college in Westerville, Ohio, refurbished the building, and in 1896, welcomed its first residents. During the next twenty-five years, OSDAA purchased over 140 acres adjacent to the home for a farm that provided most of the residents' nutrition and some income besides. It built various facilities as the demands for them grew. Until 1977, the land, its buildings, and all of its affairs were managed by the OS-DAA board of governors consisting entirely of Deaf people. The situation changed in 1971, when a consulting firm did a study that it presented without charge to OSDAA. The report urged OSDAA to expand Columbus Colony, using funds from the Department of Housing and Urban Development (HUD). Plans were drawn for replacing the existing structures with a nursing home and apartment complex to be financed by mortgages totaling over $10 million.

To get the funding, HUD asked OSDAA to form a board of trustees that would make the day-to-day decisions about operating the enterprise. (Some of the OSDAA officers at that time stated in later interviews that they regarded HUD's "request" as a requirement to obtain the funding.) The trustees would consist of two representatives from OSDAA and eight from among professionals interested in deafness. The government agencies and the mortgage company apparently felt that OSDAA's board did not have the experience this enterprise required—after more than eighty-one years of profitable management! The condition amounted to OSDAA deeding control of Columbus Colony to people outside of its organization, the majority of whom were not deaf.

Once hiring for the new development began, the arrangement's true meaning dawned on OSDAA, and sparks flew. OSDAA representatives attended board of trustee meetings at which vital decisions were made, but they were unable to follow the discussions or to actively participate. The outside trustees could not understand why they were mistrusted, though they made almost no efforts to gain the confidence of the Deaf members. They treated Columbus Colony as they would any other business, being concerned for its fiscal soundness and general adherence to health and welfare standards but not to the feelings of a group that had nursed the enterprise along for over eighty years. OSDAA had consistently rejected land developers' offers for their land, whose strategic location contiguous to the border of the state's capital had skyrocketed its value. Their proud determination to hold the property for the welfare of Deaf people was threatened by grandiose scenarios in which they could only be minority players.

Though the four-to-one representation has been unaffected, the Colony's board of trustees did amend its bylaws to permit members of the OSDAA board of governors (all of whom are deaf) to simultaneously serve as trustees. For several of the OSDAA members, this experience confirmed their fears about working with the general community. Perhaps its new administration, led by a dynamic young Deaf leader, Cecil F. Bradley, will restore to Columbus Colony the original position of pride it once held for Ohio's Deaf community.[22]

ECONOMIC ASSESSMENT OF
THE DEAF COMMUNITY

Deafness clearly exacts an economic penalty. In the marketplaces, communication problems and public prejudices against disabled people act to depress the earnings and the purchasing power of Deaf people. Because of their relative scarcity in the population, Deaf people do not have much commercial appeal. They do not impact heavily on many merchants, so their economic clout is weak. They cannot, therefore, fight economic discrimination with economic reactions; their purchases would in most instances not be missed should they elect to boycott or take other actions against those who discriminate against them.

Like all of the economic trends just described, change can be anticipated. But whether the changes are for the better or worse requires an unclouded crystal ball. More lawyers, dentists, and other professionals are advertising that they or members of their staffs have signing skills. As the actual numbers of Deaf people grow, their economic power will likely improve. To have a market—a group of people toward whom sales efforts can be directed profitably—requires sufficient numbers. The Deaf community is approaching that size for some services, though it remains marginal for many products.

The long-term economic trends promise little relief for Deaf people. Unemployment rates continue to favor the physically unimpaired, and there is little to suggest that Deaf people will achieve parity, either in the amount or level of employment. The earnings discrepancies between the Deaf and general populations have worsened over the last half century. A major factor has been the decline of skilled occupations in which Deaf workers excelled and of comparative earnings of semi-skilled occupations. The increase in service, sales, and clerical occupations with their emphasis on communication has worked to the disadvantage of Deaf people. Economic conditions, employer prejudices, communication constraints in negotiating the labor market, restricted social contacts that limit job networking—all of these factors concatenate to influence the future of Deaf workers.

The laws against employment discrimination have proved difficult to enforce, and the requirements of due process are especially hard on Deaf persons. Legal assistance through the National Center on Law and the Deaf has been a vigorous force in trying such cases, but so far the results, in many instances, have been disappointing, leaving Deaf people discouraged about the protection of their rights. Certainly, no one seriously argues that federal action to aid physically disabled workers should cease, that rehabilitation programs should be abandoned and laws supporting their equal access to employment be repealed. Nonetheless, the sum total of these efforts has not appreciably raised the economic position of Deaf people in the United States. One can understand the discouragement of Deaf people who find that in a depressed economy their condition worsens disproportionately, while in a flourishing economy their condition improves only mildly. The Deaf community, then, will most likely continue to be economically underprivileged.

Notes

1. Ries, 1980, 10. See also the same source for 1962–63 and 1971. Though the percentages vary somewhat from study to study, as would be expected, the basic finding is the same for the three surveys.
2. Among the first systematic efforts for Deaf children ever recorded are those of Juan Pablo Bonet and Pedro Ponce de León. Their pupils came from royal and other highly placed families (Schein, 1984a). That selection of students was only natural, since public education for the nondisabled masses had not come into vogue in sixteenth- and seventeenth-century Spain.
3. Fraser, 1976. Since wealthier people do not need to apply to the state for assistance, deafness in their families may escape notice more often than in those who do need public assistance. Conversely, the U.S. Bureau of Census undercounts the most economically deprived persons. The two tendencies may, or may not, counterbalance each other. More likely, they lead to rates that are comparatively higher among the middle-income groups and lower at the two extremes of the income continuum.

4. Instead of auditory hearing aids, some deaf children may be given vibrotactile aids. These devices convert sound to vibrations transmitted to a sensitive area of the body, such as the sternum. The children learn to interpret the vibrations as representing sounds occurring around them. They are intended principally to supplement lipreading cues. Pickett and MacFarland, 1985.

5. Parents may find that some of the preceding expenses are already covered by their health and hospitalization policies or by union or company benefit plans. Services may be available at minimal costs from government and voluntary agencies in the parents' area. The same agencies may also provide hearing aids to deaf children at reduced or no cost. To locate such resources, parents should consult with their local and state welfare agencies, audiological clinics and hospitals, and Gallaudet University's National Information Center on Deafness (800 Florida Avenue N.E., Washington, DC 20002). Lions International has added deafness to blindness as the two major disabilities for which it provides financial aid. Other civic and fraternal groups, like Sertoma, Optimists, and Rotary, may have similar programs that provide aid to families with deaf children.

6. Best, 1943; Christiansen and Barnartt, 1987; Mitchell, 1971; Schein and Delk, 1974.

7. Schein and Delk, 1974.

8. Christiansen and Barnartt, 1987, find the greater proportion of Deaf people who are finishing college encouraging since college graduates are far more likely to enter white-collar positions than people who have not attended college.

9. Schowe, 1979.

10. This information comes from *Vibrations*, 1986, 14(3), 3–4.

11. Schein, Bowe and Delk, 1973; Schein, Delk and Hooker, 1980. A study of a large and a small federal agency showed that, even though required to do so by law, these agencies did not make accommodations that would enable Deaf workers to be employed as often as they could be.

12. Schein and Delk, 1974. Figures shown are rounded. Note also that some of the variation in the rates may be due to differences in the age-sex-race composition of the two populations.

13. Schein and Delk, 1974, 1978.

14. Schein and Delk, 1974.

15. Christiansen and Barnartt, 1987; Schein and Delk, 1974, 1978. The rates by race and sex are even more depressing; nonwhite workers earn less on the average than white workers, and nonwhite Deaf people earn even less than either group and for either sex.

16. Crammatte, 1968, 1987.

17. Schein, 1988.

18. Most of this section is based on Schein, 1977c.

19. Garretson, 1980, 1.
20. From testimony before the Federal Trade Commission, *In the matter of hearing aids*, CR 8096. Washington, D.C., 13 April 1976, 170–178.
21. Schein, 1977c.
22. Under a contract between Columbus Colony and Deaf Community Associates, in 1981, Marcus T. Delk and I conducted a study of the organization. Additional material is from Jamieson, 1980. I am deeply indebted to Cecil F. Bradley, administrator of Columbus Colony, and Richard Huebner, chairman and president, for correcting some misimpressions and bringing the account up-to-date. The opinions, however, are mine alone.

7

Medical, Legal, and Interpreting Services

Another perspective on the Deaf experience can be gained from an examination of three services—medical, legal, and interpreting. The treatment that Deaf people receive from those who provide these services illustrates further the relations between the Deaf and general communities.

MEDICINE

Deaf people have expressed serious reservations about the quality of medical care they receive.[1] Their complaints revolve around three faults—inadequate communication, ignorance about deafness, and poor attitudes toward Deaf people. The physician's inability to communicate with a Deaf patient can be annoying, but it can also have life-threatening consequences for the Deaf patient. A Deaf college professor satirized medical treatments he received in which he was expected to lipread after drops were put in his eyes or in which he was told to hold his breath but never to start breathing again. About medical treatment in general, he says,

> I am what is generally known as a good lipreader. My doctor, like so many others, is of the opinion that since I speak clearly, I must lipread equally well. I assure you that his diagnosis is wrong. . . . Many a time I have struggled to lipread him, pretended vast understanding, and then gone home to have my wife call his nurse to find out what the diagnosis was. The main reason for this lack of

rapport between the doctor and his deaf patient appears to be the nonorientation of the medical profession to deafness and its non-medical complications, and the ever-present communication problem. I once asked a young doctor just what he had learned about deafness during his training. He said he could recall learning quite a bit about the causes and diagnosis of hearing loss and the anatomy of the ear. But as far as he could remember, nothing was ever said about the possible problems inherent in the doctor–patient relationship.[2]

Treatment in hospitals sometimes takes on nightmarish qualities for Deaf patients who find themselves subjected to procedures they do not comprehend and, even worse, being ignored when they need medical attention. A professor of nursing related a story of a young Deaf woman who was alone when she recovered from anesthesia following the birth of her child. She panicked when no one was around to tell her what had happened. Being unable to hear or speak, she could not make the nurses understand her fears.[3] Deaf patients confined to a hospital bed can push a button to get nursing attention, but it aids them not at all when the nurse responds over the intercommunication system. Even if they have clear speech, Deaf patients cannot know when to respond to a loudspeaker.

A survey of Deaf officers in state associations revealed a wide communication gap in hospitals.[4] For all their modern equipment, few hospitals provide communication aids for Deaf patients—TDDs, interpreters, communication boards. Only 8 percent of respondents to the 1980 survey had interpreters available at some time during their hospital stays. They preferred interpreting over writing notes back and forth, but writing was the most prevalent means of communicating between themselves and hospital staffs (83 percent). Consequently, the Deaf leaders felt that they understood only a relatively small percentage of what was told to them and, conversely, that only a small percentage of what they tried to say was understood by medical and nursing personnel. These results are particularly discomfiting when it is recalled that the Deaf leaders who were questioned had higher educational levels than the Deaf community's average and, being leaders, they tended to be more aggressive and better communicators than the average Deaf person.

The problems continue when Deaf patients leave their beds for other services, where their charts are unlikely to make clear that they cannot hear. A note saying "patient is deaf" often provokes useless shouting from technicians. Because hearing and speech are so intimately linked in most people's minds, Deaf persons with fairly good speech have trouble convincing the hospital staff that they cannot hear, which leads to situations that are silly, at best, and dangerous, at worst. Magnetic-resonance imaging (MRI) is particularly discomforting to Deaf people because it requires the patient to lie inside a machine in semidarkness. MRI technicians constantly talk to patients, reassuring them and urging them not to move, all of which is wasted on deaf people. Deaf people report this experience is like "being buried alive."

When Deaf persons undergo eye surgery, they literally become deaf-blind. One elderly Deaf man spent five days in the hospital with his eyes bandaged. His wife, realizing how he would feel and being able to communicate with him by fingerspelling in his hand, stayed with him every minute, even sleeping in a bed next to his so she would be available during the night. When her husband was discharged, she was dismayed to find she was also charged for a hospital bed! The hospital administrator relented when, on advice from her lawyer son, she told the hospital she planned to send a bill for her nursing services.

Sometimes physicians object to the presence of interpreters while they are examining or counseling patients; other times, they insist upon them, even when the Deaf person would prefer not to have one. In the first instance, some physicians take it as a matter of pride that they can communicate, and they see use of an interpreter as calling their qualifications into question. They may also regard an interpreter as breaching confidentiality and disturbing the doctor–patient relationship. When a certified, professional interpreter is being used, confidentiality is assured by the interpreters' code of ethics, something about which most physicians are unaware. The opposite situation can occur; some physicians insist that a family member interpret when the Deaf person would rather they do not. A hearing boy told me about being forced to sit in on his mother's examination and relate matters of feminine hygiene that he could not understand but that embarrassed him and his mother. Why? Because the physician asserted he was too busy to write notes.

Lay people often expect doctors to know everything. Their idols' clay feet and empty heads disappoint them. Ignorance about deafness can be particularly disturbing to well-educated Deaf adults. A Deaf teacher related what happened when she sought out an obstetrician for her pregnancy. She was shocked when the physician tried to schedule an abortion. "You don't want to bring a Deaf baby into the world," he said to her. That both she and her husband were adventitiously deaf had not been elicited by the physician, though she was not sure that such information would have mattered to him. Needless to say, she found another obstetrician who saw her to term, at which time she delivered a healthy, normally hearing baby.

Judgments by psychiatrists can be equally uninformed. Called upon to determine if a Deaf adult's behavior indicates psychosis, the examining physician who has little or no experience with Deaf people and who cannot communicate manually may make a tragic error—tragic for the Deaf person. Anecdotes about Deaf adults incorrectly diagnosed as psychotic appear so frequently that one wonders if constant reviews of all confined mental patients should not be made by professional panels whose members are chosen because they have extensive educational and experiential backgrounds in deafness.[5] Otherwise, Deaf people remain at risk of gross misjudgments that can lead to lifelong imprisonment as "mental patients."[6]

Hugh Kenner, a writer who was deafened at five years of age, does not look kindly on medical practice, even as it applies to hard-of-hearing people. Referring to the experiences of a friend who is losing hearing he observes:

> [Physicians] disallow a hearing aid because then she'd stop paying real attention. Never mind that we're all allowed glasses before we're blind. Deafness is the one disability to get written off as an attitude. As that, or as sheer dumb idiocy.[7]

Hearing parents of deaf children usually do not find much solace from consulting with their physicians. One study found that 8 of 10 parents were not informed of the causes of their children's deafness by their physicians nor given the opportunity to discuss this troubling issue when etiology was unknown or uncertain.[8] Harassed pediatricians with enormous caseloads will still be called upon by most parents to render judgments that go far beyond their expertise. A Deaf father of a Deaf daughter warns them "to be aware that the medical and educational aspects of deafness are two horses of a different color."[9]

The Deaf community looks askance at the medical conception of genetic deafness as a pathological condition rather than as a normal deviation. Few physicians can deviate from their training and look upon a Deaf person as being healthy and socially well adjusted. Because of their views of Deaf people as "disabled," the medical practitioner often deals with them in a condescending manner that betrays their inherent belief that "deaf and dumb" is not a misnomer.

It is important to add that Deaf people make up a tiny fraction of most physicians' practices. Seeing a Deaf patient only rarely, they are prepared neither by experience nor education for the difficulties that often arise. Most medical personnel conscientiously try to accommodate to a Deaf patient. Some even find their way to sign classes, only to find that an hour or two worth of lessons will not provide them with the communication competence necessary for good patient care. Nor should the expectations of Deaf people be regarded as unreasonable. They are aware of the problems and make efforts to avoid the situations described above. When they encounter problems, they generally meet them with patience, ingenuity, and good humor.

LAW, THE COURTS, AND THE POLICE

Historically, Deaf people have done poorly before the bar of justice. Being unable to understand what is being said, they are often powerless to defend themselves.[10] In instances in which they appear as plaintiffs, they have similar difficulties due to the arcane nature of the proceedings and the difficulties they have in expressing themselves other than in sign language. In the past two decades, federal courts and most state courts have held that Deaf participants are entitled to the same interpreter services granted to non-English-speakers. That this essential provision is not always granted by the courts should sadden all citizens who respect the constitutional guarantees of justice. Yet, slips do occur, as can be seen by a recent case in Miami, in which a Deaf man was given an indeterminate sentence without benefit of an interpreter and without the aid of counsel. (See "Justice Should be Blind . . . and Deaf?")

Even less tolerable are instances in which the interpreter is incompetent. Courts usually have no way of assessing the communication abilities of foreign-language interpreters. If a secretary or relative says they understand Greek or Swahili or whatever language is needed, the court often accepts the individual as an interpreter. So in the case of ASL, it is not unusual to find that the Deaf person cannot understand the court-appointed interpreter and vice versa. A few years ago in New York, a graduate student in social work was observing in the courtroom when a deaf youngster with whom she had been working was arraigned. The graduate student quickly determined that the interpreter was misrepresenting the

JUSTICE SHOULD BE BLIND . . . AND DEAF?

A man who cannot hear or speak spent 41 days in jail on an open-ended sentence he received in a case in which he was not represented by a lawyer, a public defender says. Judge Murray Meyerson had given the man, Monroe Halcomb, 31 years old, an indefinite sentence for a probation violation. Mr. Halcomb was discovered in jail by Kenneth Marvin, an assistant public defender, and was released two days before Christmas. Mr. Marvin said he learned of Halcomb's case "purely by accident" from another prisoner.

"He could have been in there forever," Mr. Marvin said. "There are safeguards and procedures built into the system to prevent this kind of thing from happening," he said. "In this case, they were totally ignored."

Judge Meyerson said he ordered Mr. Halcomb jailed because the defendant's mother, Ethel Halcomb, said she and her family feared the 290-pound man when he was drunk. She also said alcoholism counselors had recommended confinement. Mr. Halcomb was never represented by a lawyer. In addition, he was not provided with a sign language interpreter when he pleaded not guilty to a charge of disorderly intoxication July 7.

"Everybody should be represented by an attorney," Judge Meyerson said. "In this particular case, his mother, who he lived with, was with him."

The case began May 10 when the manager of a doughnut shop complained of an unruly customer. Mr. Halcomb was charged with disorderly intoxication, a charge that carries a maximum penalty of 60 days in jail. Judge Meyerson ordered him to participate in an alcohol and drug abuse program, but his mother said he quit after a couple of sessions. On September 5, Edward Cooke, supervisor of Dade County's alcohol and drug abuse program, asked Judge Meyerson to sentence Mr. Halcomb to treatment. The judge sent Mr. Halcomb to jail November 13, saying that the indefinite sentence was treatment rather than punishment. When an administrative judge signed the release, he ordered Mr. Halcomb to appear before Judge Meyerson next week. A lawyer will accompany him. (*The New York Times*, 3 January 1987, A24)

boy's answers to questions and that the boy did not understand the interpreter. When the graduate student interrupted the court proceedings to advise the judge, his response was, "Sit down and be quiet, or I will hold you in contempt of court." She left the courtroom in tears. However, the story does not end at that sad point. With the assistance of the New York Society for the Deaf, the court was made aware of the interpreter's incompetence and agreed to only use qualified interpreters in the future.

Once in prison or in a mental institution, the efforts of Deaf adults to communicate are often misunderstood as "assaultive" or "crazy" behaviors that lead to further difficulties. Their signing, pantomiming, gesturing, and poor vocalizations confirm the verdict or diagnosis. And who can say how many Deaf people become unbalanced as a result of improper confinement? Being the only Deaf person in an institution, unable to communicate with one's caretakers, could be ego-destructive in relatively strong-minded individuals. Long-term solitary confinement can cause incalculable psychological damage.

There are, of course, Deaf criminals. By pointing to injustices against Deaf people, I do not mean to embrace the naïve point that Deaf people are blameless. What the crime rates are in the Deaf community has never been systematically studied, so whether the average Deaf person is more or less likely to commit a criminal act is a matter for speculation. My guess is that their crime rates are lower than those of the general population. One basis for that assessment is the study of deaf drivers. The least-biased sample of deaf drivers' records was compared to those of hearing drivers living in the same area and showed that deaf drivers had fewer moving violations and far fewer accidents.[11] That and other favorable evidence notwithstanding, the Department of Transportation persists in denying permission to deaf truck drivers in interstate commerce.

The National Center for Law and the Deaf (NCLD), at Gallaudet University, has done a great deal to provide the Deaf community with their own advocacy. Under the leadership of Sy DuBow, NCLD has published several editions of *Legal Rights of Hearing-Impaired People* (Gallaudet University Press, 1986). It contains information about court decisions and related matters of concern to the Deaf community. NCLD multiplies its influence by providing consultation to attorneys defending Deaf clients and by filing friend-of-the-court briefs in actions of importance to the Deaf community.

CHALLENGES TO DEAF PERSONS' RIGHTS TO PARENTHOOD

Chilling to any Deaf parent are those instances in which a court has ruled that their deafness makes them unfit to raise children. Such cases have been brought by social agencies seeking to take children out of Deaf homes, while others have arisen when Deaf persons have sought permission to adopt a child. One of the most horrifying cases involved a California Deaf couple seeking to adopt a boy for whom they had already been foster parents.

In 1966, Wayne and Madeline Christensen appeared in Los Angeles Superior Court for purposes of adopting a child that the county welfare agency had entrusted to them. The Adoption Bureau had investigated the prospective parents and determined they were qualified. The matter appeared routine until Judge A. A. Scott interrupted the hearing and stated on the record,

> I am sorry, I can't go through with it [the adoption procedure]. . . . These people adore this child. . . . From all reports they are wonderful people. . . . There is no question . . . it is a happy home, but is it a normal home? Is the Court doing right by giving a healthy normal child to handicapped people?[12]

The Christensens' attorney, Ivan Lawrence, obtained a continuance of the case. He returned with seventeen witnesses, including a professor of pediatrics, but to no avail. Five months prior to the hearing, Judge Scott had written a letter in which he said, in part, "I believe this adoption should be nipped in the bud . . . in my opinion, we are not doing right in approving an adoption to deaf-mutes."[13]

At the continued trial, Judge Scott ordered the baby to be taken from Mrs. Christensen at once. He further reprimanded the representative of the Adoption Bureau, saying that its actions in approving these handicapped people as parents was gross misconduct. The frightened child was wrenched from Mrs. Christensen's arms in the courtroom to the great distress of all present, except Judge Scott.

The Christensens' attorney appealed the ruling. In due course, the Appellate Court ordered a new trial and also took the unusual step of reprimanding Judge Scott for his prejudicial behavior. The new judge speedily approved the adoption, and the Christensens emerged with Scott legally their son. The coincidence of names—the baby's first name and the judge's last—may seem ironic. But a further irony occurred, one that would have been worthy of that master of the surprise ending, O. Henry. A few months after Scott's last court appearance, the Christensens discovered that he was hearing-impaired! He had a severe deficit in one ear and a milder one in the other. Chance had brought Scott to the parents most likely to understand and care for him.[14]

Looking back on this case, one might conclude that legal precedents had built an adequate bulwark against future assaults on Deaf parents. Two recent examples make clear that misconceptions about deafness remain a problem of serious proportions. In 1986, Joe and Shirlene Timmons, of Okeechobee, Florida, prevailed against the state Department of Health and Rehabilitation Services, which three years earlier had taken away their normally hearing toddler. The state court ordered the agency to return the child to the Timmonses and "to stop harassing them." At about the same time, Miguel Lozada, a father of two hearing daughters, who himself was born deaf, endured the longest trial in the history of Queens (New York) to retain the children's custody after their nondeaf mother had deserted the family. Concluding the eighteen-month trial, in which the state argued that Lozada's deafness disqualified him as a parent of hearing children, the judge ruled in his favor. Sadly, the list of cases could continue. In Georgia, juvenile court took hearing children from a Deaf mother (reversed on appeal, in 1978); in Michigan, a court awarded two hearing children of Deaf parents to the nondeaf grandparents (reversed on appeal, in 1985). The continued evidences of judicial prejudice must surely add to the sense of alienation Deaf people feel when they learn of them.

POLICE ACTIONS

Over the years, a number of instances have occurred in which innocent Deaf people have been killed by police officers. One incident during the Watts riots, in Los Angeles, illustrates the point. A young Deaf boy was on his way home. He was unaware of the rioting. As he walked through a looted area, he was stopped by a police officer. The boy reached for his pad and pencil. The officer, believing he was pulling a gun, shot him.

Many police agencies have taken steps to avoid repetition of such tragedies. They have put in short training courses, issued bulletins to their personnel about deafness, and developed cooperative relationships with local agencies serving Deaf people. Despite these efforts, mistakes continue to occur. The distressing newspaper account of another unprovoked attack on a Deaf person (see "A Mistake") is not recounted to embarrass police officers who may be acting with good intentions. Rather than being indignant, hearing readers might put themselves in the place of Deaf adults and feel the chill from the realization that the next unfortunate happening might involve themselves.

What makes these accounts of difficulties between Deaf adults and law enforcement agents even more troubling is that deafness is a rare condition, so encounters between police and Deaf people should seldom occur. That may be one reason why efforts by various police departments to educate their officers about deafness and Deaf people apparently have not had too much success. The incident recounted in "A Mistake" occurred in a department that had recently had an orientation to deafness. Of course, such negative outcomes must not inhibit efforts to solve this problem, but more ingenuity, more enthusiasm, or more creative techniques are needed to assure that future encounters between Deaf people and the guardians of the law will not result in misfortune.[15]

INTERPRETING[16]

Before 1964, interpreting was a favor that hearing persons did for their Deaf friends and relatives. The Registry of Interpreters for the Deaf (RID) changed the status of interpreting from an unpaid courtesy to a paid profession. While RID is not a commercial enterprise, interpreting now is. A large share of interpreters are independent contractors, earning all or a substantial part of their income from serving Deaf people. They may enjoy the freedom that this arrangement gives them, but interpreters often find it economically unsatisfactory. They obtain no benefits—health insurance, retirement, unemployment—and they frequently have cash-flow problems, either having to wait long periods for government agencies to pay them or not collecting at all. To assist them in overcoming these problems, interpreter services have sprung up around the country. A typical one is the New York Society for the Deaf (NYSD). It assumes the role of a broker, receiving requests and locating the interpreters to fill them. NYSD pays the interpreters promptly in accordance with an agreed-upon fee schedule and collects that fee from clients plus a percentage to cover its overhead. The agency is able to guarantee interpreters their pay, keep them busy, spare them the expenses of advertising their availability, and provide them with other employment security. In turn, NYSD assures the purchasers of interpreting that the services will be of high quality,

A MISTAKE

Three weeks after an organization for the Deaf offered to provide police with special training, a Deaf man was mistaken for a
suspected auto thief and clubbed with a nightstick. "They never
stopped to think or check that this man is Deaf," said Mae Bell
Bogner, executive director of the Deaf Service Center of Tampa.
"This is a problem facing all Deaf people everywhere, and something has got to be done. Someone could be easily killed."

Jeffrey Johnson, 21, suffered shoulder bruises Monday night.

"We made a mistake, no doubt about it. I don't know what
went wrong," police spokesman Steve Cole said Tuesday. "Sometimes in the heat of trying to catch somebody, it's going to happen
and it's unfortunate that it did. I think [the officer's] main concern
was he thought he had somebody that was going to get away from
him."

When Police Chief A. C. McLane met with Bogner three
weeks ago, he turned down her offer to train officers, Cole said.
Instead, McLane took packets of information on the subject, Cole
said. The packets were distributed to division commanders, who
were supposed to pass the information on to their officers.

Johnson's sister, Betty Matthews, filed a complaint with the
police department Tuesday. "The main thing is he doesn't understand why he was struck. He keeps asking why," she said.

Police said officer Delier Diaz gave chase to a car that had refused to pull over. The two occupants pulled into an apartment
complex, parked the vehicle and fled. Johnson had just helped two
maintenance workers at the complex free a tractor from a ditch
when Diaz arrived. The officer approached Johnson, who raised
his hand to his ear—the signal used by the Deaf to indicate they
can't hear. "Jeff put up his hand and the cop just started hitting
him," said apartment resident Elizabeth Borreo. "He hit him with
his stick on the leg. Jeff bent down to grab his leg, and he hit him
again on the left shoulder. Then the cop pushed him down."
Apartment manager Iris Cox told police: "You got the wrong guy.
He lives here and I saw him not five minutes ago." A crowd gathered. Within 30 minutes, the officers released Johnson. Later Monday night, [two men were arrested for the car theft.] (*Miami Herald*,
2 March 1988, 15A)

something they can seldom determine and can rarely enforce on
their own. The brokers of interpreting services create the market,
such as stock exchanges create securities markets. A few attempts to

provide this service on a proprietary basis have failed, largely because the volume is not yet sufficient to justify the overhead. Most of the nation's interpreter brokers are voluntary agencies which, like the NYSD, incorporate this service along with the other social and rehabilitation services they regularly provide. In that way, they are able to support their own efforts as well as contribute to the preservation of a service vital to the Deaf community.

Interpreters are in short supply throughout the United States. Paradoxically, interpreters often have difficulty scheduling themselves, either being without any assignments or having to choose among two or three. The newness of interpreting as a profession creates some confrontations with older Deaf persons who have been accustomed to interpreting as a favor. Having to pay for the service affronts some and puzzles others. The Rehabilitation Act Amendments of 1973 further altered the situation. Title V of the act mandated interpreting in many situations in which Deaf people had previously been ignored. Federally supported activities could no longer ignore Deaf people. They had to be given equal access, which almost always means being provided with interpreters. As a result of this new source of referrals, interpreters found themselves in greater demand than ever.

In 1973, it was estimated that the United States had only about three hundred interpreters. Only six institutions had programs training interpreters, with a combined annual graduation of fewer than one hundred. The National Interpreter Training Consortium (NITC), a five-year demonstration project, was formed with federal funding in 1974. It developed a curriculum, evaluated candidates for interpreter training, and provided those selected with sufficient instruction to enable them to begin serving as interpreters. NITC also undertook the preparation of teachers, something not previously done, and encouraged other institutions to initiate similar programs. In the five years that it existed, NITC graduated more than twenty-five hundred interpreters, at an average federal subsidy of about three hundred dollars each. At the end of the five-year project, Congress enacted legislation to fund interpreter training programs around the country.

In spite of the continuing efforts to recruit and train interpreters, they remain in short supply, especially in the less-populated regions. What do Deaf people do when they cannot find a qualified interpreter? What they did before 1964; that is, they find a hearing child of Deaf parents who is willing to assist them, or else they do without, use paper and pencil, or attempt to speak and lipread. Admittedly, these are seldom satisfactory options. Volunteers are not bound to maintain confidentiality, and they may intrude themselves in the situation rather than interpret. Writing is slow, Deaf speech is frequently unintelligible, and lipreading inexact.

When qualified interpreters are available, all problems are not resolved. As noted in the discussion about physicians, not all hearing people readily adjust to having an interpreter present at private meetings. They need to be instructed to speak to the Deaf person, not to the interpreter, and to speak normally, as if the Deaf person could hear. If the hearing person says, "Tell her that . . ." the interpreter will repeat, "Tell her that . . ." Older Deaf people also need to learn how to use interpreters. The younger generations will be accustomed to having professional interpreters, but their presence in the Deaf community is relatively new. A few years go, it was not uncommon for Deaf college students to say to an interpreter, "I won't be in class tomorrow, so take notes, and if there is a test, take it for me." Interpreters then had to explain that they only interpret. They do not fetch coffee, substitute on examinations, or do other chores. Such instances would be rare today, though older Deaf adults may still ask their interpreter's advice about the matter at hand, whether it is how to respond to a question in court or what to pay for an automobile. The professional interpreter, of course, must politely refrain from giving any opinion.

Almost no research has been done on the attitudes of Deaf people toward interpreters and vice versa. The intimate nature of the relationship would seem an attractive area for study by psychologists, yet such studies have not been reported. A recent exception is a survey undertaken by the NAD. A little over half of those surveyed said they cannot get an interpreter whenever they want one, and more than 7 out of 10 said they cannot get an ASL interpreter (some interpreters are able to sign only in Manual English). The majority of Deaf respondents said they were satisfied with interpreter fee schedules, but this judgment is tempered by the more than two-thirds of respondents who received all of their interpreting without charge to themselves. Regarding their satisfaction with the interpreting services they had received, 30 percent were always satisfied, 59 percent were sometimes satisfied, and 70 percent were never satisfied. Of those not always satisfied with interpreting, only 23 percent said they ever conveyed these assessments to the interpreter. Most respondents (72 percent) did not know about the RID's complaint procedures. Importantly, only 39 percent knew about the RID Code of Ethics, and only about 1 in 5 understood such critical ethical tenets as confidentiality and impartiality.[17]

NAD plans to develop a nationwide evaluation and certification program for interpreters. The respondents recommended that NAD sponsor courses in how to use interpreters. From the foregoing evidence, an important component of such training should be to encourage Deaf people to learn to defend their rights in dealing with interpreters. It would be unusual to find that no friction, no negative feelings, no awkward situations develop in the delivery of interpreting services. But until they are made explicit, they will remain as potential sources of discomfort to Deaf people, without immediate actions to relieve them. Too many respondents to NAD's survey stated that they did not complain about poor interpreting because "I did not know I could." The dependency relationship fostered by the situation makes Deaf people reluctant to criticize lest they endanger a critical service. Perhaps sessions bringing together Deaf people and their interpreters in a setting that encourages a free exchange of complaints about each other—interpreters do have criticisms of their clients—would aid in improving this vital communication link.

SUMMARY

The preceding material has been presented largely from a Deaf person's perspective. Wrongs have been committed against Deaf people. Too often they have not been treated fairly in doctors' offices, hospitals, courtrooms, and in encounters with the police. Yet from a professional's point of view, the nature of deafness—its rareness and its impediment to communication—causes the unhappy situations that arise. The problem is not ignoring Deaf people but being ignorant of them, or so many physicians, attorneys, and police officers would claim. Like so much of society, they contribute to the Deaf community's sense of alienation. Reflecting on those instances described, the reader can empathize with Deaf persons who regard themselves as living in a hostile world in which the Deaf community provides a sanctuary.

NOTES

1. Schein and Delk, 1980.
2. Jordan, 1971.
3. Douglas, 1971.
4. Schein and Delk, 1980.
5. For an excellent, detailed account of a landmark case see Petersen, 1973.
6. For example, Rainer and Altshuler (undated) quote a psychiatrist who has spent years working with deaf patients: "We have seen several patients, however, who, at the very least, were misdiagnosed and, at the very most, have remained up to 6 or 8 years in a hospital without the necessity for continuous hospitalization" (p. 58). Later, in the same volume, another psychiatrist notes that 2 percent of patients in state mental hospitals are deaf "and some of these are involved in misdiagnoses" (p. 148). Dubow and Goldberg (1981) put the situation plainly: "Despite some progressive reforms, mentally ill deaf people suffer neglect and abuse in many state mental health systems. These abuses can range from misdiagnosis and improper intake procedures, to inadequate treatment once hospitalized, to a lack of suitable aftercare" (p. 195).
7. Kenner, 1986, 12.
8. Schlesinger, 1971.
9. Newman, 1971. For a further discussion of relations between parents and the medical professions, see chapter 4.
10. A notable exception is Massieu's plea for the Abbé Sicard's life made by his Deaf students before the French National Assembly during the Reign of Terror (Lane, 1976, 83). His speech epitomizes the best persuasive writing.
11. Schein, 1968.
12. Lawrence, 1972, 2.
13. Ibid., 3.
14. Ibid.
15. A police official I interviewed emphasized the difficulties of the officer on the line: "When you must act in a second, you act on instinct. The man on the beat does not have time to reflect on far-out possibilities— like the guy is deaf—when faced with someone who is running away or who does not respond in expected ways to commands given him. . . . You can blame the officer in hindsight, but you need to be on the scene to understand why things happen the way they do sometimes." Asked what could be done, he shrugged and added, "We try to educate cops as best we can, but there is so much to learn and so little time to learn it. Still, we just have to keep trying."

16. Except as otherwise indicated, the following material is drawn from Schein, 1984a.

17. From 1987–88 National Study of Deaf Adults' Satisfaction with Interpreters. *NAD Broadcaster*, May 1988.

8

A Theory of Deaf
Community Development

Whether the Deaf community is regarded as a linguistic, ethnic, social, or other community, it clearly exists. That leaves the task of explaining why. Because the Deaf community plays so large a role in the lives of almost half a million Deaf citizens of this country, delving into the factors that have led to and shaped its development appears well justified. Furthermore, an understanding of why Deaf people have moved in the directions they have may assist other disabled and ethnic minority groups to plot their own courses more effectively. Those engaged in education and rehabilitation can better serve Deaf people if they appreciate the pervasive influence the Deaf community exerts on the lives of most early deafened people. Deaf leaders, too, might gain from a theory about what is for them a daily reality. In dealing with an abstraction, they might discern useful strategies that might otherwise remain obscure or unseen.

REVIEW OF THEORIES OF DEAF
COMMUNITY DEVELOPMENT

In recent years, a number of theorists from several disciplines have become interested in the phenomenon that is the Deaf community. Some scholars have proposed that segregated education underlies the development of the Deaf community. Like Alexander Graham Bell, they conclude that the residential schools provide the basis for the formation of Deaf society. For those holding this view, main

An Early Theory of Deaf
Community Development

While the deaf person may be found to be an active component in the economic and industrial life of society, yet his inability
to hear accompanied by his general inability to speak fluently and
intelligibly stand in the way of his prompt and continuous partak-
ing in its social life. He may, and does, have many friends among
his neighbors and acquaintances, but in the discourse between
man and man which forms such a large part of the interest and
delight in living, he is for the most part unable to join. There is
usually at hand no ready and rapid means of communication as
there is between two hearing persons in their conversation; and
his intercourse must necessarily be slow and tedious. The privi-
leges of his church he cannot enjoy; in his lodge he misses the
fellowship which is one of its fundamental ends; in few forms of
convivial entertainment can he take part. Thus seeking an outlet
for those social instincts which surge through his being, the deaf
man finds himself among men, but as though surrounded by a
great impenetrable wall against which their voices break in vain.

Placed, however, with his deaf fellows, the deaf man discovers
himself in a different situation. He soon learns that by the use of
that language of signs so largely employed by other deaf, and of
which he has in a short time become master—in fact probably
from school days—he is able to converse with an ease and quick-
ness fully as great as by that means of which he has been deprived. Hence he ceases in large measure to carry on his social
intercourse with the hearing and turns to his deaf comrades; in
them he builds up a quite congenial companionship and fellowship; and to them he looks largely for his means of social diver-
sion. With them he feels a close bond of sympathy, and is moved
to cooperate with them, and to stand with them when their mutual
interests are concerned. In time, associations of rather formal nature come to be organized among them. In such wise is realized
the desire of the deaf as of all men to commune with their
fellows.[1]

streaming tolls the Deaf community's death knell, or at least signals
its imminent decline. Others have suggested that the Deaf community has emerged as a reaction to mistreatment by the majority community. The argument runs somewhat along these lines: Deaf

people prefer to be a part of the larger community, but the larger community, through indifference or downright hostility, rejects them; reacting to this frustration, Deaf people turn to each other.

Still other theorists have pointed to the ease of communication between prelingually Deaf individuals as the principal reason for the Deaf community as we know it. They describe the Deaf community as a linguistic community, emphasizing the common mode of communication and the common language. Observing the swift, fluent interchanges between Deaf people, one understands intuitively as well as cognitively the attractiveness of one Deaf person for another.[2]

Two deaf experts in rehabilitation, Boyce R. Williams and Allen E. Sussman, also see the Deaf community in linguistic terms. They explain that "the subculture of deaf persons has its roots in their urgent need to nullify the communication barrier,"[3] and that

> unlike some other disability groups, deaf people have always taken care of their own social needs. It is not a grammatical error that leads them to call their organizations clubs *of* the deaf. It is their way of emphasizing that they are not the recipients of other people's charity, that the disability of deafness does not foster incompetence.[4]

Ben M. Schowe, himself deaf from his teens, resents any implications that the Deaf community is not real. He regards it as a force that scientists have "glossed over without illumination, without any serious attempt to define or delimit, and with scant perception of its dynamic role and function in the lives of the Deaf." In his view, "the Deaf society is of prime importance. It is in the milieu of this social structure that the Deaf gain a self-respecting image of themselves and a productive relationship with others."[5]

Ethnographers Anedith and Jeffrey Nash focus on three distinguishing features of the Deaf community—sign language, shared experiences, and consciousness.[6] The latter refers to the perceptual shaping that occurs from awareness that, as a Deaf person, one is outside the larger community; in other words, a sense of isolation from the larger community.

Probably the most thorough description of the Deaf community has been written by a sociologist, Paul C. Higgins.[7] He considers membership to be based on shared experiences, identification, and involvement. Sign language binds Deaf people together, as does the common stigmatization they have suffered. They participate together in many activities. Thus, while language is an important element, it does not wholly explain the Deaf community. Furthermore, Higgins would insist upon pluralizing the term, believing that it is important to emphasize the separate nature of the many geographically separated Deaf communities. On this latter point, he is joined by Carol Padden,[8] who similarly emphasizes the diverse nature of local Deaf communities. With Tom Humphries, another Deaf linguist, Padden has written a comprehensive exposition of Deaf culture, emphasizing the influence of ASL on the thinking of Deaf people.

My own reading of the evidence evinced so far is that *all* of these theorists are correct. Their insights are valid and provocative. However, like most social-psychological phenomena, the development of the Deaf community is multiply determined. No single factor determined the emergence of the Deaf community in the United States. The evidence suggests that the Deaf community's genesis and subsequent growth required the interactions of at least five factors.

THE THEORY

The theory of Deaf community development presented here hypothesizes five factors—*demography, alienation, affiliation, education,* and *milieu.* These factors and their interactions account for the unique social-psychological behavior of Deaf people that resulted in the development of the phenomenon called the Deaf community. If the proposed theory appears complicated, it should be noted in defense that the Deaf community is multifaceted, so a satisfactory explanation for its developmental course is apt to be complicated.

DEMOGRAPHY

A precondition for the development of a Deaf community is the attainment of a sufficient number of Deaf people in relation to their basic characteristics—age, sex, and geographical location. Borrowing from physics, this qualification of necessary size could be referred to as "critical mass" (that is, the size required for an action to occur). This size factor has two aspects—actual and relative. Both are needed to understand the Deaf community.

Actual Size

For a Deaf community to emerge, the actual size of a group of Deaf people must reach some number larger than two. Precisely how much larger is an open question. The number of people who constitute a viable community (one that continues over more than a generation) can be approximated empirically. Such research must take into account age, sex, and other socially relevant characteristics, because the overall number would certainly vary depending on the makeup of the community. Another factor of importance to the Deaf community is geographical dispersion, since the number of people needed would vary with the amount of distance over which they are scattered.

A preliminary study suggests that, for a widely dispersed geographical area, about a thousand Deaf people are needed to generate a state association. Wyoming, for example, was the last state to establish a state association, in 1979. In 1970, I estimated its Deaf population at a little over nine hundred, while in 1960 it was less than six hundred. The theory does not suggest that the nine hundred or a thousand Deaf people will all join the association; some will be too young, others too old, others not interested, and so on. Having a sufficiently large base to draw from is the essential point. The Union League, discussed in chapter 3, began with only seven members; however, it had more than a thousand Deaf people in New York City from which to draw. These approximations illustrate one approach to testing this portion of the theory.

In 1830, the Deaf population in the United States, about six thousand, was not large enough to develop a Deaf community. By 1850, the Deaf population had grown to almost ten thousand (see Table 6). At about the same time, the New England association came into being. In 1880, when the National Association of the Deaf was founded, the Deaf population of the United States exceeded thirty-three thousand, apparently a sufficient number for establishment of a national organization.

The theory considers not just whether a community does or does not form (and survive) with particular numbers of people, but also how size influences the way in which the community develops. Assuming that a community can begin with as few as a handful of

Table 6 Total Population and Deaf Populations: United States, 1830–1930

Year	Total Population[a]	Deaf Population	Rate of Deafness per 100,000 People
1930	122,795,046	57,804	46.5
1920	105,710,620	44,885	42.5
1910	91,972,266	44,708	48.6
1900	75,994,575	24,369	32.1
1890	62,947,714	40,592	64.8
1880	50,155,783	33,878	67.5
1870	39,818,449	16,205	42.0
1860	31,443,321	12,821	40.8
1850	23,191,876	9,803	42.3
1840	17,069,453	7,678	45.0
1830	12,866,020	6,106	47.5

SOURCE: Adapted from Jerome D. Schein and Marcus T. Delk, Jr., *The Deaf Population of the United States* (Silver Spring, MD: National Association of the Deaf, 1974), 18.

[a]Population figures from *Statistical Abstract of the United States* (Washington, DC: GPO, 1988).

members, it will conduct itself much differently than a community with twelve hundred members. Economic considerations alone limit the smaller group in ways that a much larger group is not limited.

The student strike at Gallaudet University did not occur when the student body amounted to less than a thousand (see chapter 5). In 1988, Gallaudet had enrolled about fifteen hundred Deaf students, a number that inspired mutual confidence among the strike leaders. They, in turn, were joined by many Deaf people from the area who provided support with their physical presence on campus and at the march on the Capitol. Membership size, then, is an important determiner of a community's behavior. A caution, though, is in order. The theory does not state that *number* of Deaf people is sufficient to forming a Deaf community. The other four factors must be considered, too. Size of the population, however, is a necessary condition for the formation of a Deaf community. In other words, a Deaf community will not form if the number of Deaf people is too small, but it will not form solely because the number is large.

Relative Size

A second demographic consideration must be the size of the Deaf population relative to the total population. If the relative size is small, it will likely spur the growth of a Deaf community. The prevalence of deafness in the United States has ranged between 32.1 per 100,000 in 1900 and 202 per 100,000, in 1971.[9] When the Deaf population was at its relatively lowest point, in 1900, the NFSD was founded. So being a very small part of the total population does not appear to inhibit the development of the Deaf community. But when the relative size is large—say 5,000 Deaf persons per 100,000—then a Deaf community will be less likely to develop. In that saturated condition, the majority would more likely make accommodations to incorporate the minority.

The latter case has been documented on the island of Martha's Vineyard. Deaf people were so large a part of the population that, as one island resident recalled, "everyone here spoke sign language."[10] In that circumstance, alienation of Deaf people did not occur. The community adapted, in important ways, to its Deaf members. Informant after informant on Martha's Vineyard expressed surprise that the investigator was interested in deafness; for them, the fact that some of their numbers did not hear was not remarkable. A reporter from a Boston newspaper, in 1895, observed that

> the spoken and the sign language will be so mingled in the conversation that you pass from one to the other, or use both at once, almost unconsciously. They [deaf islanders] are not uncomfortable in their deprivation, the community has adjusted itself to the situation so perfectly.[11]

Would too large a proportion of Deaf people arouse the majority to assault the Deaf community? In a personal communication, Paul Higgins conjectures that as the number of Deaf people increases, the majority might perceive them as a threat. While that did not appear to be the case on Martha's Vineyard, where the relative proportion of Deaf people became very high, it is a possibility. On the other hand, relatively small numbers of Deaf people may be more vulnerable to the overt hostility of the general community. The Deaf community was attacked at its core, in 1880, when the proportion of Deaf people to the general population was much less than 100 per 100,000. In that year, the second International Congress on Education of the Deaf (only eight countries were represented) met in Milan, Italy. Its organizers were committed to the oral method of instructing deaf children. Edward Miner Gallaudet, then president of what is today Gallaudet University, argued that the congress was unrepresentative because many countries were not present and because Deaf people were not permitted to address the body. Nonetheless, the first resolution adopted by the congress had a strong, pervasive impact on the education of deaf children. It proclaimed,

> The Congress, considering the incontestable superiority of speech over signs, (a) for restoring deaf-mutes to social life, and (b) for giving them greater facility of language, declares that the method of articulation [oralism] should have the preference over that of signs in instruction in education of the deaf and dumb.[12]

The resolution, known thereafter as the Milan Manifesto, passed 160 to 4, with the four dissenting votes coming from the United States delegation and one from England. The reaction of Deaf people in the United States was to found the National Association of the Deaf, in defense of sign language (see chapter 3). In the succeeding eight decades after its passage, the manifesto was invoked again and again to frustrate efforts to use sign in the instruction of deaf children. Only since the 1960s has the tide begun to turn in support of manual communication in deaf students' classrooms. Once more, the majority frustrated Deaf people in their effort to manage their affairs; the majority decided "what was good for" Deaf people, and they disagreed with the prescription. Milan was not solely a reaction to the growing size, hence the greater visibility of Deaf people; it was a raw exercise of the majority's power. Still, it illustrates a potential danger to the Deaf community, the danger of growing large and affluent.

With regard to relative size, then, we propose that being a very small proportion of the total population will not inhibit the development of the Deaf community and, within limits, stimulates it. When the relative number of Deaf people grows past some critical amount—as it probably did on Martha's Vineyard—the likelihood of a Deaf community developing diminishes. The reason is that, with so many Deaf people, the society makes adjustments to them. Between the extremes, the relative size of the Deaf community seems to have less significance than the actual size. Finally, it is important to repeat that actual and relative population sizes together make up only one of the factors influencing the Deaf community's development.

Alienation

Alienation is the motor that drives the Deaf community. The experiences of rejection, of not fitting in with hearing deaf people, act as a centrifugal force pushing Deaf people away from general society. One word can hardly carry the weight of meaning intended. A close second to "alienation" is "rejection." But Deaf people also encounter antagonism, aversion, disaffection, enmity, estrangement, hatred, hostility, negativism, opposition, repugnance, repulsion, resistance, and stigma. The latter was the preferred term by Goffman (1963). Perhaps a better choice might be oppression, rejection, or marginality. "Alienate" is transitive; it means "to make indifferent or adverse; estrange." In some respects, it seems too strong, since the general public is often indifferent to, unaware of, and ignorant about Deaf people. With respect to sign, Deaf people have been oppressed, witnessed by the Milan Manifesto cited earlier. As an adjective specifying their status, "marginal" seems apt. Simply classifying Deaf people as "marginal" or "outsiders," however, does not connote the active opposition that Deaf people have often faced in history—and occasionally encounter today. The choice of "alienation" sacrifices elegance for comprehensiveness.

The majority of Deaf people first encounter passive alienation in their own homes. Certainly, their parents wish them no harm, but, as noted in chapter 4, most Deaf children's parents have normal hearing and, therefore, cannot depend upon empathy to guide their child-rearing practices. Many parents do not accept their child's deafness, and they strive to make the child "normal." Roger Carver and Michael Rodda, having studied a large sample of parents, concluded that these efforts "are harmful and stressful, and can be classified among the adverse circumstances which can affect the child's normal development, especially in language and cognition."[13] They and other authorities[14] recommend that parents concentrate on providing their children with a warm, supportive environment and eschew the role of taskmasters who impose difficult chores on the child without regard to the emotional consequences. "Normal" for many Deaf people is a passive form of rejection.

Consider a well-articulated view of the Deaf community that was prevalent in the mid-twentieth century:

On the part of a certain portion of the public, societies composed exclusively of the Deaf have been opposed, or at least looked upon with disfavor. This is because it has been felt that it is not well in general for a segment of the population, whether the Deaf or any other group, to be segregated from the rest of their fellow men, and to form a class apart in the community. A particular objection that has been advanced is that unless discouraged the practice will cause intermarriage among the Deaf, which may result in an increase in their number.[15]

What can any group of persons believe about society's attitudes toward them when that society wants to prevent "an increase in their number?" Preventing deafness may seem a benign objective, but how can it be regarded by those who are already deaf? Society says, We don't want more like you around here. From a speech by a young Deaf researcher to his colleagues in a government agency, a similar message comes through:

> If I had to put in a nutshell what is the worst thing about being Deaf, it's not that I am not able to hear music. It's not that I am not able to hear a voice. It's not that I can't use the telephone. It's not that I can't enjoy a movie or a play. What is it then? Attitude. That is my biggest handicap. Not my attitude; your attitude. . . . Society has placed a stigma on deafness. Parents of Deaf children feel guilty because they "produced a Deaf child." Deaf people are often referred to as "deaf and dumb," or more recently, "deaf-mute." I guarantee you, if you call any person, deaf or not, "dumb" they are going to be insulted. And rightly so![16]

Active alienation results from overtly hostile acts of majority members; for example, refusing to hire them, calling them pejorative names, making fun of their signs. These deliberate assaults on Deaf people may occur at any time in their lives, which makes them worse, as they are unexpected. In schools, for example, a child may be branded "an oral failure" for not developing good speech and lipreading skills. Deaf students often encounter "can't-can't" teachers who emphasize their limitations. The teachers may have the best of intentions, wishing only to acquaint them with the "real" world, but the net effect is alienation of the deaf student from the general community.

Whether in private conversations, public speeches, or in publications, Deaf people have increasingly made plain their views of the oppression they feel. If "oppression" seems too strong a word to express the assault they experience from society in general, a more appropriate term might be "isolation"—a feeling of being cut off from the main body of society, separated from it by "a glass wall," through which they can see but cannot participate in the activities of the general community.

Some Deaf people regard their circumstances differently. They accept the fact the world is designed by and for people who can hear. Like left-handed people, they realize that the majority rules. As former NAD president Mervin Garretson has explained, "From daybreak when greeted by a flashing light at bedside to the end of the day each Deaf person encounters all kinds of subtle little problems or inconveniences."[17] These difficulties may be accepted with humor or resignation, but they must be accepted, because "that's the way the world is." As a result of dealing with these unintentional barriers to Deaf people, Garretson is "grateful for a community that knows sign language, where you can relax in your own culture and even be perceived as knowledgeable and expert in your own language. But the nagging tendency to feel inferior because it is different from the majority culture remains." How insightful that last sentence!

The net result of alienation, whether in passive or active forms, is to drive Deaf people away from the general society. To what, then, does it drive them?

AFFILIATION

The counterforce to alienation is affiliation. The action of alienation is centrifugal, while that of affiliation is centripetal. Affiliation is the tendency of people to seek each other out and to establish conditions that facilitate their opportunities to intermingle. Historically, Deaf people in the United States have reacted to the expressed and implied hostilities of the general community by developing their own resources. The most extreme form of that response emerged in the mid-nineteenth century, when a Deaf man named J. J. Flournoy proposed the establishment of a state or territory exclusively for Deaf people. He suggested that the new state be called Deaf-Mutia or Gesturia. A contemporary of Flournoy wrote in response to Flournoy's proposal:

> Let me say to Mr. Flournoy that the idea of a community of deaf-mutes is to me nothing new. In the year 1831, William Willard and five or six others, including myself, formed ourselves into an association with a view of purchasing land in some favorable spot in the West, and so arranging that we might, through life, live in close neighborhood and continue to enjoy the friendships we had formed in Hartford. At that time, we were pupils of the Asylum, and all, except myself, were to leave in a few weeks or months. By election we added a sufficient number of past pupils to make our

whole number thirteen. It was a sort of secret society, as we preferred to put it into practical execution rather than have the project
dissipate in mere talk. Time went on, and we all found ourselves
compelled to attend to the stern realities of life—procuring a self-
support—before we could attend to carrying out what Mr. Willard
afterwards, in one of his letters to me, called our Don Quixotic
scheme. Mr. Willard became a teacher in the Ohio Institution, I in
Hartford; the rest of us were scattered over New England, and the
project gradually died away.[18]

The debate about a Deaf state persisted in the letters column of
the *American Annals of the Deaf* for some time, revealing the deep
sense of alienation from the general community felt by a group of
well-educated Deaf people and their strong desire to maintain affiliation. Deaf people sometimes have been chastised for their clan-
nishness, their "we-they" attitudes, as if they had rejected the
general population, a patently ridiculous notion. It is a bit like the
bully who starts a fight and then blames the person he is hitting for
being in the way.

Why the strong tendencies to join with other Deaf people? Is it
merely to escape the inhospitable society? A brief look outside of
deafness provides a useful insight. The Nobel laureate, Gabriel
García Márquez, has written the true story of a sailor who survived
the outer limits of isolation and brutal exposure on the ocean. When
he is at last rescued, Márquez describes what the sailor thought on
meeting the first man to reach him.

> The starved, sun-baked, semidelirious sailor, at last granted hu-
> man contact, discovers within himself a primary aesthetic impulse:
> "When I heard him speak I realized that, more than thirst, hunger,
> and despair, what tormented me most was the need to tell some-
> one what had happened to me."[19]

How better to express the strength of the need to communicate
than in that taut phrase, "more than thirst, hunger, and despair?"
As humans, we appear genetically predisposed to interchange
thoughts and emotions with our fellow beings. This need appears
as strong in Deaf as in hearing deaf persons. It contributes the ob-
verse to the alienation factor, which is that general society tends to
frustrate Deaf persons' efforts to communicate. Yet this deep need
persists. So, on the positive side, they find satisfaction with other
Deaf persons who have the patience, as well as the same wish, to

communicate. The way in which Deaf people prolong their meetings when they do get together is another manifestation of the "need to tell."

Another facet of affiliation is belonging. Ben Schowe tells his own "at home among strangers" story (see "Belonging"). He makes the point forcefully that it is not sign, but sign and the sharing of deafness that attracts Deaf people to each other. This position, of course, reflects that held by Paul Higgins and several other theorists, like Carol Padden, who recognize that signing is the tip of the iceberg. The iceberg itself is *culture*. When joining the Deaf community, Deaf people acquire an entire heritage, one based on conditions they can share and build upon.

Three conditions foster affiliation—relaxation, empathy, and recognition. When in conversation with other Deaf people, a Deaf person can relax, empathize with what is being discussed, and recognize and identify with those in the group. Deaf people's backgrounds enable them to predict with fair accuracy their friends' reactions. Having shared similar experiences, they can empathize with each other. Because they tend, like most human beings, to be suspicious of those who are unlike them, recognizing others as being the same provides a feeling of safety. People like them will not hurt them and, best of all, will not ignore them. Being with other Deaf people is like being at home.

EDUCATION

Education did not cause a Deaf community to develop in the United States, but it exerted a strong influence on it—it shaped it. We are not talking here only about formal instruction that Deaf children receive in school, important as that is. We also include here the myriad experiences that Deaf people have in common during their developing years—experiences of communication difficulties, of embarrassments, of rejection by playmates and some adults, and of joyous moments when they meet other Deaf children and occasionally Deaf adults.

Schools as the Seedbed for the Deaf Community

The idea that education alone gave rise to the Deaf community is an example of the logical fallacy *post hoc ergo propter hoc* (after this,

Belonging

Ben Schowe tells his "at home among strangers" story as follows:

Gradually sinking into profound deafness does not ease the shock. There is always some hope that the steady deterioration will be arrested. . . . Psychologists who have looked into the subject say that "progressive deafness" is the most trying of all to the human spirit . . . and that adolescence is a particularly trying time to sustain it. I would not know about that. All I can state of my own knowledge is that the world seemed to be receding farther and farther away as I approached manhood, not only in sound production but also in its camaraderie. My childhood playmates all had new fields of interest where I could not easily follow. . . .

Memories of this period I would rather forget. But you had better believe me when I say that at nineteen years I was fast approaching a state of complete demoralization. Then in one last desperate venture I got together the money for a trip to Washington to find out if Gallaudet College, which I had heard about, had anything to offer. . . .

[Unbeknownst to Schowe, he had arrived during a convocation, so he thought the campus was deserted. As he was despairing his lack of luck, the program ended.]

Then suddenly the rear doors to old Chapel Hall flew open and here they came. Wave upon wave of handsome boys and girls my own age as gay and electric as if they had never heard of the terrible blight of deafness!!!

That they talked-on-their-hands was merely incidental. The only question in my mind, if there was a question, was how long it would take to learn it. These fine young people, scores upon scores of them, had everything that I had longed for—or so it seemed.

The big thing was to *belong* somewhere really![20]

therefore because of this). France had a school for Deaf students before any other nation. It did not, however, develop a vigorous national association of Deaf people before the United States. Similarly, Germany, England, and Sweden had schools for Deaf students before the United States but not national associations of Deaf people. Apparently, more is needed to encourage the Deaf community to emerge and strive for the degree of self-determination that Deaf people in this country sought during the nineteenth century.

One philosopher cites the thinking of the French physician-researcher Jean-Marc-Gaspard Itard at the outset of the nineteenth century to reinforce the notion of a Deaf community as a natural outgrowth of deafness.

> So Itard came to see a great institution for the Deaf for what it really is, a society with a language of its own. He even imagined what society would have been like if it had developed so that men expressed their ideas and emotions by moving their limbs and faces rather than their tongues. In such a society, vision would be the main source of learning, and hearing and Deaf people would be perfectly on a par. Writing might have been invented sooner, he decided, for it is easier to imagine representing signs than drawing sounds. Once this was accomplished, mankind would have embarked just as promptly on the glorious career that written language made possible. Suppose everyone in that society were Deaf; apart from lacking a few ideas concerning sound, people there would be what speech and hearing have made them in our society. Man realizes his potentialities by dint of his genius, not by the suppleness of his organs.[21]

But deaf children do not live in a world only with other Deaf people. They live at least some of the time with people who are not deaf and who usually are inept at, if not completely incapable of, communicating with them. Yet the deaf child realizes that these people are in control. The power rests with those who can hear. Seldom does the deaf child encounter a Deaf successful adult, not that there are none or so few, but because their families are usually unaware of them and the schools are not staffed by Deaf teachers and administrators. Hence, as noted in a preceding chapter, deaf children tend to develop poor self-concepts—when those self-concepts mirror the majority views of them—and to achieve poorly in academic subjects, selected by the majority and, most often, taught by representatives of the majority.

Deafness versus Blindness

Another way of testing the proposition that the schools accounted for the growth of the Deaf community is to look at the parallel case of blind people. While blind children also were educated together, frequently in residential schools, they did not develop a similar community. There have been ample organizations *for* blind people, but almost none *of* blind people until about 1960. Even then, the organizations of blind people do not compare in number or strength to those of Deaf people. While the reasons for this difference are probably numerous, a salient factor is communication. Deafness interrupts communication with the general public, blindness does not. Anyone can discuss and commiserate with the blind person, but not with the Deaf person. Blindness evokes sympathy; deafness tends to evoke frustration and hostility. Thus, blind people have long had supporters who have been willing to do for them what they would have difficulty doing for themselves. Deaf people, on the other hand, have tended to be ignored by the general public, which seems to prefer to avoid contact with them because social interchanges are so difficult. "The blind leading the blind" seems ludicrous, while the Deaf communicating with the Deaf does not. Blindness interferes with mobility, something that sighted people can assist blind people to overcome. But deafness inhibits communication with those who cannot communicate manually, something with which Deaf people can assist each other. This factor may be the critical one in accounting for the differences between these two admittedly gross sensory disabilities. The one has brought support from the general public and the other has caused its members to seek each other for support and companionship.

The Later Entries

As the first two quotations in this book have shown, Deaf people enter a Deaf community at whatever age they encounter it. Meeting other Deaf people instantly triggers the desire to come home. The recollections of an Australian Deaf man, who was raised largely apart from other Deaf people, illustrates that the phenomenon is likely to be replicated across nations (see "Fellow Sufferers").

(As an aside, I remind the reader that we are speaking here of Deaf people, not deaf people. Confusing the early and later onset deafness occurs commonly enough. As discussed earlier, the situation for those who acquired deafness in adulthood differs considerably from those who were born deaf or become deaf early in life.)

Schools contribute to the shape of the Deaf community. What Deaf students learn about organization they apply in adulthood. Their education helps them to decide how the Deaf community will be organized, how it will be managed, what its objectives will be, and much more. In the Deaf community, the presence of Gallaudet University and, in recent years, a supplementary network of postsecondary programs have given a sophistication to Deaf leadership

FELLOW SUFFERERS

An Australian, deaf from birth, muses about his adult reaction to his early education. He lives and works in Australia as a youth worker with the Adult Deaf Society of Victoria, Melbourne.

Because I went to a normal school, I was the only Deaf person there. Often I thought I was the only one around. It wasn't until after I finished school that I had the opportunity to meet others with a similar disability. Now most of my closest friends are Deaf people. Why? Because we share common ground. I can relax with them. When I talk with hearing people, I have to concentrate to hear.

My friends and I help each other with difficulties, and we teach each other about relationships and life. We've developed into self-accepting, more confident human beings. And it is with this confidence that I am beginning to make in-roads into communicating with hearing people.

It doesn't rest there . . . together we are working toward developing in others a better recognition and understanding that we are people who happen to have a hearing loss, that we are capable of doing most things anyone else can do, sometimes as well or better, and that we can and should be involved in the decision-making processes that affect Deaf people. Like everyone else, we want to be the masters of our own destinies [ellipsis in original].[22]

that it might not otherwise have had. The success of the organizational underpinnings of the Deaf community must be attributed in large measure to the educational preparation that Deaf people in this country receive. Thus, we conclude that the schools can hasten and strengthen the development of a Deaf community, but they are not essential to it.

THE MILIEU

Those who instruct parents are correct in noting that "deaf people must live in a hearing world." What they fail to mention is the range of adaptations to that point. It is not only possible, it is common, for most of us to create environments within our environments. We are citizens of the United States, of a particular state, a county, a city or town. Within the city or town, we are not a part of everything that happens. Instead, we select aspects of the total activities in which we choose to participate. Similarly, Deaf people selectively respond to some, but not all, of the surrounding community's events.

Other disability groups have not banded together in the same way as have Deaf people. There is no comparable "blind community" or "arthritis community." Disabled people certainly share interests based upon their particular physical problems.[23] Yet until very recent times they have not organized on the basis of these disabilities. True, organizations for blind people date back many years, antedating organizations of Deaf people.[24] But the blind organizations have been *for* blind people, while the Deaf organizations have been *of* deaf people. The prepositions indicate crucial distinctions: who controls the organizations, who sets its priorities, who dispenses its favors, who accepts its burdens.

We must also ask why the Deaf community developed in the way that it has, in order to make predictions of how it will react to changes around it. The Deaf community differs not only from other groups of disabled people, but also from Deaf communities in other parts of the world. Throughout the world, Deaf people appear to share the same affiliative tendencies,[25] but in France, Germany, Great Britain, and the Soviet Union, the government dominates the social structure. Control of the United States' Deaf community rests in the hands of Deaf people. Is it deafness that differs from nation to nation? No, deafness, in the sense of an inability to hear and understand speech, is the same from country to country. What differs, then, are the countries—the milieus—in which deaf people reside.

The United States' attitude toward its minorities stimulated the development of the Deaf community. Ethnic groups that have immigrated have been encouraged to retain their cultural identities to some extent, though they have also been expected to "melt" in the melting pot. Another major factor favoring a strong Deaf community has been the rapid population growth. The actual numbers of Deaf people in this country are huge, compared with those in most other nations. Of course, Deaf communities are not a uniquely United States phenomenon. What evidence we have indicates that wherever Deaf people are they tend to gravitate toward each other and to affiliate in some manner. But the United States Deaf community differs from other Deaf communities in the elaborateness of its organizational structure. This point, too, is typical of this country.

Over a century and a half ago, in his classic treatise, *Democracy in America,* Alexis de Tocqueville wrote,

> The emigrants who colonized the shores of America in the beginning of the seventeenth century somehow separated the democratic principle from all principles that it had to contend with in the old communities of Europe, and transplanted it alone to the New World. It has there been able to spread in perfect freedom and peaceably to determine the character of the laws by influencing the manners of the country.

These words seem to have equally forceful application to the Deaf community in the United States. The Deaf community that evolved here formed in the way it did for the same reasons that the larger community took the shape it did. Whatever conditions shaped the country influenced in much the same ways the smaller community. The fifth factor, then, reduces to saying that a Deaf community does not grow in a vacuum. The manner of its growth and the nature of the structure it adopts depend upon the soil in which it is planted. The milieu influences its inception and development.

Returning briefly to Deaf-Mutia, we can set Deaf people's ambitions for a community of their own in the context of that period in United States history. Their ideas were not unique; various religious groups did, indeed, set up separate communities, most notable among them being the Mormons. The Amish, Shakers, and others bought land communally and succeeded in varying degrees to live apart from the surrounding communities. In Canada, thirty-six Deaf colonists settled with their families in Wolselley, Manitoba on three hundred acres purchased from the Canadian Pacific Railway, with the encouragement of the national government. So the phenomenon appears to have pervaded North America. However, the melting-pot philosophy was growing stronger and stronger, and the majority views of separatist groups became increasingly hostile. Within that setting, the strategy of Deaf people shifted away from physically separate communities to strengthening their organizational structure, hence the growth of the national societies and their continued blossoming into the twentieth century.

INTERACTION OF THE FIVE FACTORS

The Deaf President Now movement at Gallaudet University, March 1988, provides an excellent opportunity to demonstrate the interaction of the five factors. The events prior to this significant week and the details of the week have been presented in chapter 5 and referred to frequently in other portions of the text. It will not be necessary to recount the details here. Let us turn, then, to the analysis, and see how the theory accords with the actual happening.

DEMOGRAPHY

Demographic conditions at the university favored strong action. The Deaf student body numbered over fifteen hundred, and it was supported from time to time by Deaf adults from the surrounding communities and across the country. During the march to the Capitol, estimates of the number of marchers ranged from two thousand to three thousand. In terms of characteristics, the students constituted a relatively homogeneous group—young, bright, and middle-class. Their supporters, most notably the GUAA leadership, shared the latter two characteristics.

ALIENATION

By its actions, the board of trustees provided ample alienation. It seemed to completely ignore the students' feelings. One trustee later remarked that he was surprised that the students were so serious about this matter. The board chair's remark that deaf people are not ready for the hearing world merely summarized what the students perceived as the board's mistrust of their abilities. Subsequent actions by the board did nothing to relieve the alienation.

AFFILIATION

The pleasure the students, and later the outside supporters who joined them, felt in cooperating toward a unanimous goal was evident from the outset. To the ease of communication was added the immense satisfaction of seeing sign play a dignified role on national television. The crushing blow to the new, hearing president was her inability to sign. Similarly, further proof of the board's invalidity was its chair's inability to sign. It was all there for the world to see, and the world accepted ASL on the Deaf community's terms.

EDUCATION

The Leadership Training Camp of JNAD had its obvious payoff in the way that the affair was managed. The student leadership knew what it was doing; they planned and executed their maneuvers with a skill that seemed practiced. It was. Only a few weeks earlier, the students had conducted their annual election for officers of the student government. These students were raised in an educationally more liberal period than Deaf students in the first half of the century, when sign had been suppressed and denigrated. Today, Deaf students see substantially greater acceptance for sign, increased opportunities for higher and postsecondary education, and more Deaf educators in supervisory and administrative positions. The students' actions in March 1988 affirmed that a taste of self-determination can be intoxicating.

MILIEU

The public switches were set in favor of the students. The play and film *Children of a Lesser God* made the case for the students. The media had little else to cover that week (the presidential primaries were unusually dull), so the Gallaudet story was a bonanza for them. For television, in particular, the whole affair made an excellent "visual." The students managed the media with great skill, and the board did little to counter them.

APPLYING THE THEORY

Let us consider what might have happened if any of the five factors had been other than it was. Little needs to be said about demography. Had there been too few students involved, the event would not have occurred. The alienation that the board aroused could have been soothed, and such a move might have put an end to the strike. Regarding affiliation, it is hard to imagine the students not cooperating, but it could have happened. Some of the normally hearing graduate students did counsel against the strike, but they withdrew quickly when the intensity of the undergraduates' movement was revealed. Without the education they had, the students might have become boisterous, destructive of property, and generally counterproductive. Instead, they were disciplined. They drew favorable public and governmental responses, garnering the press's sympathy and becoming the darlings of television.

From the foregoing, it would seem that the theory would have predicted the students' action. At least, the theory does not argue against their taking the actions that they did. Whether the theory can be as effective in predicting other actions in the Deaf community remains to be seen.

All that has been written up to now does not support a purely mechanistic concept in which Deaf people are merely elements that are acted upon. Deaf people react. They can accept hostility or rail against it. They can build the Deaf community's resources to a level that demands the respect of the general population, or they can recoil from the oppression they feel and assume a purely defensive posture in the face of any assaults launched on their positions. In each of the five factors, there is ample room for a variety of responses by Deaf people to the circumstances in which they find themselves.

Deaf people, as individuals and in groups, obey the general laws of psychology and sociology. Deafness does not make one less human. It does accentuate characteristics that lead to patterns of behavioral organization that differ, in some respects, from those of persons who are not deaf. As a practical matter, those who deal with Deaf people—whether parents, educators, rehabilitators, psychologists, social workers, employers, policymakers, administrators or others—need to be aware that Deaf people often react in unexpected ways and that their behaviors are associated with their deafness. Whether these behavioral differences arise from alterations of basic physiology due to deafness or to conditions imposed upon Deaf persons because they are unlike the general population in a significant way is an issue that this text alone cannot resolve, but it is an issue that badly needs to be addressed by future research. In anticipation of future research, however, we have assumed for purposes of this text that there are regularities in the behavior of Deaf people that are nontrivial, that are associated with (but not necessarily caused by) their deafness, and that these behavioral aspects are worthy of close scientific scrutiny.

Developing a better appreciation of the interactions between the factors in this one theory will foster improved predictions about the Deaf community's future and give Deaf people better control of their future. At this stage of knowledge, little empirical data support predictions about the Deaf community over the next few decades. Nonetheless, science demands that its employees do its business, chief among which is to predict and then to test those predictions. The next chapter will endeavor to put the theory to work in just that fashion.

NOTES

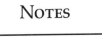

1. Best, 1943, 351–52. Higgins 1980 and Winzer 1986 adopt similar views, but with significant additions.
2. Schlesinger and Meadow, 1972. Padden (1980) regards ASL as the cement that binds the Deaf community, and she highlights its distinct culture as a further element in its definition. Jacobs (1974, 1980) certainly accepts the linguistic links that bind the Deaf community when he characterizes it as a "natural consequence of uninhibited communication." Rutherford (1988) joins these theorists in emphasizing the Deaf community's unique language.
3. Williams and Sussman, 1971, 22.
4. Ibid., 23.
5. Schowe, 1979, 36–37.
6. Nash and Nash, 1981.
7. Higgins, 1980, 1987.
8. Padden and Humphries, 1988.
9. Schein and Delk, 1974; Schein, 1987b.
10. Groce, 1985. The criticisms by linguists about inadequacies and inconsistencies in the book do not deflate the point being made here (Crouch, 1986; Weiss and Wilcox, 1986; Yau, 1986). It is possible to find other dense concentrations of Deaf people (e.g., Adamarobe, Nigeria) and to observe the same result: when Deaf people make up a substantial portion of the total population, a Deaf community does not develop that is independent from the larger community.
11. Quoted in Groce, 1985, 57.
12. Brill, 1984, 20.

13. Carver and Rodda, 1987, 87.
14. Freeman et al., 1975; Naiman and Schein, 1978; Schlesinger and Meadow, 1972.
15. Best, 1943, 352.
16. McGrath, 1982, 18.
17. Garretson, 1980, 5.
18. Booth, 1858, 72–73.
19. Cited in Updike, 1986, 105.
20. Schowe, 1979, 87–88.
21. Lane, 1984, 141.
22. Harper, 1983, 19.
23. For examples, see Roth, 1981, and Thomas, 1982.
24. An early organization for the blind was the Boston Guild, founded in 1824. No organization *of* blind people emerged until 1961.
25. Garretson, 1980, states, "In my visitations of over 25 foreign nations I find, like in the United States, the deaf community is related through their language, their signs, a chain of local, state or province social and athletic clubs or associations, and usually a national organization. They will have a regular newsletter, newspaper, or published journal—much like an ethnic, religious, or linguistic group within a major country." See also Andersson (1981) on a comparison between Swedish and United States Deaf communities. Flynn (1984) notes that the first deaf president of the Adult Deaf Society of Victoria (Australia) took office in 1983.

9

THE THEORY AT WORK

It is time to put the theory to work—to make predictions about the future. That, after all, is the *raison d'être* of a theory. It must expand our knowledge by anticipating the outcomes of future events. In so doing, a useful theory generates research by suggesting otherwise unexpected relations and stimulating efforts to alter circumstances so as to generate particular results. Indeed, as the logic of science contends, theories cannot be valid or invalid; they are merely more or less useful. Their value depends on whether or not they generate fresh insights and lead to more research. A theory should not be backed against a wall and forced to account for every development in the subject it chooses to explain, but its coverage must be sufficiently broad to encompass the subject's principal aspects.

In taking up the challenge to predict, the theory begins with possible changes in its five factors. How will alterations in the demographic composition of the Deaf population affect the Deaf community? What will be the effects of a differing mix of attitudes of the general population toward its disabled members? Will the relatively new approach of linguists to American Sign Language affect the Deaf community in significant ways? How will new developments in education and technology influence the course of the Deaf community's development? And what will happen when the milieu changes?

DEMOGRAPHY

Consider three possibilities—the number of Deaf people decreases, stays the same, increases. What would the theory say about each case? The first instance is unlikely, though it could occur either by reducing the causes of deafness or by curing deafness. The only chance of the latter on the immediate horizon is the cochlear implant, which will be discussed later in this chapter. As for reducing the causes of deafness, that is always possible, though unlikely. If deafness decreases, the Deaf community would persist until it reaches the point below which it cannot support its organizational infrastructure.

Considering that the Deaf community came into being when there were fewer than 10,000 Deaf persons in the United States and that there are presently about 500,000, the chances remain remote that a decline so large that it prevents the Deaf community from continuing will occur on a national level. However, local conditions could certainly change drastically. An area that had a number of Deaf people adequate to maintain a local Deaf community might lose a large portion of its Deaf population. Recalling that Wyoming did not have a state association until its Deaf population reached about a thousand people, one can readily imagine situations in which a state's population dwindles below an adequate number to maintain its statewide Deaf community. Under such circumstances, the theory would predict that the remaining Deaf people would, to the extent they were able, move to an area more populated with Deaf people—either within the state or in another state. The affiliation factor, the desire for companionship with other Deaf people, would be expected to operate.

There is a possibility that, over the next half century, the size of the Deaf population will decline or remain about the same as it is now, though an increase in the number of Deaf people over the next few decades is more likely. Hearing impairment has grown dramatically in the United States and indications are that it will continue to increase. Many more people will be deaf and hard of hearing in the next few decades than ever before. The number of Deaf people will increase, too.

The estimated size of the total hearing-impaired population can be calculated by considering the changes in rates over the last thirty years and projecting them forward along with the estimated growth in the total population (see Table 7). The figures for late-deafened and Deaf segments are derived by applying the ratios of those conditions to the total hearing-impaired population. The ratios used for the calculations are 1:1.15 for hard of hearing, 1:9.85 for late-deafened, and 1:32.59 for Deaf. Applying these ratios to the estimated rates for all hearing-impaired persons yields the rates shown

Table 7   Current and Projected Rates for Impaired Hearing, Deafness, and Early Deafness: United States, 1980–2050

| | Rates per 100,000 | | | |
Year	All Impaired Hearing	Hard of Hearing[a]	Deafness[b]	Early Deafness[c]
1980	7,900	6,855	802	243
1990	8,400	7,289	853	258
2000	9,000	7,810	914	276
2025	10,900	9,459	1,107	334
2050	11,800	10,240	1,198	362

SOURCE: Adapted from Jerome D. Schein, "The Demography of Deafness," in *Understanding Deafness Socially*, ed. Paul C. Higgins and Jeffrey E. Nash (Springfield, IL: Charles C Thomas, 1987).

[a]All ages at onset. Deafness not included. Ratio to total = 1:1.15.
[b]Ages at onset nineteen years and over. Ratio to total = 1:9.85.
[c]Ages at onset before nineteen years of age. Ratio to total = 1:32.59.

in Table 7. The rate for Deafness will grow from an estimated 243 per 100,000, in 1980, to 362 per 100,000, in 2050. While rates are shown, rather than actual numbers of people, it should be clear that substantially greater numbers are expected in each of the three divisions. If the population grows to an expected 300 million people by 2050, then the rate for that year translates into over one million Deaf persons. The effect of that huge number would be to greatly increase options for Deaf people, opening many more opportunities for groups within the Deaf community to have their own organizations. The political importance of Deafness would be increased, particularly if, as will be discussed below, early and late-deafened people cooperated on matters of joint interest.

Let us examine a major factor accounting for the projected increases—the aging of the U.S. population. The average age of U.S. citizens is increasing, as people live longer. The estimates rely on the observation that the older one becomes, the more likely one is to have impaired hearing. The largest portion of the projected increases in the rates of hearing impairment and deafness will be among older people who have recently, in their lives, become hearing impaired (see Table 8). Even the data in Table 8 will be misleading, if one overlooks the fact that each successive decade's increases come, again, largely from the larger proportions of older persons—more people over seventy-five years, say, in the next decade than in the previous decade.

Table 8   Current and Projected Rates for Impaired Hearing Among Persons 65 Years of Age and Over: United States, Selected Years

Year	Rate per 100
1960	37
1980	43
2000	46
2050	59

Source: Adapted from Jerome D. Schein, "The Demography of Deafness," in *Understanding Deafness Socially*, ed. Paul C. Higgins and Jeffrey E. Nash (Springfield, IL: Charles C Thomas, 1987).

Alterations in the balances between young and old Deaf people will affect the Deaf community. The domination by older people will be greater because the proportional share of the Deaf population will be in the older age groups through at least 2010, perhaps longer. With older people at the helm, the organizations in the Deaf community will probably take a more conservative approach to those affairs of interest to Deaf people. This could mean fewer dramatic events like the recent strike for a Deaf president at Gallaudet University.

Changes in the geographical concentrations of Deaf people will certainly alter Deaf communities. A decline in population has already been discussed, but increases are more likely, at least in some areas. For example, southeastern Florida is experiencing a boom in Deaf retirees. Tending as they do to settle in the same general towns—though not in contiguous neighborhoods—they naturally bring with them their affiliation tendencies. Elderly Deaf people have sought out their friends and acquaintances in the northern area of the state, around the Florida School for the Deaf and Blind. They find their volunteer support welcomed by the school authorities and, in return, they gain from the contacts they make. In the Miami—Fort Lauderdale area, they have developed a host of social groups, again reflecting their prior associations. Similar population shifts throughout the country can be expected to have the same results in altering the ways in which local Deaf clubs function. The influx of new members may create some temporary turbulence in social relations that should subside quickly.

What will growth in absolute size of the Deaf population mean? For one thing, its economic and political stature should improve. The increased number of Deaf people will mean greater visibility. One person among a thousand can be easily overlooked, but, oddly enough, one hundred people among one hundred thousand are much less likely to be missed. The general effect of the increased size of the national Deaf population is likely to be a political strengthening of the Deaf community. Or, put another way, a greater likelihood exists that Deaf people will be able to improve their position in society.

Will increases in the size of the Deaf population keep pace with the consistent growth in the general population? In asking this question, we are concerned with the relative size of the Deaf community, rather than its absolute size. The theory would predict that the Deaf community would be strengthened if the relative number of Deaf people declined. As noted in chapter 8, a lower ratio of Deaf to general population tends to bolster the Deaf community, due, of course, to the alienation and affiliation factors being brought more strenuously into play. Since an increase in the relative numbers of Deaf persons to a point that would favor elimination of the Deaf community—say, ratios as high as 1 Deaf person per 100 population—is highly unlikely, another possibility must be considered. If Deaf people reach out to and embrace late-deafened people, the size of the Deaf community would be radically altered. It could approach the conditions found in Martha's Vineyard, in which a substantial portion of the population was deaf. By 2050, there would be over 1,500 per 100,000 deaf/Deaf people, or 1.5 percent of the population—a gargantuan hunk! In actual numbers, they would amount to over 4.5 million persons. Is that likely to happen? Are Deaf and deaf—that is, early and late-deafened—people likely to come together? The theory says no. For a discussion of the reason, see "Affiliation." The tiny probability of that occurring, however, should be given some thought.

Opportunities for cooperation between the Deaf and hard-of-hearing organizations can greatly alter the fortunes of each. If their leaders work together, their combined organizations will become a powerful political force. With political power in hand, the combined groups can open doors previously barred against them. Within the coming decade, deaf, Deaf, and hard-of-hearing people will combine to form a single, politically powerful organization.[1]

ALIENATION

The public interest in sign classes and the dispersion of Deaf students into regular classes in public schools might be harbingers of greatly changed attitudes toward Deaf people. To the extent that they are, they will act to lessen the pressures on Deaf people to move away from the general community, but they will not lessen the pull toward the Deaf community. Two or three hours a week of sign instruction for sixteen weeks does not develop competence in ASL any more than the same amount of time spent on learning Chinese or Japanese would. Meeting an occasional Deaf student in class will not convey sufficient understanding of Deaf culture to enable a nondeaf person to share it with a Deaf person.

Deaf people, for the most part, are aware of the feelings they engender in a portion of the general population. The responses are not actively hostile, but passively so. Hearing people avoid Deaf people because they are difficult to communicate with. Misunderstandings quickly arise; situations become awkward. Many Deaf people reciprocate the desire to escape prolonged interactions with hearing people. Alienation in these terms is unlikely to subside in the near future. Unless dramatic, unforeseen changes occur, the centrifugal force will continue to drive the majority of Deaf people away from the general community.

AFFILIATION

The centripetal force will likely gain strength, even more than it already has, from the recognition of ASL and the accompanying improvements in Deaf people's self-images. Raymond J. Trybus, a noted researcher and former head of the Gallaudet Research Institute, believes that feelings of inferiority will "diminish rapidly and then disappear as Deaf communities struggle for and begin to achieve self-determination and linguistic self-respect."[2]

The revolution at Gallaudet University, and other successes like it, will add immeasurably to the prestige of the Deaf community. One immediate response to the selection of a Deaf president and all of the attendant national publicity has been an increase in applications for enrollment. The intimate relationship between Gallaudet University and the Deaf community, then, suggests that the latter will certainly be stronger as a result of the self-determination it achieved in March 1988. Success breeds successes, so the Deaf community can look forward to more achievements of this kind.

What about an influx of late-deafened people into the Deaf community? It is unlikely. Some deaf individuals will join the Deaf com-

THE CASE OF THE LINGUISTIC HYPOCHONDRIAC

This case study was reported by Raymond Trybus, former dean and director of Gallaudet University's Graduate Research Institute.

Among the patients with whom I worked clinically some years ago was a young Deaf woman who complained of anxiety and nervousness about the future, and an inability to make personal vocational decisions or progress. As our initial sessions probed into this problem, the young woman began to explain that a major component of her difficulties was that, as a result of her deafness, she was unable to comprehend or follow instructions in the English language. This, she indicated, meant that she was unable to profit from reading instructional and self-development manuals in her vocational specialty of accounting, as well as in a variety of other areas. For example, she could not understand written materials on the basic workings of automobiles and thus could not diagnose or remedy minor difficulties with her own car. In the course of our discussions, she acknowledged frequently that she was very fluent and respected as a master of Sign Language, and was in constant demand as a teacher and tutor of signing. However, she dismissed this as "kid stuff," and indicated that all that really mattered in life was the ability to perform linguistically in English. What became more and more apparent as our sessions continued was that her English language abilities were in fact very adequate. By all the formal and informal measures I was able to devise, she was perfectly able to read, understand, write, and speak perfectly grammatical, idiomatic English. There was, in fact, not the slightest factual basis for her complaint of inadequacy in English. It finally became clear that the source of the difficulty was that she had internalized a message which she had heard frequently during her years of growing up: Deaf persons depended for success on their mastery of English, but that at the same time Deaf persons were unlikely to be able to master the English language. At the same time, she dismissed her competence in American Sign Language as of secondary importance at best, as a kind of "crutch" for those benighted souls like herself who were unable to achieve mastery in the *proper* language, that is, English. This young woman's difficulty, in other words, was at root a deficiency in her sense of power and significance as a Deaf person, which expressed itself most pointedly in her complaints of linguistic inability.[3]

munity; they already have, but in relatively small numbers. The greater likelihood is that late-deafened people will be more attracted to organizations of their own, like Self Help for Hard of Hearing People.

When a late-deafened person attempts to enter the Deaf community, they confront a new language, ASL, so they do not find themselves relaxed. Their early lives as normally hearing persons do not provide an empathic reaction to Deaf people, nor can they readily identify with people who have practiced a lifelong adaptation to not hearing. The deaf people will experience some alienation, but not the affiliation tendencies that would draw them to the Deaf community. With so many of those who are late-deafened being persons past fifty-five years of age, the likelihood of moving into a new community further diminishes. Those are the reasons why the theory does not predict that late-deafened and hard-of-hearing people will join the Deaf community. There is another possibility, however; for which see "Milieu."

EDUCATION

To the extent that Deaf people can become more actively involved in education of deaf children, the Deaf community will be strengthened. The example of Gallaudet University, however, is not apt to prove applicable in many other educational settings. The Deaf student body at Gallaudet University now numbers a little less than two thousand. That number bulks large on a television tube, and more cogently, it encourages bold actions that lesser numbers would not support. There were many individuals to share the tasks and keep up the cheering. The size of the group generated a substantial power, enough to instigate bold action and sustain morale. Could this happen in state residential schools? By the numbers, no. Most state residential schools have either no high school or a tiny one, with fewer than fifty students. A huge day school, like JHS 47 in New York City, has no high school class. Concentrations of Deaf students of a mature age are limited to only one other setting in the United States, The National Technical Institute for the Deaf, in Rochester, New York, with about five hundred Deaf students.

The only way that a Gallaudet-type revolt could succeed at the state or local level is if the Deaf community initiated it. Such was the case in Louisiana several years ago. The Deaf community marched on the state capital and convinced the government to appoint a Deaf superintendent of the school. Barring such actions, the likelihood is low that local authorities would grant any substantial influence over educational policies for Deaf children to the Deaf community.

As of today, few schools even seem aware of Deaf culture. They know about an aspect of that culture, ASL, but of little beyond that. Insofar as ASL is concerned, it is not taught to deaf children in public schools. Instead, they are instructed in pidgin sign, Manual English, or other varieties of English on the hands, such as Seeing Essential English. Instruction in these forms of English concerns some authorities. Paul Higgins asks,

> [A]s different sign language systems proliferate in educational programs for hearing-impaired youths, will potential members of deaf communities use mutually understandable sign languages? Might these variations in sign systems lead to social distinctions among members of deaf communities as has the preference for signing and speaking? Or, as fewer hearing-impaired children are educated in residential programs and as more are mainstreamed with hearing children, will these hearing-impaired children develop the identification, experiences, and ties to other hearing-impaired people that will lead them to the deaf community?[4]

The theory would predict that these concerns will not prove more than bothersome. ASL has been preserved despite the lack of a written form, despite the lack of formal instruction in its use, and despite active opposition from some normally hearing school administrators.

Mainstreaming

Enrollments in the traditional residential schools for Deaf students have declined steadily from the seventies into the eighties.[5] With the majority of Deaf students in day classes and unspecialized educational facilities, some Deaf people believe that this arrangement will decimate the Deaf community. The theory predicts otherwise. While education certainly has a substantial effect on the shape of the Deaf community, the existence of the Deaf community does not depend upon any particular educational setting. Experience has shown that Deaf youth join the Deaf community whenever given the opportunity, so declines in numbers should not be affected by this factor. It is more likely to affect the organizational structure, but

not in the sense of weakening it. Organizations in the Deaf community may be improved by young Deaf leaders who have fresh ideas.
On the dark side, those coming late into the Deaf community will
be disadvantaged in language learning and cultural knowledge. It is
the penalty they will pay, but, as in the past, most will catch up.

MILIEU

General attitudes toward minorities tend to shift with the state of
the economy. When economic conditions are good, the political climate tends to be liberal—welcoming programs to improve conditions for minorities. When a general decline in fortunes occurs,
minorities are most likely to suffer. In the short run, then, the Deaf
community cannot expect great changes for the better in the regard
the public has for it.[6]

Organized religions, too, are affected by economic conditions.
In turn, their lessened good fortunes can be expected to be reflected
in their programs for Deaf people. Several years ago, an official of
the Catholic Church sounded a warning about the role of religion in
the Deaf community's social life.

> As the church today faces greater fiscal problems as a result of de-
> clining membership, there will not be funds available to continue
> programs that are now servicing the Deaf under religious aus-
> pices—schools, homes for the aged, rehabilitation centers, social
> agencies, hospitals, etc. The leadership of the church would do
> well to shift its policy from programming in some of these areas to
> an advocacy role whereby it will work and fight if need be to see
> that necessary programs are established by others and, if already
> established, to ensure that the Deaf have their rights protected.
> Such an advocacy role should be developed in partnership with
> the leadership of the Deaf so that it does not become a paternalis-
> tic role.[7]

What will happen as a result of new technologies? Can the theory help us to assess the likely influences on the Deaf community
from cochlear implants, captioned television, and other advances?

TELECOMMUNICATIONS

Captioned film brings Deaf people together. Captioned television,
to some extent, keeps them apart. For the former, Deaf people travel

to their clubs; for the latter, they stay home. Will the ascendancy of television over movies destroy the Deaf community? Hardly. It will alter face-to-face relations somewhat. TDDs, too, act to distance Deaf people from each other. They can now use the telephone to get information for which they had to travel to a friend's house or visit the club. What about computers? Electronic mail also reduces face-to-face interactions. These changes will not, however, seriously affect the Deaf community. People do not long remain in isolation. Surrogate communication will not permanently replace direct communication.

Telecommunications devices will encourage Deaf people to improve their English. Some scattered research evidence already suggests that is happening among younger Deaf students. Television may also homogenize ASL, much as it and radio did for English. As ASL receives more national exposure, Deaf people in different parts of the country will have to learn variations in ASL's vocabulary and syntax, and they are likely to adopt the versions that are used by the most prestigious, most attractive signers whom they see. In these regards, telecommunications and the adaptations that make them available to Deaf people will, in the long run, add another dimension to the Deaf community. They will not diminish its role in the lives of Deaf people.

COCHLEAR IMPLANTS

Recently, medical engineering has produced the cochlear implant. To assess its impact on the Deaf community one must first be clear about what it is. A cochlear implant does not provide or restore hearing. It especially does not enable the individual to hear and understand speech. It stimulates the cochlea with low-level electrical current. Since the cochlea is not designed to process electrical impulses, individuals who have received implants usually characterize what they first perceive as "buzzings and static." In time, some learn to associate the incoming electrical impulses with environmental sounds and to improve their lipreading. A few have developed the ability to interpret the signals as speech. These nontrivial advances are welcomed by some people who have been deafened in adulthood. Deaf people, however, have not leaped to the opportunity to have the operation. The official position of the NAD has been cautious, if not hostile. Here are a few lines from its lengthy policy paper:

It is the position of the National Association of the Deaf that while research is necessary and needs to be supported, it is equally important not to move prematurely with surgery which may be irrevocable. The NAD believes it is too early to place the cochlear implant in young children. . . . The NAD takes the position, further, that clinics performing implant surgery need to cease projecting to the public an image of deaf people as unhappy, fearful, maladjusted, and in desperate need of the faculty of hearing. Such negative stories create misconceptions and inappropriate attitudes toward deaf people which tend to linger and to overlook the fact that many deaf persons lead happy, successful lives.[8]

What the NAD's statement does not explicitly say is that many Deaf adults prefer to be deaf. Hearing has no attraction for them. They have lived all their lives without sound, and the offer of hearing brings with it apprehension rather than pleasant anticipation. This certainly is not true for all Deaf persons; many are at least curious about what it would be like to hear. But others are not. Carol Padden, who chaired a GLAD committee studying the cochlear implant, expressed refreshing thoughts about deafness, thoughts that challenge typical medical and popular opinions.

The committee expressed concern that the medical profession has little knowledge of, or ignores, the different attitudes held by deaf people about their deafness and consequently about implants. . . . The public seems fascinated with the implant because it promises a modern, medical approach to a "problem," of hearing impairment, but the committee observes that deaf people vary with respect to how they view their "problem." Some do not view implants as a "tool to fix a defect, but to add to the repertoire of tools that an individual has available. Some individuals will choose to have such a tool, and others will not."[9]

Many years ago, H. G. Wells, the novelist, responded to the popular notion that "in the Kingdom of the Blind, the one-eyed man is king." The idea that sight, which the majority has and prizes, would not be welcomed by those who never had it intrigued him. His story reveals a point of view similar to that expressed by Padden and the NAD (see "In the Kingdom of the Blind").

Changes in the Environment

Environmental trends can only be dimly discerned. Whatever social and political developments occur, they will certainly have an effect

IN THE KINGDOM OF THE BLIND

In H. G. Wells's story, Nunez, a normally sighted man, falls into a valley where all the inhabitants are blind. They regard the sighted man as disabled. He talks crazily about "seeing" things; he foolishly wants to go outside in the hot time of day, when everyone else sleeps. The elders call upon their greatest physician to examine Nunez and attempt to diagnose what they regard as his weird behavior.

"His brain is affected," said the blind doctor.

The elders murmured assent.

"Now, *what* affects it? *This*," said the doctor, answering his own question. "Those queer things that are called the eyes, and which exist to make an agreeable depression in the face, are diseased, in the case of Nunez, in such a way as to affect his brain. They are greatly distended, he has eyelashes, and his eyelids move, and consequently his brain is in a state of constant irritation and distraction."

"Yes?" said old Yacob. "Yes?"

"And I think I may say with reasonable certainty that, in order to cure him complete, all that we need to do is a simple and easy surgical operation—namely, to remove those irritant bodies."

"And then he will be sane?"

"Then he will be perfectly sane, and a quite admirable citizen."

"Thank Heaven for science!" said old Yacob, and went forth at once to tell Nunez of his happy hopes.[10]

upon the Deaf community. The Deaf community, on the other hand, is not solely a reactor in the arena, it is also an actor capable of exerting its own influence on the environment. In an article on the Deaf community, Paul Higgins concluded with some queries about the Deaf community's future. He speculated about improvements in job opportunities and social services and asked,

If that greater acceptance and wider opportunity develop for deaf people, that will be due in part to the efforts of deaf communities and their supporters, to their lobbying, legal action, leadership, and determination. It is even possible that in their own successes, deaf communities may alter, even diminish, themselves. Whatever happens, deaf communities face a challenging and uncertain future.[11]

WORK TO BE DONE

When the factors of the theory of Deaf community development were first presented, terms from physics were used—critical mass, centrifugal and centripetal forces. The implication behind this practice should be made explicit: It is my hope that, to some degree, future development of the theory will attach mathematical values to these factors. It is not visionary to speak about determining the numbers of Deaf people who are necessary to the formation of a Deaf community, to determine the number that makes up the "critical mass." The problem should be amenable to empirical research.

Quantifying alienation and affiliation will be more difficult, but not beyond present-day psychometrics. The negative valences that apply to various forms of passive and active hostility and the positive values associated with a common language and other aspects of affiliation should be capable of calculation, though with suitably modest precision. Having the numbers, even if they are imprecise, will greatly facilitate the study of the Deaf community. What takes paragraphs to convey now could be expressed in a number or a brief formula.

To assess education and milieu, again, does not stress available techniques. Rating scales can be developed to metricize the qualitative distinctions between prevailing conditions. As with alienation and affiliation, rubrics can be made to characterize positive and negative environments, practices, and so forth. These rating scales can be applied by competent judges, the results compared for reliability, and adjustments or corrections made as indicated. It then remains to correlate the measures with assessments of the Deaf community, its size and strength, and other aspects of the social behavior of Deaf people that are of interest.

These steps will facilitate the study of the interactions among the factors. In this presentation, each has been discussed without much regard to the others. The reader is already aware of how awkward that can be from the preceding discussions; it is also incorrect, since the five factors are not independent. A change in any one of the factors potentially affects the others. Alter the size of the Deaf community and its affiliation values will likely change. How? That needs to be determined, and it can be through research. The techniques of miltifactorial analysis are well advanced and can readily handle the calculations.

Theories are judged by their attractiveness to researchers, by the success with which they generate hypotheses for empirical testing. At this preliminary stage in its development, the theory only hints at possibilities for exciting and, it is hoped, practical findings about the Deaf community. It remains to be seen if others will be sufficiently challenged to confirm or deny its premises—either would be welcome, since both would stimulate more research on the Deaf community.

A CLOSING NOTE

Several years ago, I surveyed the evidence about the Deaf community then available to me. Little that I said at that time bears repeating. However, I am convinced of one observation that I believe is worth reiterating here:

> Whatever factors intrude to accentuate or attenuate the trends, Deaf society will be worth close study. It offers society more than it takes from it culturally.[12]

NOTES

1. Trybus, 1987.
2. Trybus, 1980.
3. Trybus, 1980, 212–13.
4. Higgins, 1987, 260.
5. Callan, 1983, 24.
6. Some authorities have recommended programs to change the public's attitudes toward various disability groups. So there is Better Speech and Hearing Week and other such designated days, weeks, and months. But are they worth the cost? Or is this approach a waste of time and money? In my opinion, it is a waste. Better to invest funds in the group that receives the hostility. Why? Because the general population forgets the message after one week—if they recall it that long. Second, these "weeks" allow the public to assuage its conscience with a cheap gesture, rather than embarking on long-term programs to effect

substantial, lasting changes. Better to invest the effort in Deaf people, teaching them to defend themselves, to cope with insults and discrimination, to strengthen their positions, and to gain whatever ends they desire.

7. Hourihan, 1979, 508.
8. *The NAD Broadcaster,* March, 1986, 1.
9. Padden, 1985, 14.
10. Wells, 1980, 149.
11. Higgins, 1987, 260. Johnson (1969, 35) adds a cautionary note: " . . . The deaf appear to be victims of their own public relations program. This has resulted in a rosy picture of the deaf in which they do not appear to have many real problems. I wish I could go along with the idea that the deaf are a pretty problem-free group of human beings, but such has not been my experience. The deaf, like everyone else, have problems, problems which are not being met. It is time that we begin doing something about them."
12. Schein, 1979b, 487.

REFERENCES

Ainoda, N., and Suzuki, S. 1976. Environmental influence upon the language development of a normal hearing child brought up by deaf parents. *Proceedings of the International Congress on Education of the Deaf* (25–29 August 1975). Tokyo: The Organizing Committee, ICED.

Alderton, H. A. 1896. The influence of deafness upon the development of the child. *Laryngoscope* 1(2): 1–16.

Allen, J. C., and Allen, Martha L. 1979. Discovering and accepting hearing impairment: Initial reactions of parents. *Volta Review* 81(5): 279–85.

Andersson, Yerker. 1981. A cross-cultural comparative study: Deafness. Unpublished doctoral dissertation. University of Maryland, College Park.

Ashley, Jack. 1973. *Journey into silence.* London: The Bodley Head.

Atwood, Albert W. 1964. *Gallaudet College: Its first one hundred years.* Lancaster, PA: Intelligencer Press.

Bangs, Don. 1987. Television and motion pictures. In *Gallaudet encyclopedia of Deaf people and Deafness,* Vol. 3, ed. John V. Van Cleve. New York: McGraw-Hill.

Banta, Elizabeth M. 1979. Siblings of deaf-blind children. *Volta Review* 81(5): 363–69.

Barker, Roger G., Wright, B. A., Meyerson, L., and Gonick, M. R. 1953. *Adjustment to physical disability and illness.* New York: Social Science Research Council.

Bartone, Paula. 1987. Facilities for helping hearing-impaired people overcome substance abuse. *Voice* 3(5): 8–9.

Beggs, Ralph. 1983. A biographical history of education of the deaf in Canada. *Journal of the Association of Canadian Educators of the Hearing Impaired* 9(1): 12–23.

Bell, Alexander G. 1883. *Memoir upon the formation of a deaf variety of the human race.* New Haven, CT: National Academy of Sciences.

Bellefleur, Philip A. 1976. TTY communication: Its history and future. *Volta Review* 78:107–12.

Bender, Ruth E. 1981. *The conquest of deafness.* 3d ed. Danville, IL: Interstate Printers and Publishers.

Benderly, Beryl Lieff. 1980. *Dancing without music.* New York: Doubleday.

Berg, Otto B. 1968. The denominational worker with the deaf in the Episcopal church. *American Annals of the Deaf* 113:891–92.

———. 1984. *A missionary chronicle.* Hollywood, MD: St. Mary's Press.

Best, Harry. 1943. *Deafness and the deaf in the United States.* New York: Macmillan.

Bishop, Ervin, and Dibrell, Benton. 1978. *The New Testament for the Deaf.* Arlington, TX: Baker Book House.

Blau, P. M., and Scott, W. R. 1962. *Formal organizations.* San Francisco: Chandler.

Boatner, Maxine Tull. 1959. *Voice of the deaf.* Washington, DC: Public Affairs Press.

Booth, Edmund. 1858. Mr. Flournoy's project. *American Annals of the Deaf* 10: 72–79.

Bowe, Frank. 1973. Crisis of the deaf child and his family. In *The deaf child and his family,* ed. Glenn T. Lloyd. Washington, D.C.: Rehabilitation Services Administration.

Braddock, Guilbert C. 1975. *Notable deaf persons.* Washington, DC: Gallaudet College Alumni Association.

Brasel, K. E., and Quigley, S. P. 1977. Influence of certain language and communication environments in early childhood on the development of language in deaf individuals. *Journal of Speech and Hearing Research* 20:81–94.

Brill, Richard G. 1984. *International Congresses on Education of the Deaf.* Washington, DC: Gallaudet University Press.

Brooks, Lester. 1986. The drama of talking hands. *Bostonia* 60(3): 44–48.

Buck, Frances. 1980. The influence of parental disability on children: An exploratory investigation of the children of spinal cord injured fathers. Unpublished doctoral dissertation. University of Arizona, Tucson.

Bunde, Lawrence T. 1979. *Deaf parents—hearing children.* Washington, DC: Registry of Interpreters for the Deaf.

Calkins, E. E. 1946. *And hearing not.* New York: Charles Scribner's Sons.

Callan, Joan C. 1983. School related attitudes toward deafness. In *Critical issues in rehabilitation and human services,* ed. G. Douglas Tyler, 22–26. Silver Spring, MD: American Deafness and Rehabilitation Association.

Caplow, T., Bahr, H. M., Chadwick, B. A., Hill, R., and Williamson, M. H. 1982. *Middletown families: Fifty years of change and continuity.* Minneapolis: University of Minnesota Press.

Carver, Roger J., and Rodda, Michael. 1987. Parental stress and the deaf child. *Journal of the Association of Canadian Educators of the Hearing Impaired* 13(2): 79–89.

Christiansen, John B., and Barnartt, Sharon N. 1987. The silent minority: The socioeconomic status of deaf people. In *Understanding deafness socially,* ed. Paul C. Higgins and Jeffrey E. Nash. Springfield, IL: Charles C Thomas.

Clarke, B. R., and Winzer, M. A. 1983. A concise history of education of the deaf in Canada. *Journal of the Association of Canadian Educators of the Hearing Impaired* 9(1): 36–51.

Clifford, Lynetter V. 1977. The problem of the normal-hearing child of deaf parents. *Special Education Bulletin* 19(2): 14–17.

Cohen, Anthony P. 1985. *The social construction of community.* New York: Methuen, Inc., Tavistock Publications.

Cohen, Betsy M., and Livenah, Hanoch. 1986. The self-help movement: Evolution of a dystonia chapter. *Rehabilitation Literature* 47(1–2): 8–11.

Collins, K. J. 1974. The deaf and the police. *Hearing* 29(12): 386.

Commission on Education of the Deaf. 1988. *Toward equality: Education of the deaf.* Washington, DC: United States Government Printing Office.

Conlon, Sara E. 1987. Alexander Graham Bell Association for the Deaf. In *Gallaudet encyclopedia of Deaf people and Deafness,* Vol. 1, ed. John V. Van Cleve. New York: McGraw-Hill.

Conrad, R., and Weiskrantz, B. 1981. On the cognitive ability of deaf children with deaf parents. *American Annals of the Deaf* 126:995–1003.

Corfmat, P. T. 1965. Some thoughts of a hearing child of deaf parents. *British Deaf News* 5:4–5.

Corson, H. J. 1973. Comparing deaf children of oral deaf parents and deaf parents using manual communication with deaf children of hearing parents on academic, social and communicative functioning. Unpublished doctoral dissertation. University of Cincinnati.

Crammatte, Alan B. 1968. *Deaf persons in professional employment.* Springfield, IL: Charles C Thomas.

————. 1987. *Meeting the challenge.* Washington, DC: Gallaudet University Press.

Critchley, Edmund. 1967a. Hearing children of deaf parents. *Journal of Laryngology and Otology* 81(1): 51–61.

————. 1967b. The social development of deaf children. *Journal of Laryngology and Otology* 81(3): 291–307.

Crouch, Barry A. 1986. Martha's Vineyard, 1700–1900: A deaf Utopia? *Sign Language Studies* 53:381–87.

Cummins, Jim. 1984. *Bilingualism and special education.* San Diego, CA: College-Hill Press.

Day, Charles. 1975. Growing up with deaf parents. *Deaf American* 27(January): 39–42.

Deafpride. 1976. *Deafpride papers: Perspectives and options.* Washington, DC: Deafpride.

DeGering, Etta. 1964. *Gallaudet: Friend of the deaf.* New York: David McKay.

Delgado, Gilbert L., ed. 1984. *The Hispanic deaf: Issues and challenges in bilingual special education.* Washington, DC: Gallaudet University Press.

Denis, Taras. 1974. Achieving normalcy. In *Deafness in infancy and early childhood,* ed. Peter J. Fine. New York: Medcom Press.

Denton, David L. 1987. Least restrictive environment. *Maryland Bulletin* 106(3): 3–5.

Diamond, Jared M. 1988. The last first contacts. *Natural History* 97(8): 28–31.

Dollard, Vincent. 1988. Evolution of an art form: Visual poetry. *NTID Focus* (Summer): 26–27.

Douglas, Ann M. 1971. A nurse looks at the health problems of deaf people. In *Medical aspects of deafness, Proceedings of National Forum IV* (Atlantic City, New Jersey), ed. Doin Hicks. Washington, DC: Council of Organizations Serving the Deaf.

Dubow, Sy, and Goldberg, Larry J. 1981. Legal strategies to improve mental health care for deaf people. In *Deafness and mental health,* ed. L. K. Stein, E. D. Mindel, and T. Jabaley. New York: Grune and Stratton.

Eastman, Gilbert. 1980. From student to professional: A personal chronicle of sign language. In *Sign language and the deaf community,* ed. Charlotte Baker and Robbin Battison. Silver Spring, MD: National Association of the Deaf.

Epstein, June. 1980. *No music by request.* Sydney, Australia: Collins.

Erting, Carol. 1987. Cultural conflict in a school for deaf children. In *Understanding deafness socially,* ed. Paul Higgins and Jeffrey Nash. Springfield, IL: Charles C Thomas.

Fant, Louie J. 1974. Louie J. Fant, Jr. tells how he felt. In *Deafness in infancy and early childhood,* ed. Peter J. Fine. New York: Medcom Press.

Fine, Peter J. 1974. *Deafness in infancy and early childhood.* New York: Medcom Press.

Finkelstein, V. 1980. *Attitude and disabled people.* New York: World Rehabilitation Fund.

Fleischman, Alexander. 1986. The deaf person and the Jewish community. In *The deaf Jew in the modern world,* ed. J. D. Schein and L. J. Waldman. New York: New York Society for the Deaf.

———. 1987. National Congress of the Jewish Deaf. In *Gallaudet encyclopedia of Deaf people and Deafness,* Vol. 2, ed. John V. Van Cleve. New York: McGraw-Hill.

Flynn, John W. 1984. *No longer by gaslight.* East Melbourne, Victoria, Australia: Adult Deaf Society of Victoria.

Forecki, Marcia C. 1985. *Speak to me.* Washington, DC: Gallaudet University Press.

Fraser, George R. 1976. *The causes of profound deafness in childhood.* Baltimore: Johns Hopkins University Press.

Frederickson, Jeanetter. 1985. *Life after deaf. Impact of deafness on a family.* Silver Spring, MD: National Association of the Deaf.

Freeman, Roger D., Carbin, C. F., and Boese, Robert J. 1981. *Can't your child hear?* Baltimore: University Park Press.

Freeman, Roger D., Malkin, Susan F., and Hastings, Jane O. 1975. Psychosocial problems of deaf children and their families: A comparative study. *American Annals of the Deaf* 120:391–405.

French, Dorothea B., and MacDonnell, Brenda M. 1985. A survey of questions posed by regular classroom teachers integrating hearing-impaired students in Nova Scotia and New Brunswick. *Journal of the Association of Canadian Educators of the Hearing Impaired,* 11(1): 12–23.

Frishberg, Nancy. 1988. Signers of tales: The case for literary status of an unwritten language. *Sign Language Studies* 59:149–70.

Furfey, P. H., and Harte, T. J. 1968. *Interaction of deaf and hearing in Baltimore City, Maryland.* Washington, DC: Catholic University of America Press.

Galenson, E., Miller, R., Kaplan, E., and Rothstein, A. 1979. Assessment of development in the deaf child. *Journal of the American Academy of Child Psychiatry* 22 (1): 23–28.

Gallaudet College Alumni Association. 1974. *The Gallaudet almanac.* Washington, DC: Gallaudet College Alumni Association.

Gallaudet, Edward Miner. 1983. *History of the college for the deaf*. Washington, DC: Gallaudet University Press.

Gannon, Jack R. 1981. *Deaf heritage*. Silver Spring, MD: National Association of the Deaf.

————. 1987. Gallaudet College Alumni Association. In *Gallaudet encyclopedia of Deaf people and Deafness*, Vol. 1, ed. John V. Van Cleve. New York: McGraw-Hill.

Garnett, Christopher B. 1968. *The exchange of letters between Samuel Heinicke and Abbé Charles Michel de l'Epée*. New York: Vantage.

Garretson, Mervin D. 1962. *Coordination and teamwork among national, state, and local organizations of the deaf*. Washington, DC: Gallaudet College.

————. 1980. The realities of deafness. Paper presented at the International Congress on Education of the Deaf, Hamburg, West Germany, 4–8 August 1980.

Gawlik, Rudolph E. 1969. The deaf man and the world of worship. In *The deaf man and the world*, ed. Ray L. Jones. Washington, DC: Council of Organizations Serving the Deaf.

Geertz, C., ed. 1975. *The interpretation of cultures*. London: Hutchinson.

Gjerdingen, Dennis. 1979. Principles of the school/family relationship. *Volta Review* 81(5): 330–36.

Glick, Ferne P., and Pellman, Donald R. 1982. *Breaking silence*. Kitchener, Ontario: Herald Press.

Glickman, Neil. 1986. Cultural identity, deafness, and mental health. *Journal of Rehabilitation of the Deaf* 20(2): 1–10.

Gliedman, John, and Roth, William. 1980. *The unexpected minority*. New York: Harcourt Brace Jovanovich.

Goffman, Erving. 1963. *Stigma. Notes on the management of spoiled identity*. Englewood Cliffs, NJ: Prentice-Hall.

Gregory, Susan. 1976. *The deaf child and his family*. New York: Wiley.

Groce, Nora E. 1985. *Everybody here spoke sign language*. Cambridge, MA: Harvard University Press.

Hairston, Ernest, and Smith, Linwood. 1983. *Black and deaf in America*. Silver Spring, MD: TJ Publishers.

Harper, Phil. 1983. Understanding deafness. *Perspectives* 3(2): 17–24.

Harris, George A. 1983. *Broken ears, wounded hearts*. Washington, DC: Gallaudet University Press.

Harris, Rachel Stone. 1983. Deaf parents' perceptions of family life with deaf and/or hearing children. In *Critical issues in rehabilitation and human services*, ed. G. Douglas Tyler, 5–9. Silver Spring, MD: American Deafness and Rehabilitation Association.

Higgins, Francis C. 1983. A seventy-five-year-old celebrates its history. *Gallaudet Today* 14(1): 21–26.

Higgins, Paul C. 1980. *Outsiders in a hearing world*. Beverly Hills, CA: Sage.

————. 1987. The deaf community. In *Gallaudet encyclopedia of Deaf people and Deafness*, Vol. 1, pp. 256–261, ed. John V. Van Cleve. New York: McGraw-Hill.

Hodgson, K. W. 1954. *The deaf and their problems*. New York: Philosophical Library.

Hourihan, John P. 1979. Church programs for the hearing impaired. In *Hearing and hearing impairment*, ed. Larry J. Bradford and William G. Hardy. New York: Grune and Stratton.

Jacobs, Leo M. 1974. *A deaf adult speaks out*. Washington, DC: Gallaudet University Press.

―――. 1980. *A deaf adult speaks out*. 2d ed. Washington, DC: Gallaudet University Press.

Jamieson, Syd. 1980. Voyage by the deaf. *Challenge!* 4(8): 16–21.

Johnson, Richard K. 1969. Personal counseling. In *The deaf man and the world of love, Proceedings of National Forum No. 2*, (New Orleans, Louisiana), ed. Ray L. Jones. Washington, DC: Council of Organizations Serving the Deaf.

Johnstone, Mary. 1984. Deafened adults living between two worlds. *Gallaudet Today* 14(3): 7–10.

Jones, James H. 1981. *Bad blood*. New York: The Free Press.

Jones, Michael L., and Quigley, Stephen P. 1979. The acquisition of question formation in spoken English and American Sign Language by two hearing children of deaf parents. *Journal of Speech and Hearing Disorders* 44(2): 196–208.

Jordan, I. King, and Karchmer, Michael A. 1986. Patterns of sign use among hearing impaired students. In *Deaf children in America*, ed. Arthur N. Schildroth and Michael A. Karchmer. San Diego: College-Hill Press.

Jordan, Jerald M. 1971. Doc, I can't hear so good. In *Medical aspects of deafness, Proceedings of National Forum IV* (Atlantic City, New Jersey), ed. Doin Hicks. Washington, DC: Council of Organizations Serving the Deaf.

Kannapell, Barbara. 1980. Personal awareness and advocacy in the deaf community. In *Sign language and the deaf community*, ed. Charlotte Baker and Robbin Battison. Silver Spring, MD: National Association of the Deaf.

Kenner, Hugh. 1986. The ghetto of unhearing. *New York Times Book Review*, 5 October, 12.

Kruger, Art. 1987. American Athletic Association of the Deaf. In *Gallaudet encyclopedia of Deaf people and Deafness*, Vol. 1, ed. John V. Van Cleve. New York: McGraw-Hill.

Lane, Harlan. 1976. *The wild boy of Aveyron*. Cambridge, MA: Harvard University Press.

―――. 1984. *When the mind hears*. New York: Random House.

Lawrence, Ivan E. 1972. *Is justice deaf: What are the legal and constitutional rights of the deaf*. Tallahassee, FL: Florida Registry of the Interpreters for the Deaf.

Lenneberg, Eric H., Rebelsky, Freda G., and Nichols, Irene A. 1965. The vocalizations of infants born to deaf and hearing parents. *Human Development* 8:23–37.

Lerner, Shirley. 1986. *The union league of the deaf—Then and now.* New York: Union League.

Letters to the editor. 1987. *Sign Language Studies* 57:371–73.

Lewin, Kurt. 1948. *Resolving social conflicts.* Part 3. New York: Harper. (See 195–96, "Leadership from the Periphery.")

Lunde, Anders S. 1956. The sociology of the deaf. Paper presented to American Sociological Society, Detroit.

Madsen, Willard. 1973. Sign on: The American Sign Language in your community programs. In *Proceedings of National Conference on Program Development for and with Deaf people.* Washington, DC: Gallaudet College, University of Maryland, and National Association of the Deaf.

Maestas y Moores, J. 1980. Early linguistic environment: Interactions of deaf parents with their infants. *Sign Language Studies* 26:1–13.

Malouf, David. 1987. House of the dead. *New York Review of Books* 34(4): 3–8.

Martin, Frederick N., Bernstein, Mark E., Daly, John A., and Cody, Janet P. 1988. Classroom teachers' knowledge of hearing disorders and attitudes about mainstreaming hard-of-hearing children. *Language, Speech, and Hearing Services in Schools* 19(1): 83–95.

Martin, Kathleen M. 1983. Vocational and economic concerns of deaf people through the turn of the century. In *Critical issues in rehabilitation and human services,* ed. G. D. Tyler. Silver Spring, MD: American Deafness and Rehabilitation Association.

Mathis, Steve L. 1975. Hearing children of deaf parents. In *Proceedings of the VII World Congress of the World Federation of the Deaf, Washington, D.C.* Silver Spring, MD: National Association of the Deaf.

Mayberry, Rachel. 1976. An assessment of some oral and manual language skills of hearing children of deaf parents. *American Annals of the Deaf* 121:507–12.

McGrath, Paul. 1982. Reflections on a not so golden silence. *Communication* 7(2): 18.

Mead, Margaret. 1970. *Culture and commitment.* London: The Chaucer Press.

Meadow, Kathryn P. 1968. Early manual communication in relation to the deaf child's intellectual, social, and communicative functioning. *American Annals of the Deaf* 113:29–41.

———. 1980. *Deafness and child development.* Berkeley, CA: University of California Press.

Meadow, Kathryn P., Greenberg, Mark T., and Erting, Carol. 1984. Attachment behavior of deaf children with deaf parents. In *Annual progress in child psychiatry and child development, 1984,* ed. Stella Chess and Alexander Thomas. New York: Brunner/Mazel.

Meadow-Orlans, Kathryn P. 1985. Impact of child's hearing loss on the family. Paper presented at the biennial meeting of the Society for Research in Child Development, Toronto, 17 April 1985.

Mendelsohn, Jacqueline Z. 1983. Families. In *Critical issues in rehabilitation and human services,* ed. G. Douglas Tyler, 2–4. Silver Spring, MD: American Deafness and Rehabilitation Association.

————. 1987. American Society for Deaf Children. In *Gallaudet encyclopedia of Deaf people and Deafness*, Vol. 1, ed. John V. Van Cleve. New York: McGraw-Hill.

Mentkowski, Tom. 1983. Why I am what I am. *The Florida School Herald* 82(6): 1–2, 5, 12.

Meyer, Marcella M. 1987. Greater Los Angeles Council on Deafness, Inc. In *Gallaudet encyclopedia of Deaf people and Deafness*, Vol. 1, ed. John V. Van Cleve. New York: McGraw-Hill.

Mitchell, Sue Hardie. 1971. An examination of selected factors related to the economic status of the deaf population. Unpublished doctoral dissertation. American University, Washington, D.C.

Moores, Donald F., and Kluwin, Thomas N. 1986. Issues in school placement. In *Deaf children in America*, ed. Arthur N. Schildroth and Michael A. Karchmer. San Diego: College-Hill Press.

Mow, Shanny. 1970. How do you dance without music? In *Answers*, ed. James A. Little. Santa Fe: New Mexico School for the Deaf.

Murphy, Albert T. 1979a. Members of the family: Sisters and brothers of handicapped children. *Volta Review* 81(5): 352–62.

————, ed. 1979b. The families of hearing-impaired children. *Volta Review* 81:265–384.

Murphy, Judith, and Slorach, Neil. 1983. The language development of pre-preschool hearing children of deaf parents. *British Journal of Disorders of Communication* 18(2): 118–127.

Naiman, D., and Schein, Jerome D. 1978. *For parents of deaf children.* Silver Spring, MD: National Association of the Deaf.

Nash, Jeffrey E., and Nash, Anedith. 1981. *Deafness in society.* Lexington, MA: Lexington Books.

National Association of the Deaf. N.d. *The NAD story.* Silver Spring, MD: National Association of the Deaf.

Newman, Lawrence. 1971. Habilitation—mental health. In *Medical aspects of deafness, Proceedings of National Forum IV* (Atlantic City, New Jersey), ed. Doin Hicks. Washington, DC: Council of Organizations Serving the Deaf.

————. 1979. Two children: A study in contrasts. In *Deafness in infancy and early childhood*, ed. Peter J. Fine. New York: Medcom Press.

Neyhus, Arthur I., ed. 1978. Deafness and adolescence. *Volta Review* 80: 263–377.

Nix, Gary W. 1981. Mainstreaming: Illusion or solution? *Journal of the Association of Canadian Educators of the Hearing Impaired* 8(1): 7–14.

Ohsberg, H. Oliver. 1982. *The church and persons with handicaps.* Scottsdale, PA: Herald Press.

Padden, Carol. 1980. The deaf community and the culture of deaf people. In *Sign language and the deaf community*, ed. Charlotte Baker and Robbin Battison. Silver Spring, MD: National Association of the Deaf.

————. 1985. GLAD publishes position paper on cochlear implants. *The GLAD News* 17(6): 11–16.

Padden, Carol, and Humphries, Tom. 1988. *Deaf in America: Voices from a* culture. Cambridge, MA: Harvard University Press.

Padden, Carol, and Markowicz, Harry. 1975. Cultural conflicts between hearing and deaf communities. In *Proceedings of the VII World Congress of the World Federation of the Deaf*, Washington, D.C. Silver Spring, MD: National Association of the Deaf.

Panara, Robert. 1987. Literature, writers in. In *Gallaudet encyclopedia of Deaf people and Deafness*, Vol. 2, ed. John V. Van Cleve. New York: McGraw-Hill.

Parasnis, I. 1983. Effects of parental deafness and early exposure to manual communication on the cognitive skills, English language skill, and field independence of young deaf adults. *Journal of Speech and Hearing Research* 26:588–94.

Pelarski, JoAnn. 1973. Tell it like it is. In *Proceedings of National Conference on Program Development for and with Deaf People*. Washington, DC: Gallaudet College, University of Maryland, and National Association of the Deaf.

Petersen, Eugene W. 1973. Theon Jackson's long confinement serves the deaf. *The Deaf American* 25(5): 3–4, 34.

Picken, Margo. 1986. The betrayed people. *New York Review of Books* 33(19): 44–48.

Pickett, J. M., and McFarland, W. F. 1985. Auditory implants and tactile aids for the profoundly deaf. *Journal of Speech and Hearing Research* 28: 134–50.

Quigley, Stephen P., and Frisina, D. Robert. 1961. Institutionalization and psycho-educational development of deaf children. *CEC Research Monograph*, ser. A, no. 3.

Rae, Luzerne. 1851. Presentation of silver plate to Messrs. Gallaudet and Clerc. *American Annals of the Deaf and Dumb* 3:41–64.

Rainer, J. D., and Altshuler, K. Z. N.d. *Psychiatry and the deaf*. Washington, DC: Social and Rehabilitative Service, Department of Health, Education, and Welfare.

Rainer, J. D., Altshula, K. Z., and Kallman, F. J. 1963. *Family and mental health problems in a deaf population*. New York: New York State Psychiatric Institute.

Rawlings, Brenda W., and Jensema, Carl J. 1977. *Two studies of the families of hearing impaired children*. Ser. R, no. 5. Washington, DC: Gallaudet College, Office of Demographic Studies.

Rawlings, Brenda W., Karchmer, Michael, and DeCaro, James J. 1988. *College and career programs for deaf students*. Washington, DC: Gallaudet University, Research Institute.

Rhoades, Cindy M., Browning, Philip L., and Thorin, Elizabeth J. 1986. Self-help advocacy movement: A promising peer-support system for people with mental disabilities. *Rehabilitation Literature* 47(1–2): 2–7.

Ries, Peter. 1980. Hearing ability of persons sociodemographic and health characteristics, United States. *Vital and Health Statistics*, Ser. 10, no. 140.

Rosen, Lillian. 1981. *Just like everybody else*. New York: Harcourt Brace Jovanovich.

Rosen, Roslyn. 1986. Deafness: A social perspective. In *Deafness in perspective,* ed. David M. Luterman. San Diego: College-Hill Press.

Roth, William. 1981. *The handicapped speak.* Jefferson, NC: McFarland.

Rowley, Clifford R. 1987. American Professional Society of the Deaf. In *Gallaudet encyclopedia of Deaf people and Deafness,* Vol. 1, ed. John V. Van Cleve. New York: McGraw-Hill.

Russo, Anthony. 1975. *The god of the deaf adolescent.* New York: Paulist Press.

Rutherford, Susan D. 1988. The culture of American deaf people. *Sign Language Studies* 59:129–47.

Sachs, Jacqueline, Bard, Barbara, and Johnson, Marie L. 1981. Language learning with restricted input: Case studies of two hearing children of deaf parents. *Applied Psycholinguistics* 2(1): 33–54.

Schein, Edgar H. 1970. *Organizational psychology.* 2d ed. Englewood Cliffs, NJ: Prentice-Hall.

Schein, Jerome D. 1968. *The deaf community.* Washington, DC: Gallaudet College Press.

———. 1970. Social services and the deaf client. In *The deaf man and the law,* ed. Robert L. Meyer. Washington, DC: Council of Organizations Serving the Deaf.

———. 1973. Model for a state plan for vocational rehabilitation of deaf clients. *Journal of Rehabilitation of the Deaf,* Monograph No. 3.

———. 1977a. *Implementation of the Model State Plan for Vocational Rehabilitation of Deaf Clients.* Silver Spring, MD: National Association of the Deaf.

———. 1977b. *Model state plan for vocational rehabilitation of deaf clients: Revised.* Silver Spring, MD: National Association of the Deaf.

———. 1977c. Psychology of the hearing-impaired consumer. *Audiology and Hearing Education* 3(2): 12–14, 44.

———. 1978. The deaf community. In *Hearing and deafness,* ed. H. Davis and S. R. Silverman, 4th ed. New York: Holt, Rinehart and Winston.

———. 1979a. How well can you see me? *Teaching Exceptional Children* 12(2): 55–58.

———. 1979b. Society and culture of hearing-impaired people. In *Hearing and hearing impairment,* ed. Larry J. Bradford and William G. Hardy. New York: Grune and Stratton.

———. 1980. From zero to Line 21. In *Proceedings Third International Learning Technology and Exposition.* Vol. 1. Warrenton, VA: Learning Technology and Expositions.

———. 1981. *A rose for tomorrow.* Silver Spring, MD: National Association of the Deaf.

———. 1982. The demography of deafness. In *The deaf community and the deaf population,* ed. P. Higgins and J. Nash. Washington, DC: Gallaudet College.

———. 1984a. *Speaking the language of sign.* New York: Doubleday.

———. 1984b. State commissions on deafness. *The Deaf American* 36(5): 16–19.

———. 1985. Advocacy: A dual perspective. In *Hearing-impaired children and* youth with developmental disabilities, ed. E. Cherow, N. Matkin, and R. Trybus. Washington, DC: Gallaudet University Press.

———. 1986a. Models for postsecondary education of deaf students. *ACEHI Journal* 12(1): 9–23.

———. 1986b. Some demographic aspects of religion and deafness. In *The deaf Jew in the modern world*, ed. J. D. Schein and L. J. Waldman. New York: New York Society for the Deaf.

———. 1987a. Council of Organizations Serving the Deaf. In *Gallaudet encyclopedia of Deaf people and Deafness*, Vol. 1, ed. John V. Van Cleve. New York: McGraw-Hill.

———. 1987b. The demography of deafness. In *Understanding deafness socially*, ed. Paul C. Higgins and Jeffrey E. Nash. Springfield, IL: Charles C Thomas.

———. 1987c. Telecommunications for the Deaf, Inc. In *Gallaudet encyclopedia of Deaf people and Deafness*, Vol. 3, ed. John V. Van Cleve. New York: McGraw-Hill.

———. 1988. Turning deaf ears to the law. *American Rehabilitation* 14(1): 6–7, 25–26.

Schein, Jerome D., Bowe, Frank, and Delk, Marcus T. 1973. Barriers to the full employment of deaf persons in the federal government. *Journal of Rehabilitation of the Deaf* 6:1–15.

Schein, Jerome D., and Bushnaq, Suleiman M. 1962. Higher education for the deaf in the United States: A retrospective investigation. *American Annals of the Deaf* 107:416–20.

Schein, Jerome D., and Delk, Marcus T. 1974. *The deaf population of the United States*. Silver Spring, MD: National Association of the Deaf.

———. 1978. Economic status of deaf adults: 1972–1977. In *Progress Report No. 12*, ed. J. D. Schein. New York: Deafness Research & Training Center, New York University.

———. 1980. Survey of health care for deaf people. *Deaf American* 32(5): 5–6, 27.

Schein, Jerome D., Delk, Marcus T., and Gentile, N. R. 1977. *Implementation of the Model State Plan for Vocational Rehabilitation of Deaf Clients*. Silver Spring, MD: National Association of the Deaf.

Schein, Jerome D., Delk, Marcus T., and Hooker, Susan. 1980. Overcoming barriers to the full employment of deaf persons in the federal government. *Journal of Rehabilitation of the Deaf* 13(3): 15–25.

Schein, Jerome D., and Hamilton, Ronald. 1980. *Impact 1980: Telecommunications and deafness*. Silver Spring, MD: National Association of the Deaf.

Schein, Jerome D., and L. J. Waldman, eds. 1986. *The deaf Jew in the modern world*. New York: New York Society for the Deaf.

Schiff, Naomi B., and Ventry, Ira M. 1976. Communication problems in hearing children of deaf parents. *Journal of Speech and Hearing Disorders* 41:348–58.

Schiff-Meyers, Naomi B. 1982. Sign and oral language development of preschool hearing children of deaf parents in comparison with their mother's communication system. *American Annals of the Deaf* 127:322–30.

Schildroth, Arthur N., and Karchmer, Michael A., eds. 1986. *Deaf children in America*. San Diego: College-Hill Press.

Schlesinger, Hilde S. 1971. Prevention, diagnosis, and habilitation of deafness: A critical look. In *Medical aspects of deafness, Proceedings of National Forum IV* (Atlantic City, New Jersey), ed. Doin Hicks. Washington, DC: Council of Organizations Serving the Deaf.

Schlesinger, Hilde S., and Meadow, K. P. 1972. *Sound and sign*. Berkeley, CA: University of California Press.

Schowe, B. M. 1979. *Identity crisis in deafness*. Tempe, AZ: The Scholars Press.

Schreiber, Frederick C. 1979. National Association of the Deaf. In *Hearing and hearing impairment*, eds. L. J. Bradford and W. G. Hardy. New York: Grune and Stratton.

———. 1980. Editoral we. In *A rose for tomorrow*, J. Schein. Silver Spring, MD: National Association of the Deaf.

Schreiber, Kathleen B. 1987. *How we are*. In *Wallpaper*. Unpublished manuscript.

Schuchman, John S. 1974. John S. Schuchman's experience. In *Deafness in infancy and early childhood*, ed. Peter J. Fine. New York: Medcom Press.

———. 1987. Silent films. In *Gallaudet encyclopedia of Deaf people and Deafness*, Vol. 3, pp. 275–279, ed. J. V. Van Cleve. New York: McGraw-Hill.

———. 1988. *Hollywood speaks: Deafness and the film entertainment industry*. Urbana, IL: University of Illinois Press.

Scott, Virginia. 1986. *Belonging*. Washington, DC: Gallaudet University Press.

Scouten, Edward L. 1984. *Turning points in the education of deaf people*. Danville, IL: Interstate Printers and Publishers.

Shroyer, Edgar H., and Shroyer, Susan P. 1984. *Signs across America*. Washington, DC: Gallaudet University Press.

Spradley, Thomas S., and Spradley, James P. 1978. *Deaf like me*. New York: Random House.

Stewart, Larry G., and Schein, Jerome D. 1971. *Tarrytown Conference on Current Priorities in the Rehabilitation of Deaf People*. New York: New York University Deafness Research and Training Center.

Stokoe, William C. 1960. Sign language structure. *Studies in linguistics*. Occasional Papers No. 8. Buffalo, NY: University of Buffalo.

———. 1987. Tell me where is grammar bred?: "Critical evaluation"? or another chorus of "Come back to Milano"? *Sign Language Studies* 54:31–58.

Stokoe, William C., Bernard, H. Russell, and Padden, Carol. 1980. An elite group in deaf society. In *Sign and culture*, ed. William C. Stokoe. Silver Spring, MD: Linstok Press.

Stokoe, William C., Casterline, Dorothy C., and Croneberg, Carl G. 1965. *A dictionary of American Sign Language on linguistic principles*. Washington, DC: Gallaudet College Press.

Stuckless, E. R., and Birch, J. W. 1966. The influence of early manual communication on the linguistic development of deaf children. *American Annals of the Deaf* 111:452–60.

Student founds national program for college peers. 1984. *The Florida School Herald* 37(2): 4.

Sullivan, Frank B. 1987. National Fraternal Society of the Deaf. In *Gallaudet encyclopedia of Deaf people and Deafness*, Vol. 2, ed. John V. Van Cleve. New York: McGraw-Hill.

Sussman, Marvin B. 1966. Sociological theory and deafness: Problems and prospects. *Asha* 8:303–7.

Sutcliffe, Ronald E. 1985. A retrospect of deaf men in power. Paper delivered to the Iowa Association of the Deaf, Waterloo, IA, 3 August 1985.

Thomas, David. 1982. *The experience of handicapped*. New York: Methuen.

Thomas, Lewis. 1987. What doctors don't know. *New York Review of Books* 34 (14): 6–11.

Trybus, Raymond. 1980. Sign language, power, and mental health. In *Sign language and the deaf community*, ed. Charlotte Baker and Robbin Battison. Silver Spring, MD: National Association of the Deaf.

———. 1987. Social trends and deafness. Paper presented at the Conference of Executives and Administrators of Schools for the Deaf Forum, Santa Fe, NM.

Updike, John. 1986. Books. *The New Yorker*, September 22. (Review of Gabriel García Márquez [1986]. *Story of a shipwrecked sailor*. Knopf.)

Van Cleve, John V. 1987. Little paper family. In *Gallaudet encyclopedia of Deaf people and Deafness*, Vol. 2, ed. J. V. Van Cleve. New York: McGraw-Hill.

Vernon, McCay. 1974. Psychological aspects in diagnosing deafness in a child. In *Deafness in infancy and early childhood*, ed. Peter J. Fine. New York: Medcom Press.

——— and Koh, S. D. 1970. Early manual communication and deaf children's achievement. *American Annals of the Deaf* 115:527–36.

Walker, Lou Ann. 1982. Vanilla Fires. *People*, 12 July: 24–29.

———. 1985. *Amy. The story of a deaf child*. New York: E. P. Dutton.

———. 1986. *A loss for words*. New York: Harper & Row.

Walters, Joan. 1979. Religious education of hearing-impaired children: The community shares its faith. *Volta Review* 81(3): 41–44.

Warfield, F. 1957. *Keep listening*. New York: Viking Press.

Wax, Teena M., and Danek, Marita M. 1984. Deaf women and double jeopardy: Challenge for research and practice. In *Deaf people and social change*, ed. Alexander Boros and Ross Stuckless. Working Papers 6. Washington, DC: Gallaudet College.

Weiss, Ilene, and Wilcox, Sherman. 1986. Review. Everyone here spoke sign language. *Sign Language Studies* 51:185–88.

Wells, H. G. 1980. The country of the blind. In *The door in the wall*. Boston: David Godine.

West, Paul. 1970. *Words for a deaf daughter*. New York: Harper & Row.

Wilcox, Sherman. 1987. Breaking through the culture of silence. *Sign Language Studies* 55:163–74.

Williams, Boyce R., and Sussman, Allen E. 1971. Social and psychological problems of deaf people. In *Counseling with deaf people,* ed. A. E. Sussman and L. G. Stewart. New York: New York University Deafness Research and Training Center.

Williams, Howard G. 1982. Curriculum in a changing society. *Proceedings for Conference for Heads of Schools and Services for Hearing Impaired Children.* Manchester, U.K.: University of Manchester, Department of Audiology and Education of the Deaf.

Williams, Judith S. 1980. Bilingual experiences of a deaf child. In *Sign and culture,* ed. William C. Stokoe. Silver Spring, MD: Linstok Press.

Winzer, Margret A. 1986. Deaf-Mutia: Responses to alienation by the deaf in the mid-nineteenth century. *American Annals of the Deaf* 131(1): 29–32.

Wixtrom, Christine. 1987. Alone in the crowd. *The Deaf American* 37(3): 12–15.

Woods, W. H., Sr. N.d. *The forgotten people.* St. Petersburg, FL: Dixie Press.

Woodward, James. 1980. Sociolinguistic research on American Sign Language: An historical perspective. In *Sign language and the deaf community,* eds. Charlotte Baker and Robbin Battison. Silver Spring, MD: National Association of the Deaf.

————. 1982. *How you gonna get to heaven if you can't talk with Jesus?* Silver Spring, MD: TJ Publishers.

Woodward, James, and Allen, Thomas. 1987. Classroom use of ASL by teachers. *Sign Language Studies* 54:1–10.

Wright, Beatrice. 1960. *Physical disability—a psychological approach.* New York: Harper.

Yau, Shunchiu. 1986. A linguistic remark on Everyone Here Spoke Sign Language. *Sign Language Studies* 53:388–90.

Yount, William R. 1976. *Be opened!* Nashville, TN: Brodman Press.

INDEX

Gallaudet, Thomas Hopkins, 24,
75, 136–137
Gallaudet University, 26, 137,
138–141
Gallaudet University Alumni
Association, 25, 59, 77–78,
104n.5
Ghetto, 14, 22n.19
Greater Los Angeles Council on
Deafness, 97–98

Housing, 60–61
Humor, 61–64

International Catholic Deaf Association, 80
Interpreting, 190–194; assessing
competence, 185–187;
availability, 190–194; by
hearing children of Deaf
parents, 125–127; National
Interpreter Training
Consortium, 192; Registry of
Interpreters for the Deaf (RID),
190

Junior National Association of the
Deaf, 82

Language. *See* American Sign Language
Law: challenges to parenthood,
187–189; National Center for
Law and the Deaf, 187; police
relations, 189–190, 191,
195n.15; rights of deaf people,
185–190
Literature, 49–51, 70n.29

Mainstreaming, 141–145, 229–230
Medical services, 181–185;
psychiatry, 184, 195n.6
Milan Manifesto, 26, 69n.9, 137,
203–204. *See also* Education
Milieu: changes in, 230–235;
in other nations, 214–215;

interactions with other factors,
18–19, 216–217; in theory, 18,
213–215, 217, 232–235. *See also*
Theory of Deaf community
development
Motion pictures, 45–46
Mutual Alliance Plan, 98–99

National Association of the Deaf,
25, 74–77
National Association of
Hearing-Impaired College
Students, 84
National Black Deaf Advocates, 83
National Captioning Institute, 27,
44
National Congress of the Jewish
Deaf, 80–81
National Fraternal Society of the
Deaf (FRAT), 26, 78–79
National Literary Society of the
Deaf, 85, 86–87
National Technical Institute for the
Deaf, 27
National Theatre of the Deaf,
47–49
New England Gallaudet
Association of the Deaf, 24–25
Newspapers. *See* Literature
Ninety-percent rule, 106–107,
131–132n.1

Opera, 48–49. *See also* Theater
Oral Deaf Adults Section, 81. *See
also* Alexander Graham Bell
Association
Organizations, 72–73; advocacy,
73–84, 89, 90, 93–94; analysis
of, 99–103; coordination,
94–99; for deaf and hard of
hearing, 88–91; effectiveness
of, 103; local, 85–88;
membership, 88–89, 100,
105n.31; national, 73–84;
parent, 118–119; participation,
100–101; priorities, 101–103;